I

Investing in Real Estate with Lease Options and "Subject-To" Deals

Second Edition

Powerful Strategies for
Getting More When You Sell,
and Paying Less When You Buy

WENDY PATTON

ISBN: 9798391324324

This book is dedicated to my mother who, in 1985, got me started in real estate investing by giving me my first real estate course. It was her belief that real estate investing was the way to financial freedom. This course led me to discover my future direction in life. She believed in real estate, and she believed in me.

I want to thank my husband, Michael, and my children, Brooke, James, Jacob, Rachel, and Sarah, for sacrificing time with me during the first edition writing of this book in 2004 and especially during the many times over the years that I was buying and selling real estate. Brooke and James, my twins, came with me to see hundreds of homes when I was a single mother. Their patience was worth its weight in gold!

My gratitude and thanks to the following:

For the first edition: My sister, Jenny, who helped me with the editing of my book - for the many long hours she spent.

For the second edition: Clare Kilgore who helped me with editing, formatting, Amazon coordination, and much, much more. She was my right hand to get this second edition completed. Kim Arata, my sister-in-law who helped with her expertise in book editing (she has also edited a few books for my brother). I could not have done it without all of you along with the many people who sent me stories of their successes.

And it wouldn't be right for me to not give God, and Jesus Christ, the credit for helping me all along the way. Everything I am, and have, is all because of him.

Thank you to you all!

Table of Contents

Table of Contents

PART 3
HOW TO GET REALTORS TO HELP YOU DO LEASE OPTIONS

PART 4
STEPS TO SELLING PROPERTIES
WITH LEASE OPTIONS

PART 5
CREATING FUTURE FINANCIAL FREEDOM—FX3

Introduction:
Lease Options Anyone Can Do It!

A fourteen-year-old named John, accompanied by his father attended a seminar I spoke at in Houston. During one segment of my presentation, I teach students to call sellers directly out of Craigslist, Zillow, Facebook Marketplace, etc. When I teach this part of the class, I often make live calls to sellers so that my students can hear how I speak with the seller and how I gather information to determine whether the seller's home is a potential candidate for a Lease Option. However, I didn't make any calls on this day—we simply talked about the best techniques for calling leads.

The next day, while John was in school, he began gathering "For Rent" advertisements. After school, he started making calls—with no training—and he got a seller lead for a Lease Option that said, "Yes, I'd like to consider it." Being only 14 and having no experience, he couldn't (and didn't know how to) enter a legal contract. He asked his father, "What do I do?"

John ended up selling the deal to an investor in his local investment group for $500. He gave me a copy of his $500 check! This was not bad, especially for a 14-year-old kid and one to two hours of work. John immediately went on to develop a relationship with this local investor, and on his next deal (while still 14!), he made 50 percent—$14,000—of the profit for his assistance. He has since done other deals for much higher profits.

How and why can a 14-year-old kid do this when most adults will not? The answer is, Fear! I believe everyone has a fear of failure or a fear of success. At 14, John was not afraid of failure. Heck, he hadn't even been dumped by a girl yet. He just took what he had learned and tried it.

You are never too old or too young to start investing. If you can do the research and pick up the phone to make the calls; you are on your way. However, many of us stop before we even get started because of our fear. We might have excuses like, "I can't possibly do that. It's a young person's game. It's an older person's game. No one will say 'yes' to me. I have no experience. I don't have a good voice. I don't have money. I don't have good credit." All these statements are negative talk and inaccurate.

What will make you successful in Lease Options or Subject-Tos is just taking the plunge. You'll make some mistakes along the way, but so what? What's the worst thing that can happen? I was financially broke when I started investing in real estate, therefore I really had nothing to lose.

Young John wasn't hampered by fear, so he could jump in, take the plunge, and make things happen—and in doing so, he set his financial future in motion. His example does not involve a huge amount of money, but it's nothing to sneeze at—and extraordinary for a 14-year-old. The money was important because not only could John pay for part of his college, but now he had choices. If he continued his path in real estate investing, he could be financially set, unlike most of his friends. Choices imply options, including personal and financial freedom!

For me, the most exciting facet of real estate investing is Future Financial Freedom—or, as I call it, FX3. Everyone has a different definition of freedom; for some, it is financial (financial freedom); for others, it means having more control over their time (personal freedom). Let me have one of my students explain this in their own words to you:

Dear Wendy,

Our financial future has literally changed within the past couple of months by applying what my husband and I learned from your boot camp and, even more importantly, what we've learned from your ongoing, personalized support—you truly are the best! Keep in mind, my husband thought that I was crazy when I signed us up for your boot camp and flew up from Florida to Michigan to hear you speak. It truly was the best thing we have ever done. Please share my personal testimonial with your classes. I'm a believer, this does work!

First off, I must mention that when we attended your seminar, we had just completed a 1031 exchange, which gave us the great opportunity to start our investing career by buying three houses. Yes, it was so great having three houses siting empty and one with a renter that lived off us for free! This renter was so nice she gave a whole room to her pet rabbits to roam freely in, after we had just rehabbed the house!

During your boot camp we had a wonderful gathering at your house, in which my name was drawn to purchase a house on a Lease Option. I jumped for joy like I had just won a prize. The next day, after the [beer] wore off, I figured out what I had just committed to—a house that is 1,000 miles away, where it snows, the pipes freeze, and they have things called basements! Yes, being from Florida, this is just what I've always wanted—not!

We were up for the challenge, and you made it so easy with your support, along with the great contacts and help that we had from others who attended the boot camp. Not only did we get a great purchase price and terms with the owner, but today we have a pending contract for a Lease Option that will cash-flow us $600 a month, and at the end of the 18 to 24-month term we will profit $107,400! Gosh, I guess that will cover the cost of the class—truly amazing!

When we came home from your class we decided "no more renters." We booted the bad renter out (and no, we didn't keep the rabbits!) and sold all our houses on Lease Options. So, on our three houses that had been sitting empty, we now cash-flow $700 monthly and we will profit within 18 to 24 months, $227,900!

Now comes the best part. I finally put your class to the test. I went out and found an owner who was willing to do a Lease Option with me. Every Realtor I spoke to (and many investors as well) told me no one in their right mind will do a Lease Option with you in this market. The Florida market is way too hot. They are right, it is hot. Appreciation in some of our areas is anywhere from 34 to 40 percent.

But I got a gorgeous house that looks brand new, on a Lease Option. I also got a killer deal on the rent at $950 a month—normal rent would be $1,425! I put $5,000 *down, which will come off the purchase price. They were asking $200,000 and it's worth $239,000, so I offered them $210,000. The terms are 14 months, enough time to refinance it if I must. My new tenants bought it on an 18-month term. We will cash-flow on a monthly basis $845 ($500 of that will be applied towards the purchase price), and we are selling it for $299,900. That is a profit of $89,900. Amazing—is this for real? I've since quit my job and I'm doing this full time. Thank you again, Wendy, for changing our lives!*

Debra and Eric Larson

That story is from 2004, yet every bit of it is still relevant to this updated version of the book. The fantastic part is that those were the numbers from a long time ago. Very few things in this book have changed since the first edition was written. Why would they change? The techniques are still the same (with a few minor differences).

Why I Personally Chose Real Estate

Deal-making may just be in my blood. I've always loved a deal, and the day I realized that real estate investing was that kind of game was the most important day of my life. My first house was a three-bedroom bungalow in a suburb of Detroit. When I bought the home, I didn't have any funds available, so I used a credit card advance for my down payment. Yes, they allowed that back in 1985. My principal, interest, taxes, and insurance (PITI) was $438 a month. I rented two bedrooms to two ladies for $250 each. I had cash flow, and I was living free! My $62 cash flow per month paid my credit card payment. I was 21 years old, and I thought this was very cool! Little did I know they would later call this "house hacking". Of course, I decided to buy another home. I bought three more my first year. I had no money or assets, but I did have good credit and a few credit cards.

At the start of my real estate investing career, I was $20,000 in debt with a student and car loan. In my mind, the worst thing that could happen was that I would go bankrupt. However, I had good credit and was able to make my down payments on homes with credit cards. It wasn't long before I had a credit line of over $250,000—and too many credit cards. Using credit cards should be the last resort for most investors, as I lost a lot of profit by having huge revolving credit card debt. Even though I faithfully made payments on all of them and somehow juggled them so that no payment ever slipped through the cracks. It was, however, an administrative nightmare. Still, I couldn't focus on that. I had to focus on what was the best that could happen: I could end up with *financial freedom* and *choices*! (which I did!)

When I started investing, I didn't know about Lease Options or Subject-To deals, and I thought what I did was a zero-down deal, and something very creative. At the time I didn't know of any gurus who focused on buying using Lease Options, so I developed my own tools and systems to buy homes with little or no money down, using the same techniques I was using to sell. Since then, I have acquired almost every course available in the market on Lease Options (and lots of other techniques also) and learned extra tips from them all to add to how I do my business. I am the only national educator in the country who teaches people how to work with Realtors to find these types of zero-down deals. Over the years I have fine-tuned the techniques that really work. Completing hundreds of Lease Option contracts and teaching this topic all over the country for 15 years, has given me the experience to share the concepts in this book with you.

I have bought and sold over 750 properties since becoming an investor in 1985. In the early 2000s I had as many as 175 properties in inventory at a time. My current and longer-term goal is to diversify my investments into companies, syndications and other real estate ventures. I have invested in several states and continue to look for new opportunities throughout the country and possibly internationally.

Whether we leave a job to pursue our own dreams of becoming a baker, a pilot, an artist, a Realtor, or an investor, we all have the same concerns and fears about starting out in a new business venture where we must rely on our own efforts to make a payday. The first couple of years can be rough. It takes a while to pay your dues in any new skill—and dealing in real estate is a skill. When doing the right deals, real estate not only has immediate cash flow, but it can also provide assets by the very nature of appreciation. This appreciation factor isn't built into most other self-employment positions. Real estate builds a tangible future that can set you up for life if you have the passion and the drive to dig in and overcome your fears of trying something new.

When can I leave my 9-5?

If you want to pursue real estate investing, and in particular Lease Options or Subject-Tos, I don't advise quitting your job and starting with nothing.

Instead, I offer two pieces of advice:

1. It is best to start this business while you are still employed at your current job so that you won't have to worry about receiving a paycheck while you are learning the business.

2. Build the second income from real estate investing, which eventually will replace your primary income. This will allow you to leave your job.

Too many people leave their jobs too early, only to find out they have to go back or can't survive without the income. Don't make that mistake.

Pursuing my dreams to be a full-time investor was the best thing I ever did professionally. When I left corporate America in the mid-1990s to pursue real estate full time, it was the best career move I had ever made. It has given me financial freedom. Do you want that freedom? Real estate can give you Future Financial Freedom (FX3) too!

In this book I share my secrets and strategies with you. I suggest you try them all and decide which work best for your personal style and your specific area of the country. As you find your niche, you will perfect it. Real estate investing changed my life, and it can change yours, too. It is my hope that Lease Options, Subject-To's, and zero-down strategies will help change the way you think and help you live out your dreams, so you have all the choices and freedom you desire!

Wendy's Words of Warning

Before we get into the meat of this book, there is one caveat; I have strong opinions, and you will get to hear some of them.

 When you're ready to learn more...

This book is a great start, but it is just the tip of the iceberg. When you're ready to learn more, I have courses packed with details on Subject-Tos, Lease Options, Working with Realtors, etc. available on my website:

WendyPatton.com

PART 1

AN INTRODUCTION TO LEASE OPTIONS AND SUBJECT-TO DEALS

CHAPTER 1

How Lease Options and Subject-Tos Work and How They Can Set You Up for Future Financial Freedom (FX3)

What Are Lease Options and Subject-Tos?

Lease Options and Subject-To's are ways to purchase real estate, usually with very little or no money down, sometimes even with money back in the investor's pocket. This may sound too good to be true, but it isn't. Can an investor end up with money in his pocket and not have to put 10 to 20 percent down to purchase real estate? Yes! These techniques are used today, and have been for years, by successful investors. This book will show you how to find motivated sellers with homes that you can purchase with little or no money down—truly the fastest way to Future Financial Freedom (FX3).

A Lease Option is a strategy that gives an investor the right to lease a home with the right to purchase the home during or before the end of the lease period. Note: I said an option, but not an obligation or requirement. Instead, it is a right or privilege. An Option Agreement is a contract that gives a purchaser the right to exercise a privilege. In the case of real estate investing, it gives the investor the right to purchase property during a contracted period. It is a technique that involves gaining control of a property without the added burden of ownership. Almost all money made in real estate is made by controlling property. *Owning* property is the most obvious way to control it, but control *is* possible *without* ownership—and control is what brings in the money. It was a dying John D. Rockefeller who shared his secret to achieving great wealth: "Control everything, own nothing." All the most successful real estate developers today utilize options in some fashion, at some time.

A Subject-To is a technique by which the investor gains the title to a property but doesn't have to get a mortgage on the property he is about to control. The seller keeps the mortgage in his own name but *deeds* the property to the investor. It is deeded to the investor "Subject-To" the existing mortgage, which stays in place with this technique. The mortgage company isn't usually made aware of the change or asked about the change. The new owner just starts making the payments on the old owner's loan.

It is important to be aware that there are some risks involved with either technique. Later in the book, I will cover these risks to help minimize your exposure. The rewards that can come with either of these techniques far outweigh the risks. Real estate investing is perhaps the quickest and best way to build lasting wealth. Many of the world's wealthiest people acquire much of their wealth through investing in real estate.

Are there risks?

There are always risks!

If anyone tells you there are no risks in a particular investing technique; they are either not being honest or they don't have enough experience yet to realize the risks.

While Lease Options and Subject-To's can build you tremendous wealth, they usually shouldn't be considered a short-term investment strategy. I define a short-term strategy as one in which the time between the start of the transaction and its completion (cashing out) is less than one year. A classic example of this would be a rehab project (fixing up a home and reselling it). The other end of the spectrum would be a *long*-term strategy, such as buying a rental property and renting it over many years. Consider Lease Options and Subject-To's to be in the center of that spectrum, usually requiring one to three years for the best payoff. However, you can always immediately sell the deal to another individual or investor for a profit; this is called *wholesaling*. It can be done if you buy the property at a low enough price, you can turn a profit by selling the deal to another investor where there is still enough room for them to profit as well. You can also wholesale a Lease Option to a retail buyer. This is what I call a Cooperative Lease Option (see my website for more information on that strategy www.WendyPatton.com).

Visualize This Scenario

In every seminar I teach, I ask the students, "Who of you would be willing to purchase a home valued at $200,000 for $100,000?" Of course, all hands shoot up. Then I continue by asking if they would still be willing to purchase the same home if the price was $150,000. Most of the hands stay up. I proceed upward with the price, increasing the increments by $10,000 each time. I always sit and watch with amazement as the hands slowly but surely drop. At the price of $180,000 almost all hands are down. At $190,000, usually, all hands in the room are down. The point I am trying to make to each of them is that most investors are not willing to pay this close to retail price for a home. When paying cash or getting a mortgage I would say they are correct.

I then re-pose the question to each of them: "How many of you would be willing to pay $200,000 for a $200,000 house with no money down, in a market that is appreciating at 10 percent per year, with a 10-year period to pay the $200,0000 to the seller with monthly payments of $1,000 per month? The rental rates are $1500 and the payments you pay the seller all go towards the purchase price." Now all their hands go back up. I ask, "Why, now, are you willing to pay more for that house that you refused to pay $180,000 to $190,000 for a few

2

minutes ago?" They respond in unison, saying, "Because you added some attractive terms!" My response is always the same: "You didn't ask the terms before!" *Terms* are the key to Lease Options. Price is only one of the terms, but sometimes we forget as investors (or we don't know) that there *are* other terms to consider (until now).

Terms make up the deal, such as price, length of time to pay, monthly payment, credits paid monthly from the rent, and other items negotiated with the seller, which are discussed in more detail in Chapters 5 and 9. Many times even experienced real estate investors don't ask, "When does the seller need their cash?" They say "no" to a price without asking the seller when he needs the money. The previous example illustrates how most investors think: They don't ask all the right questions about the property before they make their decision. Wholesalers are notorious for this. They look at the surface, but they don't dig deeper for other possibilities.

Wendy's Note to Wholesalers

Consider wholesaling the Lease Option to an end Tenant-Buyer – using a Cooperative Lease Option - or find out if the seller will do a Subject-To. For those wholesalers reading this book, you will now have a few more solutions in your pocket for motivated sellers. More to come on these ideas…

Lease Options provide a creative solution that allow you to negotiate terms that can increase your profits and provide a great investment opportunity. You can pay a higher price on a home if you can get reasonable terms, and having this tool at your disposal allows you to open new possibilities and make money on deals that were before completely ruled out. I am not suggesting that you pay $200,000 for a home worth $200,000, but you can if certain market conditions and terms previously described exist. If your market is flat (not appreciating) and you have only two years to exercise your option to buy the home, then maybe the price you offer should be much less. It's all about *terms*!

When doing any Lease Option or Subject-To deal, one of my mottos is that "Everyone must win, or we don't do the deal." There are three people involved: the seller, the investor, and the Tenant-Buyer. It must be a win-win-win; otherwise, walk away.

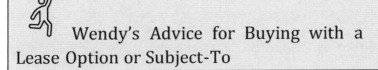

Wendy's Advice for Buying with a Lease Option or Subject-To

If it isn't a win-win-win for the seller, the investor (you), and the Tenant-Buyer; then walk away from the deal. There are plenty of deals out there where everyone can win.

Standard Lease Option Deals

My typical strategy is to Lease Option *from* a seller and then to Lease Option that home *to* a Tenant-Buyer. This is called a "Sandwich Lease Option."

How Lease Options Work

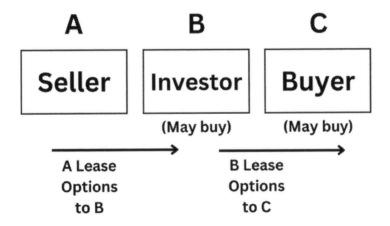

The above illustration depicts a Sandwich Lease Option. In a sandwich, the meat is in the middle—that's the best part. You (the investor) are in the middle of this transaction; your reward is the meat—the difference between what you can pay for the home and what you can sell it for. There are other ways to make this deal even better and more profitable, which I discuss in Chapters 5 and 9.

Wendy's Ethics Rule

Don't do Lease Options with potential Tenant-Buyers who have no way of ever being able to get a mortgage. That's just being greedy and taking advantage of someone. It is not fair to the Tenant-Buyer. If the Tenant-Buyer messes up, shame on them! If *you* mess *them* up, shame on you!

A variation of the Sandwich Lease is the Lease Purchase. While a Lease Option gives the investor the right to purchase real estate, the Lease Purchase *guarantees* that he or she will purchase the property during a given period. Under some circumstances I will commit to buying certain homes using this technique—for instance, with specific Realtors, with deals that have a very good potential for profitability, when I have a solid buyer lined up, with high appreciating markets, and with very long-term deals. I do not use Lease Purchases much when I'm selling, because they are hard to enforce. If your buyer defaults, you must sue him specifically for nonperformance to get him to buy your home. It is costly and very time consuming to do this. If your buyer cannot get a mortgage, it is also a waste of time. Because of the legal battle that could be involved, normally I would recommend you move on and find another buyer (much like a Lease Option).

How Lease Purchases Work

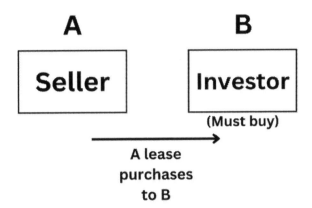

A **B**

| Seller | Investor |

(Must buy)

A lease
purchases
to B

Wendy's Ethics Rule

Don't do Lease Purchases if you don't intend to follow through on the transaction. Do what you say you will do when you say you will do it. Help keep real estate investing an honest profession.

Standard Subject-To Deals

If I can't get a Lease Option or Lease Purchase from the seller, or if it doesn't make sense from a business perspective, then a Subject-To is another way to acquire the property. However, it is important to note that a Subject-To is a buying strategy only. Though I may acquire the property Subject-To, I could still sell it on a Lease Option. (Again, can be just an acquisition technique like above)

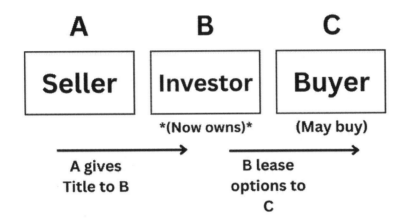

Here's a great real-life example from my files of a Lease Option deal from start to finish— a true win-win-win:

The Seller: Janet

> Company looking for 3-4 homes in this area, on long- term lease. Call 123-222-2222.

Janet, a seller, answered an ad I had placed online. Janet's home had been listed on the market for $189,900 with a Realtor and the listing contract had recently expired. She saw my ad and decided to call me. She was exactly the kind of person I was looking for: willing to sell and willing to do a long-term lease. I still had to determine some other factors to make sure it would be a win-win-win.

Janet's most important area of concern was her price. It was set at $185,000, and she was not going to budge on that portion of the deal. Price was her most important "term". Therefore, I would need to look at the rest of the terms to see if I could still make this a win-win for my side of the deal. Now that I have much more experience in real estate, I do not say "no" as quickly as I used to; I look at the entire deal now, instead of getting caught up with the traditional price-alone deal structure. Janet had fixed her price, so I had to look at monthly payments and the available timeline. By having all the facts, I was able to analyze the entire deal and thus make sure I would still obtain *my* bottom line of *profitability*.

At the time of this deal, we were in a strong appreciating market—approximately 6 to 7 percent per year. I figured that a 6 percent growth rate on $185,000 would mean approximately $10,000 per year just in appreciation. I had really hoped to get the property for $175,000. Even with the $10,000 in appreciation after the first year, I would still only be where I had originally wanted to be in the first place. I did end up buying the house and putting $4,000 of improvements into the property (basic carpet and paint). I now had $189,000 into the property, including the improvements. Anything above the $189,000 that I could sell it for would be pure profit.

Janet was not in trouble financially, but she was motivated to sell. She had a severe shoulder injury that was preventing her from doing the maintenance around the property. She made great money and could have hired someone to do the maintenance, but she decided that with 20-plus surgeries under her belt and more to go, she just wanted some time off from dealing with her large home and yard. She didn't need to pull her money out of the property, but she did ask for $1,000 up front so that she could go rent a lakefront home in the area. The $1,000 I gave her for the option fee, plus the $4,000 for improvements, was a total of $5,000 out of my pocket for this home, which is less than 3 percent down—a small amount for this home.

The Buyer: Roberta

I knew that Janet and I were going to come to terms and do the necessary paperwork on a Sunday, so I started to market the home on that same Sunday, and I got a call from Roberta. I told Roberta that she could drive by the home, but that she could not go in or on the property yet, because someone still lived there. Roberta didn't even know I didn't have the deal tied up—I just wanted her to drive by and see if she liked it. There wasn't even a sign in the yard yet.

Roberta had some minor credit problems and seven dogs. Most landlords will not ever rent to someone with seven dogs, and someone with poor credit to boot. Also, mortgage lenders won't do a mortgage for someone who has credit issues. With an inability to get a mortgage and rent from most landlords; what was she going to do? No one would rent to her, and no one would give her a mortgage. There are many people seeking a solution to this kind of situation. These are the people I am trying to help. They want the American dream, yet they are unable to obtain it in the usual way. Lease Options give people a second chance to improve their credit while working toward the purchase of the home they desire to own.

If you're a landlord, all you get up front on any of your rentals is the security deposit, and that is just not enough cash to take on the risk of someone with poor credit and seven dogs. You can change this scenario by converting these people from tenants to Tenant-Buyers; then the risk that once was on you is shifted to the Tenant-Buyer, which is where you want it. With

Roberta putting a lot of money down (option fees are not refundable), she was taking the risk.

Let's look at how the deal unfolded:

My out-of-pocket costs:

Option fee to seller	–$ 1,000
Improvements	–$ 4,000
Option fee from Roberta	+$10,000
Positive amount in my pocket	+$ 5,000

Without even owning this home I now had $5,000 in my pocket. Roberta was the one risking $10,000 with her option fee, as it was nonrefundable. If she didn't, or couldn't buy, she'd walk away from a lot of money.

Janet asked me for $1,100 per month for rent, and I in turn asked Roberta for $1,450 per month for rent. I was able to have cash flow of $350 per month, which would add to my profitability in the deal. In this case Janet had a lot of equity in the home, and I was able to leverage that equity to get her to accept the lower monthly payment of $1,100.

The option sale price I set for Roberta was $225,000. How did I get that figure? I put a 10 percent option premium on top of the retail price (see Chapter 5), plus I added an additional 6 to 7 percent appreciation rate at 18 months, which was approximately another $20,000. I then rounded it up a little to get to $225,000.

What was the property worth? Value is always determined by what a buyer is willing to pay. Roberta later had the house appraised at $267,000. Wow is all I can say, however many times unique properties with acreage, on the water, with views of the mountains/city, have more flexibility to appraise. Did I lose $42,000? I don't think so. After all, I did make about that much. Was Roberta happy with the appraisal? Of course! Janet was happy because she got the price she wanted, and Roberta was happy because the appraisal gave her an additional $42,000 in equity that she can utilize if she wants. Janet won, Roberta won, and I won. This demonstrates what a classic win-win-win deal is all about.

Here's the profit at closing—not bad for not actually *owning* the home (except for two hours), but just *controlling* it

Front-end cash	$ 5,000
Back-end sale	$31,000
Tax prorations (a MI thing only)	$ 2,800
$350 cash flow × 14 months	$ 4,900
Total profit	$43,700*

*It is not exactly $43,700. There are transfer/deed revenue s in some states, and title insurance fees/closing fees.

Now, want an even better ending to this story? 2 years later Janet called me wanting to do a Lease Option with me on one of my other properties. Life had changed for her, and she had a credit blip that needed some time to heal, and she was ready to own again, but for a home with a much smaller lot. Go figure!   Is that a win-win-win-win? You bet!

A Subject-To Deal

Here's a great real-life example of a Subject-To deal from start to finish, another win-win-win.

The Sellers: John and Sally

Bob, one of my students placed in ad in West Palm beach to find motivated sellers. John and Sally, sellers, answered the ad. I helped Bob structure the Lease Option portion of this deal to make the numbers work. Here is the ad:

> Tired of monthly payments? We can help. We will make your payments. Call today. Call 123-222-2222.

The sellers were three months behind on payments of $2,100 each. They saw the ad and called. Their house was worth between $385,000 and $400,000. They owed $268,000 on the first mortgage, which didn't include the three missed payments (one of which was only two days late); a second mortgage of $15,000; and a small assessment fee of $2,000, which could be paid at closing in a year or two. Total owed on the home was $285,000 (not including those back payments). These sellers had attempted to sell this home twice in the West Palm Beach market, but both buyers had backed out prior to closing. The sellers had since moved out and rented a place in a better school district for $2,200 per month. They didn't have any savings and could not afford both payments. The home was in pristine condition and needed nothing, unlike many homes in this situation.

These people wanted to work out a deal so that they would be able to get some of their equity out and not lose it all. They wanted to collect their equity when their current one-year lease expired so that they could buy a home in the new school district, though they didn't need the equity out immediately. They were in a bad situation, though, where they couldn't refinance the property, even *with* their equity, because with the missed payments they no longer qualified financially for a mortgage; they had no one they could borrow from. These people were in a difficult situation, which required a solution.

An ad like ours will attract some Lease Option sellers, but also Subject-To sellers; this couple was a Subject-To seller. They were behind on payments. They were willing to take much less than the current value of the house, and to receive payment later. They did not need their equity immediately. What they needed was a solution.

Bob offered to give the sellers $40,000 for the equity in their home, but not until he sold the property. There would be no interest on the $40,000. This would bring his total investment in the home to $331,000 (acquisition cost of $291,000 + $40,000). He also offered to make the three late payments that would bring their mortgage current—a total of approximately $6,300. From this point forward, he agreed to continue making their mortgage payments. This

15

would prevent them from going into foreclosure. Their credit score would improve as he continued to make their house payments on time. While the late payments of 60 days on the mortgage were a negative indicator, they could be explained by the couple's move and the two previous deals falling through.

Bob could have either made their payments until he refinanced the home at a lower rate or until he lease-optioned it out. He had several choices. The biggest issue on this deal was the payment amount; it was a bit high for a rental, which many times can be a problem for Subject-To deals. If the mortgage payment you are taking over is too high, you need to refinance the property at a lower rate or work out a better deal with the seller. On this home he lease-optioned it out.

The Buyer: Frank

Bob found a Tenant-Buyer, Frank, with an ad for a Lease Option for the market rental rate of $1,600. The problem was that this rate left Bob $500 negative per month! He now had two choices: (1) See if Frank could pay more, or (2) do the refinance.

Bob and I came up with an offer that Frank couldn't refuse: He offered Frank 50 percent on his investment (I will take a 50% return on my money any day of the week). Frank was a high-tech type of guy who had credit issues from the year before when he had suddenly lost his job. Since then, he had become reemployed and was making very good money. He could easily afford the payment and more. Bob offered to give him $500 a month credit plus an additional $250 credit if he paid $2,100 instead of $1,600 per month. He jumped at it. The most it would cost Bob was $750 per month for the 12 months Frank was in the home, if he bought it. If he didn't buy, it would make Bob the $500 per month cash flow, which he could keep, and because he would not have to refinance, he avoided the costs related to that. Frank also had $8,000 to put down as his option fee. He would have liked to put more down, but that was all he had saved since he had been so recently out of work.

Let's examine expenses so far:

Investor's out-of-pocket costs:

Three months of payments	-$6,300
Improvements	$0
Option Fee from Frank	+$8,000
Left over in Bob's Pocket	+1,700

Bob already had $1,700 in his pocket/profit. Frank was the one risking the $8,000 option fee because it's nonrefundable. If he didn't buy it, he'd walk away from a lot of money.

The Lease Option sale price we set for Frank was $425,900. How did we get that figure? Bob put a 5 percent option premium on top of the retail price (he started at $385,000 on this one, but it could have been higher—see Chapter 5 about determining the profitability of deals), plus an additional 5 percent appreciation rate at 12 months, which was approximately another $20,000. This was a very conservative appreciation rate for that market. I would have gone higher on the appreciation calculation. The appreciation rate at the time he sold the home was 10 to 15 percent in his area. This deal was very good; I just did not like the monthly payment left from the owners' mortgage. Also note, since this deal there are some potential conflicts with the Dodd Frank Act, and I personally don't give option credits from the rental payment for a Tenant-Buyer. Because of that option credit change, I likely would not recommend doing a deal like this with the buyer. Think creatively to figure out how you can do it without offering monthly credits. Maybe offer to give him $9,000 credit towards buying if he decides to purchase? Just think about how you can get Frank what he wants and you what you want.

Here is the profit at closing—not bad for not getting a mortgage on a deal. He technically put nothing down. Great profitability!

Front-end cash	$ 1,700
Back-end sale	$417,900
(Less the $8,000 Frank put down $425,900 - $8,000)	
Option fee credits given away	-$ 9,000
($750/month x 12 months)	
Cash flow (break-even)	$ 0
What Bob owed the owner/lender:	$324,600
($331,000 - $6,400 paid)	
Total profit	$ 86,000*

It is not exactly $86,000 profit. There are deed transfer fees in some states as well as title insurance and closing fees, however, principal paid down on the mortgage during this time period is always kept by the investor.

The *sellers* in this example were thrilled that their credit rating was improved and restored during the deal. They could once again buy a home after some time with their improved credit (gained from your paying their mortgage payment on time). The *purchaser* was thrilled that he could buy a home in a beautiful town and restore his credit. *Bob* was thrilled with his profit on this deal. This is another classic example of a win-win-win.

The main thing that has changed since this book was written the first time and this deal was done, is the Dodd Frank law. This book will not go into detail on that law. It is a law that few still understand fully, however, my personal legal research all led to one thing - DON'T give monthly option credits (or part of the rent credited to the purchaser). It can change a deal to make it look more like seller financing and cause real issues if you ever have to evict the Tenant-Buyer. I haven't given any Tenant-Buyer monthly credit since this law came out.

Not all Subject-To deals or Lease Option deals are that profitable. It depends on where you start with the seller, how motivated they are, how strong the market is (appreciation), and the price range of the home. If you're looking at a $50,000 home versus $500,000, 10 percent makes a huge difference. The starting number will have a big impact on the total profitability. This is discussed further in Chapter 5.

Most of my Subject-To deals, I rent or wrap with seller financing, but sometimes I will Lease Option them. Here are the things to consider so you can pick the exit strategy with a Subject-To:

How to Pick the Best Exit Strategy for Subject-To:
Option # 1: RENT
If the mortgage has been paid down a lot or has a lot of equity going towards the principal balance, then I might want to rent it and let the equity build up. Also, if you want to build a portfolio and you can make monthly cash flow on a property, this is a great way to build up your property ownership.
Option # 2: WRAP
If the mortgage rate is low and the payment is low, then I might want to sell it on seller financing for a higher rate and therefore a higher payment. Seller financing is when you, the investor, become the lender for who you sell it to (a wrap). The spread on some deals can be significant – i.e. 2.5% interest rate with your seller vs. 8% interest rate for your buyer. Do that math on a $300,000 mortgage with this scenario. It's over $1,000 per month difference in payments!
Option # 3. LEASE OPTION
If you don't want to build up a portfolio and wrapping the mortgage doesn't make sense, then Lease Option to a Tenant-Buyer just like you would with a purchase with a Lease Option. It's just that you would own it when you do a Subject-To with the seller.

Financial Freedom

You Can Get There!

These examples show you how Lease Options and Subject-Tos can be very profitable. The previous examples are simple versions of the Lease Option and Subject-To techniques, as there are many other creative ideas you can implement to make them as profitable and complex as you choose (covered in Chapter 9). Remember, you may need several deals just to lay the groundwork for your Future Financial Freedom (FX3). It doesn't happen with one deal, and it doesn't happen overnight. However, with persistence it *will* happen!

There are at least three paydays using these techniques:

1. Upfront Option Fee
The upfront option fee from your buyer—or anything that your seller pays you to take over a mortgage on a Subject-To deal.
2. Monthly Cash Flow
The monthly cash flow—the difference between what you pay a seller and what your buyer pays you.
3. Back End Profit
The backend profit—the difference between what you are paying for the home and what you sell it for. This is your check at the closing table, therefor accounting for what you have already paid and received.

While the option fee is nonrefundable, don't get excited on your first few deals by immediately going out and spending it all. What if something happens six months down the road? In owning or controlling real estate, things come up that are completely unexpected: broken furnaces, leaking roofs, unpaid rents, and so on. It's just like owning your own home. Things happen, difficulties can arise. Plan for those things and you will be safe. If you have held the option funds in reserve, you will be able to cover your unexpected expenses. That's just good business sense. Yes, the option fee money is yours, but be wise with it. You might want to put it aside entirely for an investor's rainy day so that you will be prepared. After the deal closes, you can take another look at the money, because you will have not only that initial option fee but also the back end from the closing.

As you are getting started in this business or any other business, it is important to be conservative with your cash flow and money. I recommend you keep your spending very tight and conservative. Also, you want to be prepared to buy the next property should a good deal be offered to you. Unfortunately, most people in our country do not have good spending habits, and these bad habits allow people to get into financial trouble. It is very important to be on a strict budget for this type of business. If this will be hard for you, then you may want to find some outside help to get you on a system, which can assist you in financial planning. I cannot stress this enough; it is the make or break for real estate investors! It's my soapbox to talk about financial freedom and about most people over-spending.

Let's say you made $30,000 overall on the deal. One positive way to use that money is to reinvest. Reinvestment will continue to bring income, but you will also want to pyramid your income. For example, if your first property made $30,000 overall and you received $5,000 in an up-front option fee, now you're going to want to look for two to three new properties, probably with the same profit ranges. You'll need money up front to pay your option fee to the seller, even though you will reimburse yourself later with the option fees from the buyer. The properties may also need repairs, and that money will have to come out of your pocket up front, so you need to have the funds available from the previous sale. During this time, you will probably keep your day job, just to keep enough cash flowing in while you are building your new business.

Reinvesting doesn't just mean pouring money into new properties. It can also mean purchasing new office equipment, software, or anything else you need to continue to build your business. Maybe it's time you trashed that clunker computer and got one that was made in the twenty-first century. Get a cell phone dedicated to your business or buy bookkeeping software. I cannot stress it enough: Be prepared for your future without overspending.

My personal minimum profit goal is $40,000 per Lease Option deal. Lease Options typically turn over every 12 to 24 months. Depending on what part of the country you reside in, the profit range should vary from $20,000 to $150,000 (Midwest to northern California). Subject-To profit ranges should be equal to or greater than Lease Options, because you are buying from distressed (usually) sellers and might be able to negotiate more on the price; however, you might also have to use more cash to purchase them. You decide how much you need to make, and then you will know how many homes you need to Lease Option or buy Subject-To. Not only can Lease Options and Subject-Tos set you up to live well today, but they can set you up for Future Financial Freedom (FX3) and retirement. Just sit back and imagine . . . how would it feel to be completely debt free? Real estate is the vehicle that can allow you to achieve just that.

 When can I leave my job?

During my first 10 years of investing, I was still working. The last few years were part-time so I could focus more and more on investing. Then finally, I took the plunge!

How can I learn more about Subject-Tos?

If Subject-Tos are a technique you would like to use for real estate investing, then I'm sure you will want to know more. There was only so much I could pack into this book; however, I have a *Course* that is much more detailed called, "Get the Deed – Subject-To". All my courses have the contracts you will need, audio training, step-by-step instructions on how to use the technique, filled out example contracts, and much more. You can find all my courses on: www.WendyPatton.com

CHAPTER 2

Success Stories of Buying with Subject-Tos and Lease Options

The best part of doing Subject-To and Lease Option deals is witnessing the end results. Unless a deal is a win for each party, walk away from it. The seller must win, the investor in the middle must win, and the Tenant-Buyer must win. When all three of these people win in a transaction, there is nothing better! This chapter contains stories shared by different investors in different parts of the country. The sellers' and buyers' names have been changed, but the numbers and details reflect the specific transactions. These deals will inspire you and show you how you too can be successful and create unique solutions for motivated sellers.

Lease Option Case: Steve's First Deal

This study is important because it describes a first deal. I like it because it highlights how each party to the transaction was able to come away as a winner. Here is how Steve described it:

> Sara had a house in Fowlerville, MI that she kept after her divorce. She couldn't stand to continue living with the memories from the marriage, so she bought another house in Fenton, MI, closer to where she works. She advertised the house as both "For Sale by Owner" and "For Rent." She wasn't excited about being a landlord, but she was looking for debt relief in a quick way.
>
> I called on her "For Rent" ad and we met to discuss some options. I agreed to start paying her $1,100 per month immediately (because that is what she needed to cover her expenses), and for $1,000 I bought an option to buy her home at $155,000 sometime within the next three years.
> I put about $300 into the house to fix a few things, plus I paid for a home inspection and a title search, so my costs were minimal, around $500.
>
> Two days after I signed with the owner, a Tenant-Buyer from my accumulated list paid me an option fee of $5,000 and the first month's rent of $1,195 to move in. The lease term was 18 months, and the buyout was $169,900. The lease started in March, and they have been paying early every single month. They have never called me with an issue of any kind, so it is going about as smoothly as I could ever hope.
>
> I liked this deal because the owner was very happy that I took the house off her hands, and she always receives rent from me by the first of the month. The Tenant-Buyers were very happy because they were able to get themselves and their three children from an apartment into a nice house on an acre of land. This is a "win" for

me also because I made money on the front end, $95 monthly cash flow, and the whole deal will make over $16,000. Not bad for my first deal.

—Steve Giroux, Michigan

Lease Option Case: Rance and Ryan's Buyers Provide Cookies

This is a fun story from two of my students who got off to a great start on their first Lease Option deal. They did such a great job that their buyer has bought additional properties from them and even sends them Christmas cards and cookies! Here's how they told it:

We attended your seminar on Lease Options in Seattle. Within one week of your seminar, we located a vacant rental in a nice Seattle neighborhood and were able to negotiate a Lease Option with the seller. We put the home under contract to purchase it for her full asking price of $175,000. We were willing to pay $190,000 but did not need to go that high. We agreed to pay $1,000 down, payable in 90 days or when we found a tenant. We negotiated 100 percent of our $900 monthly payment going towards principal reduction. We had three years to cash her out.

We sold it on a one-year Lease Option in about 10 days for $200,000. That was a great deal for our buyers. We're confident we could have sold it for $220,000. We took $10,000 down, leaving us $9,000 after paying the $1,000 to our seller. We received $1,295 a month from our tenants with no rent credit and none going toward reducing their principal. We got a $395 per month positive cash flow for one year that added up to $4,740 plus $25,800 after one year when our tenants exercised their option.

After making $30,540 on our first deal using the strategies you taught us at a half-day seminar, we signed up for your next three-day Lease Option Boot Camp and ended up acquiring 19 more properties the following year; two of them were clients referred to us by our first buyers, who have now acquired two more properties from us. Our buyers still send Christmas cards and cookies and continue to thank us for helping them buy a home when no one would loan them money because of a previous bankruptcy.

Thank you for sharing your Lease Option strategy and inspiring us to jump out of our comfort zones.

—Rance and Ryan Barclay, Washington

Wendy's Key Note:

When buying with a Lease Option it is great to get option credits from the seller, but when you are selling it isn't recommended to give option credits to Tenant-Buyers.

Lease Option Case:
Jim Reaps What He Sows

This is a great story from one of my most successful students, Jim Aydelotte:

When I began my real-estate investing business in 2006, my education consisted of some training materials doing other types of deals, and there was no one in the area that I lived in to seek help or network with. But 5 years later, and after working exclusively in creative financing with Lease Option-type deals, I learned about a REIA group in the metro-Detroit area (over an hour's drive from me). I was so excited to attend that first meeting to see what I could learn, and network with other like-minded investors. It was there that I met Wendy.

What I learned, which has since been a HUGE blessing to me, was that Wendy Patton, not only the head of MREIA (Michigan Real Estate Investors Association), was the Lease Option Queen! WOW – that's all I needed!

I bought her course immediately, went to every meeting I could possibly go to, and began attending her bootcamps. After the very first one, I gained some of the most valuable information from the very beginning that is still paying dividends to me in my business today – many years later!

While I was doing some deals before, her teaching turned my entire business around, which helped me learn what I was doing right, but more importantly doing WRONG! That was such a major turning point for me, and I could not wait to get back out there and do deals.

I took her training and ramped up - the week after that first bootcamp – and went home and did 6 deals in 6 weeks – including the time between Thanksgiving and Christmas! The information that Wendy shared was everything and more that I needed to make real progress in my business.

One of the earliest lessons Wendy taught me was to avoid paying self-employment taxes on lease-option closings. This strategy allows the investor to place a debt instrument (i.e. – Performance Mortgage) on the property being sold for the Seller. Therefore, when the Tenant-Buyer cashes out the investor - not only does this avoid paying self-employment taxes, but the back-end profit only gets hit with long capital gains taxes which is a HUGE savings.

The first deal that I applied Wendy's strategy to was a Sandwich Lease Option deal. I took control of the property for nothing down, made $5,000 up front, cashed flow it for 26 months for $7,150 total, and the back-end profit (equity spread balance) of $13,200 – for a total profit of $25,350. But the 'cherry on the top' was that I saved over $3,200 in income taxes. 'WOW, I thought, this thing really works!'

Since I've met Wendy, my portfolio grew to 7 figures investing part-time. I cannot be more thankful to Wendy and her gracious and generous teaching and help, and it's an honor to consider her my friend.

It's been my privilege and honor to teach with, and for Wendy for several years now, and her influence in my business, and my life for that matter, has been greatly enhanced, and certainly blessed.

Wendy has been, and continues to be, one of my mentors, and the value that she has shared with me, along with so many countless others, shows her love for the business, but also for others.
Thank You Wendy!
Jim Aydelotte
www.LeaseOptionCoach.com

Jim, and his wife Kathy, have not only become successful real estate investors, but they have also become some of our dearest friends. Jim is such a great educator and investor; he does all the Lease Option coaching for my students. See my website for more information on Jim.

Lease Purchase Case: Cleberto Has Multiple Exits

This situation shows that even though Cleberto and his partner had an exit in mind when he bought the property, market conditions in combination with the nature of buying on a Lease Option opened additional opportunities. Cleberto found a property listed with a Realtor. It was in a nice area of Orlando, where he holds most of his properties. He has a good understanding of the market and home prices there. Recognizing the below market price per square foot, he followed up on this property.

It was a seven-year-old home in a nice, gated community in Orlando. It had been listed for two months at $339,000. The following drew our attention:

- *The price per square foot was below the subdivision average.*

- *MLS remarks: Motivated seller, $2,000 bonus.*

Driving by the property, we noticed a recent "For Rent" sign. Now it was becoming attractive. We figured the owners must need some cash flow soon, and we wrote our offer accordingly.

After some negotiation, the following was accepted:

- *A Lease Purchase at the $339,000 full price (to get their attention) for a two-year term.*
- *We would advance three month's rent and $2,000 of the listing agent's commission (towards purchase price). These two items would be payable to*

27

the owners within 60 days.

- *$500 in escrow (toward first month's rent).*
- *Rent of $1,895.*
- *We also requested that the $2,000 bonus offered by the owners be paid to the listing agent (that way the agent would have $4,000 of his commission paid pretty much up front).*

We had previously experienced problems taking too long to rent or rent-to-own a property and had decided for this one to have a fallback plan in case it took too long to market.

Our Lease Option plan to find a buyer was as follows:

- *Rent $1,995 (to move it fast).*
- *Option fee of $10,000.*
- *Price: $379,000 for a 12-month term or $389,000 for an 18-month term. This should give us a profit of more than $35,000 and $45,000 for the 12 and 18-month periods, respectively.*

To our surprise, along came someone offering us $2,295 for a straight 12-month lease. We accepted it because it increased our monthly cash flow by $300/month, and there was an uptrend in our real estate market. We believed that trend would continue over the next couple of years.

As the end of the current 12-month lease with our tenant approaches, the market has experienced the tremendous appreciation that we expected.

At this point, these are some of the alternatives we are considering:

- *Sell this property for at least $390,000 and realize more than $40,000 in profit. Comparables are already there to support the price.*
- *Put it back on the market as a Lease Option with a price increase of $40,000, providing a future $70,000 or more in profit.*
- *Buy it early from the owners and hold it longer. Since we would be closing earlier, we may request some breaks from them.*

—Cleberto Copetti, Florida

Subject-To Case:
Scott Finds a Deal

Scott describes his transaction in terms of the numbers as well as the paperwork involved in this Subject-To deal. He goes on to tell of his Lease Option exit with another investor. Other investors can be your best sources of deals as well as your best customers. Keep your eyes open and stay creative.

The owners bought the home new for $155,000. They had paid the mortgage down to $150,000 when we bought it Subject-To. The deal was as follows:

The purchase price was $150,000 (we took over the loan Subject-To a 6 percent interest rate). In addition, we gave them a check for $1,500 upon signing the warranty deed and we'll give them another $3,500 when the house sells with a new mortgage. We had them sign a warranty deed (notarized), seller's acknowledgment agreement (two-page disclaimer that they initial), a due-on-sale acknowledgment (telling them that the property is taken Subject-To the existing financing and could be called), a notarized general power of attorney, and a purchase and sale agreement. We recorded the warranty deed and now own the house.

Scott offered the sellers $3,500 at the point in the future when the house closes. His objective was to provide them with additional incentive to follow through with the closing. He goes on to describe the sell side to another investor. Because of the fast appreciation in this current market, he negotiated a slice of that beyond the profit that he locked in at the time.

Within one month of doing the deal, a slightly smaller house sold in the same community for $205,000.

We sold this property on a Lease Option, using your techniques, to another investor for two years with $3,000 down, a positive monthly cash flow of $150, and a sales price of $188,000. We will also receive 25 percent of anything above the $188,000 that the investor sells it for.

—Scott Teerink, Arizona

Subject-To Case:
Marti Helps a First-Time Buyer

This next case shows how an investor was able to use the Subject-To approach to create happy and satisfied buyers and sellers while creating a nice profit for herself. Note: this deal is from my first edition, but the concepts and details are the same today (just larger numbers).

In June a couple responded to my ad and asked what they needed to do for me to make their house go away. They had bought it on Land Contract (a type of seller financing primarily in the Midwest), and when they moved, they wanted to give someone else the same opportunity that they had. So, they tried renting it with the option, but even the fourth renter with $11,000 down (from an insurance settlement) didn't work out. They'd had enough. It was a mess. They took out 2,000 pounds of trash and cleaned it from top to bottom, so we wouldn't have a reason not to take it.

We took the deed (their idea!) on November 19, leased it to a Tenant-Buyer on December 15, and evicted him on February 29. My renters from South Bend moved in the same day with the idea of buying it on Lease Option. However, on March 30 we had cleaned up their credit enough that we closed their loan.

The balance on the mortgage was $46,000. We sold it for $75,000, having put $4,836.64 into the rehab, holding, and my closing costs. It appraised for $78,000. The buyers needed help with their down payment and closing costs, so they paid $78,000 which covered both. My net profit was $28,037.77.

The sellers' nightmare ended, and the buyers' dream began, and we made money in the process! The buyers had been married 16 years and had always rented because no one had shown them how they could own a home. What was great was that no one in the husband's family had ever owned a home. Don't you just love this business? Too cool!

—Marti Bentley, Indiana

Subject-To Case: John Partners

This next case shows how an investor got over the hurdle of completing his first deal by partnering with someone else. You don't have to do everything yourself. John found a good deal and shared it with some people at his local investors club. John worked with one of the investors who expressed interest in the deal. Together they negotiated the transaction, remodeled the home, and then sold it for a generous profit that they were happy to divide.

I was excited that Monday when we came back from Wendy Patton's March seminar with other speakers in Houston.

I caught up on all my work and then went to my list of For-Rent classifieds. We marked everything that was interesting and after class started calling. One house was listed way below the property tax appraisal and in a decent part of town. I got a ride to look at it, and then went to a small group meeting that the local investors club had that same night. When we talked about it, three people immediately asked to buy it. The first to speak, Kerry, signed an offer and negotiated a good price.

Six weeks later we sold it to the same contractor we used for remodeling.

Our profit, net of all costs including interest, closing, insurance, contractors, and everything else, was almost $30,000. Fidelity Title Company gave me a check for $13,845.01.

The contractor himself made another $30,000 after he finished it and retailed it through MLS a few months later.

—John Ward, Texas

Subject-To Case:
Lyle Uses Creativity and Flexibility

This next case is interesting in the various lessons that are displayed. It shows how Lyle was able to help someone even when it didn't appear to be a great deal for him personally. It highlights how investors can frequently solve a seller's problem creatively where it doesn't make sense for a Realtor to list. It also shows that the first Tenant-Buyer won't always be the one to close on the deal. Each deal takes creativity and flexibility from beginning to end.

I received a call from a Realtor I know who had a friend going through a divorce with a small child involved. Since this seller had no equity in the property, my friend was unable to help her, so she brought me in, hoping we could find a creative solution to this dilemma. We paid her $500 to help with moving expenses—she was moving back home to her parents'. These were the numbers:

First mortgage balance	*$109,000*
Second mortgage balance	*$ 26,000*
Total owed	*$135,000*
Arrearages	*$ 4,200*
Cash to seller	*$ 500*
Repairs	*$ 500*
Fair market value	*$144,000*
Gross equity spread	*$ 3,800*

The only reason we did this deal was I made the mistake of letting my heart think, not my head. It was very thin, but I felt bad for her and her daughter. If we could help her, even without any profit, we would be doing a good deed. The home was only about four years old and needed nothing other than a good exterior cleanup and carpet cleaning with minor paint touch-up in the interior. We were able to take over Subject-To, with no guarantees we could save it from foreclosure. We put it in writing that we would do the best we could, but no payments would be made until we found a buyer.

Lyle was not able to effectively use signs to advertise this house because of the homeowner's association restrictions. By running an ad, he found a couple who wanted to buy on a Lease Option. The terms for his Tenant-Buyer were as follows:

- Purchase price (within two years): $149,900.

- Option fee: $5,000. The Tenant-Buyers paid Lyle $3,000 down and an extra $500 for four months. He applied all of this money toward the arrearages.

- Monthly rent: $1,495 with monthly cash flow of $50.

Lyle continues to the outcome of this case:

> *This buyer was in the property for about 16 months when the husband lost his job. They knew the terms and they agreed to vacate the property peacefully, leaving all their money on the table. This is a very important point: Make sure you have good, strong paperwork for Tenant-Buyers (like Wendy's courses). We went back in and cleaned up the property and decided to sell outright because our market had turned into a strong seller's market.*
> —*Lyle Reichenbach, Arizona*

Lyle's seller was able to rid herself of a difficult situation that would have required her to pay money out of her pocket in order to sell conventionally. She was able to avoid foreclosure and move on with her life. His Tenant-Buyers were able to build their credit as they worked toward owning a nice home that otherwise would not have been available to them.

Lyle was able to take control of a nice property and market it for very little cash out of pocket. He ultimately sold it for a profit of $28,000 after managing it for less than two years.

These stories are just a small sampling of transactions completed by investors who have used the techniques described in this book to raise their income levels while creatively solving problems for buyers and sellers. The first step in this rewarding process is to find motivated sellers. That's where we're heading in the next few chapters.

Most of these people started out exactly where you are. You can realize the same type of success and find the same types of deals. These success stories are from some of the hottest and strongest markets in the country, and these people have been successful with the techniques that you will learn about in this book.

Congratulations on starting today toward your Future Financial Freedom—FX3.

How can I learn more about Lease Options?

If these stories piqued your interest and you're ready to learn more about Lease Options – I have compiled my knowledge and experience into two much more detailed Courses "Buying with Lease Options" and "Selling with Lease Options." All my courses have the contracts you will need, audio training, step-by-step instructions on how to use the technique, filled out example contracts, and much more. You can find all my courses on: WendyPatton.com

PART 2

STEPS TO BUYING PROPERTIES ON LEASE OPTIONS AND SUBJECT-TO DEALS

CHAPTER 3

Finding Motivated Sellers for Lease Options and Subject-Tos

Motivated sellers are out there in every city, every town, every state. Finding a seller who will work with you on a Lease Option or Subject-To isn't as difficult as it might seem—if you know which techniques work to attract their attention.

For Lease Options, I recommend looking for motivated sellers with nicer homes that require little or no work. This way you spend less time working on the house and less time working to find a good buyer. It's also a lot more fun to work on nicer homes for more profit than on dumpy homes in rough areas for less profit—especially when you can buy the nice ones for little or no money down. Also, primarily with Lease Options, this is key because you do not own the home yet and putting a lot of money into a home you don't own could be risky. The other thing I consider is the price point of the property. With over 35+ years of investing, one thing I have found to be true with my properties; The lower the price point, the less likely a Tenant-Buyer will close. The *higher* the price point, the *more* likely a Tenant-Buyer will close. This is probably because the Tenant-Buyer in the *lower* price point is more likely to have a "tenant" mentality and not a homeowner mentality.

What Makes a Motivated Seller?

A person's need to sell their home can arise from a variety of circumstances and situations. These may include a job transfer, bankruptcy, foreclosure, death/family illness, moving out of the area, upgrading to a larger home, etc. However, the circumstances of the sellers may also be affected by the state of the two vying markets—buyer's and seller's—which also affect their motivation. For real estate investors it is crucial to buy homes from truly motivated sellers— sellers who have an extra urgency or need, usually financial, to sell. It's rare to get a good deal from an unmotivated seller who has no pressing reason to negotiate or give in on any part of a transaction.

There are different degrees of motivation and different reasons people need to sell their homes, but overall, there are two basic categories of motivated sellers:

1. Desperate and distressed (bad debt)—someone in trouble financially, behind on payments, going in a bad direction, lost their job, going through a divorce, delinquent property taxes, foreclosure, and so forth. These types of sellers are better for Subject-Tos, or other outright cash purchase offers.

2. Not desperate or distressed (good debt)—someone not in trouble financially or behind on payments, but motivated for *other reasons*: two house payments, inherited

a home, burned-out landlord, job transfer, moving out of the area, etc. These types of sellers are good for Lease Options *or* Subject-Tos.

Most real estate investors only go after the first category of sellers, but there is also huge profit potential with sellers that fall in the second category. Generally, Lease Option sellers should be people in the second category, while Subject-To sellers will be part of either category, though this is not a concrete rule. In this chapter we will discuss how to find motivated sellers of both types. In Chapter 4 you will learn the appropriate *techniques* to use for each kind of seller.

A final factor likely to affect a seller's levels of motivation is the state of the economy itself.

What You Need to Know about Buyer's and Seller's Markets

The economy plays a big role in finding motivated sellers no matter where you are in the country. I discuss this further in Chapter 6, but for now it is important to understand how the economy affects motivated sellers.

First let's define these two terms:

1. A *buyer's market (slower market)* is one in which real estate is not moving very quickly. There tends to be little or no appreciation, and possibly even depreciation. Sellers tend to be more open-minded about creative ways to sell their homes. There also tends to be higher unemployment in the surrounding area, longer average time on the market, less new construction, and overall, not a very good economy.

2. A *seller's market (faster market)* is one in which available real estate is moving very quickly. There tends to be high appreciation. Sellers may be getting multiple offers in one day on their homes, and bidding wars are common. There tends to be a low unemployment rate in the surrounding area, short time on the market, lots of new construction, and an overall good economy.

When the market is very strong (seller's market), people can sell their homes more easily, even if they are in the "desperate and distressed" category. In a buyer's market, it is more difficult to sell a home. No matter what kind of market, motivated sellers are always available; You just need to look harder, and you might find fewer in a strong seller's market, whereas they're much easier to find in a strong buyer's market.

Techniques for Finding Motivated Sellers

The kind of motivation you are looking for is not just someone wanting to sell their house, but someone who needs to get rid of their debt. These sellers won't come knocking on your door however, nor are they ever real obvious. You should try several different approaches and determine what works best in your area. It's a bit like fishing: Try a spot and a lure and see if they work. If they don't work, move to a different spot and try a new lure. Here are some tools that have worked for my students and me over the years:

- Bandit signs. These are the small signs you often see on street corners or telephone poles around your city. They are called *bandit signs* because in many cities posting them is illegal and you can be fined, but investors still put them out and risk incurring a fine for the sake of the potential profit of a deal they may bring. The signs might say, "Cash for Your Home," "Stop Foreclosure," etc. An advantage of buying a house on a busy street is the ability to advertise with a bandit sign in your own yard, which is generally legal (check your city ordinances). An investor I know who owns 30 houses in a subdivision deliberately bought the one on the busy entrance corner so that she could advertise on the lawn and pull people back into the subdivision to look at the other homes. Many companies make these signs, and they are not expensive, so if someone removes them or they blow away, it's not a great loss. There are HOA (Home Owner Association) rules that might restrict these types of signs, however they are an option to explore.

- Social Media Ads. With social media ads you can target certain criteria (behind on payments, probate or back taxes). I am not a social media expert, but there are tons out there and you should seek them out to see if this is a way you will try to find motivated sellers. Lots of wholesalers find leads online.

- Word of Mouth. There isn't much out there stronger than word of mouth for me. People *know* I am a real estate investor—People in my real estate office, my neighbors and of course my entire real estate investor group www.MichiganRealEstateInvestors.com. The people who tend to bring the most deals are from investor groups, especially the wholesalers. They run across deals all the time that don't fit their criteria for enough profit. Get on their lists, get to know them, tell them you are also looking for prettier deals or tighter deals then other investors might consider, IF, the sellers can consider creative financing like a Lease Option or Subject-To. My top 2 deals ever have come from real estate agents in my office in Michigan. Deals they didn't know what to do with or who to sell them to. Although those were cash deals, I ended up borrowing 100% of the money from other people. In other words, keep your eyes peeled for any type of "deal" as there is always a way to make it happen.

Ready to dive in?

If you're ready to learn more about how to get started with a Lease Option/Subject-To coach, you can visit my website at WendyPatton.com. If you have any questions, email me at Info@WendyPatton.com

- <u>Tear-off flyers</u> posted in public places like local drug stores, convenience stores, party stores—wherever you can get them posted. Yes, these are old–school, but they seem to still be hanging around in some places. These flyers can say the same things as the bandit signs and ads. The tear-off parts should have your phone number, your web address, and a short statement like "We Buy Houses." Better yet, put a QR code on them to lead them to a website. It might sound out-of-date, but this works and it is *free*!

- <u>Letters to Realtors.</u> Inform Realtors about what type of homes you buy and how you can help them sell their listings. This is one of my favorite ways of finding deals, however, it works much better in a buyer's market. I discuss working with Realtors in more detail in Chapters 10 and 11.

Ads to Attract Motivated Sellers

The ads below can be posted in Craigslist (not as before, but try it), social media, etc. *This* ad will draw in sellers who are considering something long term and those who want to rent their homes out.

> Company looking for 3-4 homes in this area for long term lease or purchase. Call 123-456-7890.

In other words, people who respond to this ad are ready to do the most important part of a Lease Option—lease—and to do it for a long period of time. This type of person does not need any cash out or they would not respond to this ad. The ones we're looking for are those who have been unable to sell their home, so they are willing to consider the four-letter word: rent. At the end of this chapter is a script that I use when calling about "for rent" ads.

> Executive looking in this area to lease-to-own a nice home. Call (123) 456-7890.

This ad will draw in the people who own nicer homes and who will more likely be Lease Option sellers than Subject-To sellers. Regarding the wording of the ad, we are executives in this business, right? I am, and hopefully you are too, so there is nothing dishonest in putting it this way. However, these sellers will naturally assume you are looking to live in the property yourself. Later, you will need to break the full facts to them. This is covered in Chapter 6 in a discussion about handling sellers' objections.

> Home not selling? We can help! We buy and lease homes. Call (123) 456-7890.

This ad will bring in sellers who are starting to get very motivated. These may be people who are behind on payments, or they may be getting motivated for other reasons. They could be either Lease Option or Subject-To sellers.

> Stop Foreclosure! Behind on payments?
> Don't lose your equity. We can help!
> Call us today! (123) 456-7890

This last ad brings in sellers in foreclosure and much more desperate circumstances. It is a stronger ad. This will be used to draw in Subject-To sellers only, sellers with bad debt. We will only buy Subject-To when a seller has bad debt—this is discussed in Chapter 4.

- **Letters in response to "For Sale by Owner" (FSBO) postings.** Many times, FSBOs (individuals selling their home without the assistance of a Realtor) think it will be easy to sell their own home. However, when they start to deal with buyers, lenders, title companies, and so on; it can become overwhelming. At that point they can start to get motivated to sell quickly. It is not always easy to sell by yourself. Many investors work with FSBOs (pronounced "fizz-bows") in buying deals. According to the National Association of Realtors (NAR), in 2021 a FSBO typically sold for 32 percent less than if sold through a Realtor, so that's a significant savings to the investor.

- **School directories, church flyers/directories.**

- **Long-term Multiple Listing Service (MLS) listings.** If you are not a Realtor, you can hire one to do a search for you of listings on the market over 90 or 120 days old. These sellers are getting motivated because their homes are taking longer to sell. Also, have a Realtor check for all the expired listings. You may be noticing that I mention working with Realtors a lot. I think becoming a Realtor is a smart move for investors. If you want to know more about that, feel free to email me: info@wendypatton.com as there are options out there for real estate schools and I would love to help you along that journey.

- **Business cards.** Your card should say that you buy or lease homes and give information about how to reach you, including your web site, etc.. With that said, I want to share that I have never had an investor website or given a business card to any owners; other than my Realtor, if the lead came from another Realtor. So don't get hung up on this one, but it *can* help share with others what you do.

- **Out-of-state owners.** Many cities have services that allow you to find all out-of-state owners, or houses where tax bills are sent to addresses other than the property itself (non-owner occupied). Because out-of-state owners are far away from their property, they may want to get rid of the faraway headache and move on with their lives. Also, they may not really know what the current market is anymore. If this information is only available to Realtors, then this would be another reason to consider getting your real estate license.

- **Vacant homes** are an indication that someone is making a payment on a home that is not being used. Write the owner a letter. You can send it to the vacant house and hope it gets answered, or you can try to find the owner through the post office, through township tax rolls, or by hiring a private investigation skip-trace service. Skip-trace services are great ways to find not only potential sellers but, later, missing tenants who owe you rent. These searches can be fairly inexpensive—check around for a good company that gives good prices and reliable service—Ask for a recommendation from other investors or a place that does background checks. You'll start to hear a few names again and again, and you'll be able to make an informed choice.

- Through <u>real estate investor clubs</u>, you can find other investors with homes they haven't sold and want to sell. Network and let others know what you do. I have bought several very good deals from other investors, either because they had their hands full at the time with their own deals, or the properties were out of their area. You should be a member of a local real estate investor club and regularly attend meetings. It is one of the best places to network. Of course, if you are in Michigan come meet me at: <u>www.MichiganRealEstateInvestors.com</u>.

- <u>Corporate relocation departments</u> have an inventory of homes that have not sold. If the company does not do a corporate buyout, the owners would be great candidates for a Lease Option. They have already relocated and need to have someone in that home and making payments.

- <u>Property managers</u> have knowledge about clients who are interested in selling. Normally the property manager is a Realtor and would receive a commission for selling a home they manage. But remember, if they sell a home out of their inventory, they also lose the monthly lease income. Be sensitive to this and figure out how to get them what they need also.

- Your <u>local chamber of commerce</u> can tell you what businesses are leaving town, who is coming in, etc. If you have a large number of properties, they might list you as a rental company and refer incoming people in the area to call you.

- <u>Word of mouth</u>. After you have been in this business and networked for a few years, you will start to find deals coming to you by word of mouth. Someone knows someone who knows that you buy homes. I have bought some of my most profitable homes by word of mouth.

Motivated Landlords

Landlords can be great motivated sellers, especially if they are burned out. If the economy is slow, they might have higher vacancies than in a fast or hot market. In my experience, I have found there are two basic types of burned-out landlords. The first type has watched a lot of late-night TV and decided to make millions in real estate. Unfortunately, many people buy real estate with no knowledge or experience, thinking they know it all after hearing a high-powered, adrenaline-rush sales pitch. There are, however, many state and federal laws that regulate this business. This type of landlord will fall for the professional tenants and their stories and experience, and often end up getting burned. Understanding how to screen tenants and select them is key not only to being a good landlord, but also the business of selling by using Lease Options. By being a member of a local real estate group, you can get the education and assistance you need to be successful as an investor. If you want to find a group in your area you can check the National Real Estate Investors Association web site. See the Resources section in the back of this book for a group in your area.

The second type of landlord is more tired than burned-out. These landlords are retiring and ready to move on with their lives. They don't need the money from the sale of a home, and in many cases, they don't want to receive it all at one time. They usually have huge capital gains to contend with and may not want to pay those gains yet, or they may want to plan for a 1031 exchange. * By optioning their home to you, they might be able to better plan for a 1031 tax-deferred exchange. There are sellers who will sell to you on an option to avoid the taxes now but gain the benefits of renting their homes. With this solution they can benefit from cash flow and avoid the other issues of being a landlord that they don't like.

When I purchase a home from a landlord, one of the benefits to him or her is that I usually assume the maintenance on the home or ask them to assume the expenses above $500 (Less than $500 I pass on to the Tenant-Buyer later on). I also take responsibility for the advertising, vacancies, showings, and so on. You can be very creative when structuring a deal with an owner of a home. The benefits for a landlord include but don't have to be limited to:

- *Maintenance*. Sellers don't have to deal with issues and calls. Even if they pay a portion of the costs, I handle the work.
- *Showings*. Sellers never have to show the home again. I do the showings, take the calls, and discuss the home with all prospective tenants.
- *On-time rent*. They don't have to worry about the tenant paying each month. Their rent check comes from me, *regardless of whether the tenant has paid me on time*. My payment is good and on time each month.
- *Advertising*. They don't have to advertise the home anymore. I pay for all the advertising, if any, and handle all the calls.
- *Vacancies*. They don't have to worry about vacancies anymore. I will pay whether the home is vacant or not. (You can negotiate this if the seller is willing—i.e., you have one-month free rent in each X any number you choose) months of the lease if you don't have it occupied. It is all negotiable. X meaning 12 month, each year, etc.

*A 1031 exchange is an IRS section that allows a person to exchange their "like kind" property for another property of equal or greater value, and therefore defer (not avoid) the capital gains on the first property. For instance, if a seller has a home that they bought 10 years ago for $180,000 and it is now worth $240,000, and they have depreciated the property from $180,000 down to $140,000, then they would need to realize a $100,000 gain ($140,000 value less the depreciated value of $40,000 equals $100,000 of gain). This would be a long-term capital gain, but with a 1031 the gain could be put off into the future.

Technically it would partially recapture depreciation for the $40,000 and the rest would be long term capital gains—But work with a CPA to make sure this is handled properly.

These benefits alone will allow a landlord to feel comfortable with selling, but also with taking in less rent than they usually charge. Talk to them about these benefits to help them see the advantage in leasing the home to you with an option. They now have fewer headaches, less overhead, and fewer fees and expenses, so they can *afford* to lease it for less. Then, because you are making a lower payment to the seller, you can also rent it to someone and have cash flow.

How to Evaluate Seller Ads

Besides *placing your own ads* to attract sellers, you can also *answer sellers' ads*. In Lease Options I find that most sellers need or want their cash out. The best way to find a seller for a Lease Option is not the FSBO section, but the "for rent" section. Your goal is to turn the landlord into a seller.

Wendy's Key Note:

One trick to finding motivated sellers is to take the current real estate ads and file them for a month. After a month, start calling those sellers. If their homes are still available, then they are getting more motivated. The longer a home sits, the more motivated they become.

The reason I don't call on ads in the "for sale" section is that 90 percent of those sellers must get their cash out and most of the other 10 percent won't consider something creative. It is not because they don't want to consider something creative—they would just prefer to cash out and be done with the property. Also, trying something unique will scare most sellers. Call the ads that are for rent, because the two main obstacles have been resolved: 1) These owners apparently do not need to sell or to cash out of the home, and 2) they are obviously willing to lease it.

With this said though, some people do have a lot of success with calling FSBOs.   Jim Aydelotte does well with this strategy.

How to Navigate Successful First Contacts with Sellers

The most effective way to contact sellers is by calling them. Immediately tell them your name to start building rapport and try to keep your voice calm and soft. Be sure to ask questions appropriate to the area you are calling. What is important to that part of the country? A basement? A pool? A fenced yard? A certain type of landscaping? Updated kitchens or bathrooms?

When you begin to regularly respond to seller ads, consider setting up another cell phone line just for your real estate investing. We'll call that the "Bat Phone", because when it rings it is a real estate deal! I prefer that callers reach a live person, so if they call my office; they get someone live. If they call after hours, they get a referral to another number where they can get a live person. However, if this is not feasible for you, be sure to check your messages frequently and return calls promptly. There are also <u>answering services</u> that answer 24/7 and will ask the questions you want to ask sellers. They do the prescreening and send you the details. You can then follow up on those that seem the most motivated. This is a great way to leverage your time when you grow your business. When you start out though, I do recommend getting the experience of answering the calls and asking the questions yourself. You can then create the guide for the 3rd party to use when answering those calls.

The third party will text or email you the responses so you can follow up when you have time. Time is of the essence though, with motivated sellers. If they called you, they are likely calling others until they get an answer.

The following script can be useful when calling the owner of a rental home. The bold words are what you say to the owner. Don't waste the seller's time asking questions that are answered in the ad or from their opening description, but *do* ask questions applicable to your area of the country, such as whether it's in a flood area, whether it has central air, whether it has ever had termites, how old the roof is, etc. You don't want to ask too many "owner" type questions until you get to that point—remember, you are calling on a *rental*. Ask whatever might be of interest to you and find out as much as you can about the home. Questions get someone talking if they are motivated. They also build rapport with the seller. This is a key to getting in the door and working out a deal—Building rapport and trust.

Hi, my name is_____. I'm calling about your home for rent. Can you tell me if it's still available?

Giving your name sounds warmer and will help put the owner at ease with you. It is a way to begin building rapport. I also use my friendliest voice for this call.

When is it available?

Can you tell me a little about the home?

Let them volunteer some information about the home or ask them to expand on some of the information in the ad. Remember, you are building rapport with the owner. You talk a little bit to let *them* talk. People warm up when they are the ones talking. Listen and sound interested.

When was the home built?

This question gives you an indication of any decorating or maintenance problems you might run into, such as the need for updates. If the house is older, ask the next question below; if not, skip to the one after.

Have the kitchen and bath(s) been updated since it was built?

If it was built in the 1970's, I often ask if the baths or kitchens are yellow/green/brown or if they have been updated. If the pictures or description show updated, don't ask if it has been updated. You can ask something more like:

I see by the photos/description (whichever it is*) **that the bathroom/kitchen** (whichever it is) ***has been updated, is that right?***

Does it have a garage or basement?

(Again, assuming that the description doesn't answer these questions, or the pictures aren't clearly showing the answer)

Is the yard fenced?

This may prompt them to ask whether you have pets. At this point they still think you are the one who will be living there. I don't change that perception until enough rapport and trust have been developed (at least with this script and approach). They may ask how many people will be living in the home. In such cases I don't want to lie but I don't want to be totally direct either. If you say, "I don't know, I'm going to rent it to someone else," you can be almost certain they will not show you the home. When this does come up, it is actually a perfect time to tell them you won't be living there, but *without* saying, "I don't know yet I won't be living there. I am subletting it." Here is how I would consider responding to them.

Well, I work with many families in the area to find nice homes to live in and yours sounds like such a nice home. It is a really nice home, right?

Then they will say, "of course it is", or something similar. This is when you move directly into your next question. In other words, you are changing the subject, but you just informed them you won't be living there. If the home sounds like something you would like to own, then pop the question. If it doesn't, just be polite and say you will call back later if you are interested.

Wow, this home sounds really nice, would you consider selling it?

If they say no, then say, **Thanks. I'm really looking for something I can buy with a lease-to-own or Lease Option**. Leave them your name and number so they can contact you later if they change their mind about selling. If they say, "yes" they are interested or they would consider it, you can ask the next question or ask the question after it about coming to see it.

Do you know how much you would want for the home?

Start to feel out the owner for the type of terms they would consider but be careful not to make any verbal offers. This isn't the time for negotiation—you are still just gathering information. Construct your offer later when you are not on the spot (unless you really know the market and are comfortable discussing those details). For me, I like to build more rapport in person, as I have found that people who like you will give you better terms and pricing. Building rapport will be a key part of being an investor.

When could I come and look at the home to see if I would be interested in it?

Make arrangements to go as soon as possible. This shows the seller that you have more than casual interest in the property. Set an appointment and keep it. If you must change your schedule, be sure to let the seller know ahead of time and make alternate arrangements for as close to the original date as possible. This courtesy will also demonstrate your genuine interest. Then be on time! There is nothing that tells someone you aren't going to do what you say than to be late for the first meeting.

My friend, and business partner Mark Jackson from the UK will show up at the front door exactly on time and say something like, "Hi, you must be _____, I'm Mark Jackson. We have an appointment at ____." He would then tap his watch to indicate a non-verbal indication that he is on time. Even before he shows up for his viewing, he might, when in contact with them, bring up some reason to call again, and at a specific time. When he calls them, he would say, "Hello _____, I told you I would call you back at 1pm today and it's 1pm. Is this a good time to talk for you?". Why would Mark demonstrate both displays of being on time? It's all about trust. The seller is going to have to trust you to pay them, or better yet, their mortgage payment. Trustworthiness and rapport start very early in these discussions, and he leverages those moments from the very beginning to tell the owner/seller that he does what he says and when he says. I love this idea and he's right. Imagine if he was late when he called, or missed the call and was late to the showing? What does that tell the seller?—He might not be trustworthy, or he might be late on his payments.

You have now called sellers, had sellers call you, and perhaps you've accumulated some leads to pursue. (like the rhyme?) Now it's time to go look at the homes, continue to build rapport with the sellers, and gather more information. In the next chapter, you will learn more about which technique to use for each motivated seller you have found.

CHAPTER 4

Lease Options versus Subject-Tos: Choosing the Right Technique for the Right Situation

Acquiring investment real estate can be handled with many different approaches. Two very popular zero-down approaches are Lease Options and Subject-Tos (also referred to as "getting the deed").

Wendy's Review of Lease Options and Subject-To's

A *Lease Option* is a technique that involves gaining control of a property, but not ownership—it is the right to take responsibility for a property and potentially purchase that property at some future date with defined terms. In simpler terms a Lease Option gives you the right and privilege to, but not the obligation to purchase.

A *Subject-To* involves getting the deed to a property without taking on a new mortgage. Instead, the seller signs over the deed to their home "Subject-To" their existing mortgage. The buyer makes the mortgage payments on the seller's existing loan but does not take out a *new* mortgage to acquire the home. It is not a formal assumption through the bank either.

Both techniques usually require little or no money down. In both, it is possible for the buyer to get money from the seller or the purchaser (or both) at the beginning of the transaction. These techniques, when used properly, can result in large profits for the real estate investor. They are very effective individually and, when used hand-in-hand by investors, are an almost unbeatable pair!

Knowing when to use which technique is important. Many times, investors try to fit one technique into every situation, which can be a very dangerous approach. Choosing the right technique—Lease Option or Subject-To—for your seller's situation can save you tens of thousands of dollars and protect not only you but your Tenant-Buyer as well.

To make a wise choice, you must have a clear understanding of two critical factors:
1. What type of motivated seller you are dealing with?

2. The techniques of Lease Options and Subject-Tos and how they best suit your seller—and you.

Know the Seller Situation

Finding a motivated seller is the first step to any good real estate deal. We tend to think of motivated sellers as people who are financially distressed, but I like to look at motivation through a wider lens. I like to divide motivated sellers into two groups:

1. **Sellers who have bad debt. Solution: Get the deed Subject-To—*no* Lease Option.** When I say no Lease Option, I mean rarely a Lease Option. When you are more advanced in understanding all the risks and solutions, you can figure out a different way to structure a Lease Option.

2. **Sellers who have good debt. Solution: Lease Option OR get the deed Subject-To.**

Sellers who have bad debt are generally in trouble financially. They might be behind on a mortgage, out of a job, down with an illness, in the middle of a divorce, etc. In these situations, *you need to get the deed,* with either a Subject-To or an outright purchase. Your main concern is that this type of seller may continue to have financial problems that could affect the title to the property if the deed is still in their name. For example, any judgments or debts against such a seller can attach to any *real estate* the seller owns—and those judgments or debts would have to be paid off before you could exercise your option to buy. That's why you want to get this type of seller off the title. Otherwise, *their* future problems could easily become *your* future problems.

Sellers who have good debt are not in trouble in the traditional sense, but they do have a reason motivating them to sell. Their problem is not financial desperation—it's simply a change in their lives. They might be transferring to a new location for a promotion, getting married (each owning their own home), building a new home, burned out on being a landlord, etc.

Once you've determined what type of motivated seller you are dealing with, the next step is to determine which technique, Lease Option or Subject-To, best suits both your own circumstances and those of the seller.

The rest of this chapter discusses the advantages of Lease Options and Subject-Tos, the risks of each, the types of sellers that will accept these techniques, the benefits to the sellers, and a comparison of the pros and cons of each strategy.

Subject-To Advantages for the Investor

Subject-Tos have at least eight advantages. Some are the same as for Lease Options.

1. Minimum or zero down. Usually, you only need to pay the seller a small amount to sign the deed over to you. It's even possible that, if they owe more than you are willing to pay, they may pay *you* to take the deed from them. Of course, this will also depend on what type of market you're in, buyer's or seller's, and their mortgage/lien situation on the home.

2. No financing required. When you do a Subject-To, you don't need to get a mortgage because you are taking over the seller's mortgage payments. Technically, you are not *assuming* the seller's mortgage. You are just making the payments on their existing mortgage.

3. Ownership. The day the seller deeds the property to you it is yours. You are the true owner of the home.

4. No qualifying. If you buy a home traditionally, you must go to a bank or mortgage company and qualify for a loan. Not so with these techniques. Also, you likely will take over an owner-occupied interest rate which is lower than an investor interest rate.

5. No income or credit checks. Not once has a seller ever asked to look at my income or check my credit. They are more concerned about *their* situation and how to get help from you.

6. You can buy them with your IRA. A few companies handle self-directed IRAs. If you use your IRA for the option payment, the rent payment and any other income goes back into the IRA. Remember, the income from a Roth IRA is tax-free for life. You can also do a Subject-To with your IRA when there's a mortgage already in place. Note, there are some things to learn about Subject-Tos and taking on debt with these types of deals. UBIT is a special tax for IRAs. Talk to your self-directed IRA company on how to handle this and how, and when, it applies to your personal deals. This book won't go into that in detail, but you can talk to your tax advisor and do your own

research.

7. <u>Great return on your investment (ROI).</u> Your ROI will be very large when you are making money and it didn't cost you much.

8. <u>The seller will love/appreciate you.</u> You will be making a positive difference in someone's life when you help them solve their problem.

Subject-To Risks and How to Avoid Them

The biggest risk for a Subject-To is the due-on-sale clause. This clause is a provision in the mortgage documents that says if the home is sold or transferred, the mortgage will be paid in full, or the lender <u>could </u>call the loan due in full. Notice the word: <u>could</u>. This does not mean it *will* be called due. This means that when the sellers deed the home to you, the lender *can* demand payment in full on the loan. However, if you make the payments on time, most lenders will never know the seller transferred their title to you and are mainly concerned with receiving their regular loan payments in full, and on time.

In a rare occurrence, a lender may, for whatever reason, choose to call the loan due on a property transferred Subject-To, instead of continuing to receive payments from an investor. You should disclose this risk to a seller and be prepared to refinance the existing mortgage in the unlikely event this happens. In my Subject-To course, I have over twenty acknowledgements the seller must agree to when I purchase their home. The due-on-sale clause is just one of the items they acknowledge.

Many educators teach their students to have the owner transfer title into a Land Trust, claiming this technique will bypass the due-on-sale issue altogether. Other educators believe that if the owner is putting the property into a Land Trust just to bypass the due-on-sale clause (i.e., covering up the breach of the due-on-sale clause), the transaction could later be considered mortgage fraud. I agree with the latter. If you always use Land Trusts with your investment properties, then it would, in theory, be okay to do so with a Subject-To. Some educators think that you should be up-front with the lender and send them a certified letter stating that you are taking the property and making the payments on loan. Most lenders will still not call the loan due (why trade payments for a foreclosure?). If the bank later tries to call the loan due, you can argue that they waived their right to foreclose by not calling the loan due up front when they were made aware of the transfer of ownership. Whichever approach you use, you should consult with a qualified attorney on the issue (although it should be an attorney who attends your local REIA, otherwise they might not understand this technique). The relevance of this issue may vary from lender to lender.

A Land Trust is roughly comparable to an entity, such as a Limited Liability Company, except that it provides no liability protection. Like most trusts, there are generally three parties: the grantor, the trustee, and the beneficial owner. The grantor is the person who puts property into the trust. In the case of a Subject-To, the seller is generally the grantor. The trustee is the person in whose name the trust's property is held. The trustee is also generally the person who administers the trust (e.g., signs deed, pays taxes, etc.). The trustee is generally an individual. In most states, the beneficial owner of the trust can be the trustee of the Land Trust. The beneficial owner is the person who gets any payments or use of the property held by the trust. You or your company is normally the beneficial owner of a Land Trust in a Subject-To transaction. In addition to making a breach of the due-on-sale clause less obvious, a Land Trust might prevent transfer fees or revenue stamps (the cost of transferring a deed) in some states. This cost can be many thousands of dollars in some states. Again, consult with a competent local attorney before using a Land Trust, because trust law varies from state to state. Also, as I mentioned, some experts do not advise concealing a breach of the due-on-sale clause. You and your attorney need to jointly weigh the benefits and risks of using Land Trusts. Personally, I rarely disclose the transfer to the lender, however I do not hide it either. If it comes up in conversation with the lender, I will share the truth, but it rarely comes up and is rarely an issue.

Instead of a Land Trust, some investors use two insurance policies to help keep the deed transfer discreet. The lender generally won't know about a deed transfer unless someone tells them, and the way they often find out is when the insurance carrier notifies them of the change in ownership. Therefore, many investors keep two policies in force: first, the old homeowner's policy with the original seller, which really is not any good since the seller no longer owns the home. Keeping this policy in place simply keeps that insurer from reporting a deed change. Second, the investor purchases a policy for himself, with the net result that he makes two insurance policy payments. Obviously, if you and your attorney decide that directly informing the bank of the transfer is the best approach, there is no reason to keep the original homeowner's policy in force. I only pay for one policy and name the lender on it and the old owner as an additional insured so the bank/lender will continue to associate the policy with the old owner. Do talk to your insurance agent to help make sure the old owner won't get anything financially should the home have a huge claim. The additional insured portion just gives them the liability protection should something happen at the home, or on the property. The goal is to have the mortgage company associate the borrower on the loan with the policy in place and yet not give them any financial benefit if there were ever a claim.

In my opinion, the best way to handle a Subject-To deal is to be completely honest. Let the lender know the ownership changed. You don't have to tell them you are the new owner, but I do tell them my LLC is the new owner. Send the lender a letter (which I have in my course) informing them of the ownership change. Keep proof of the letter in your file. If the lender doesn't respond (most won't), then the law may hold that they have accepted the change by ignoring your letter. If they try to foreclose, then you may need to pay off the existing mortgage and refinance the property into your own name. Also, you can partner or borrow from someone else. If the property doesn't have enough equity to justify refinancing into your own name, then it probably is not a worthwhile deal for you. Although I typically do not do it this way, if you choose to use this approach you must be able to refinance if the lender does call the loan due. If you choose to use this approach, then confirm with a lender how long you need to have it in your name before you can officially refinance the loan.

Wendy's Advice

Don't hide things or get involved in any type of fraud. Subject-Tos are getting more attention. Do business by being honest and up-front, and without hurting anyone, and you will make money while making others very happy.

The big risk of using a Land Trust to hide a due-on-sale transfer, or of double-paying insurance for the same reason, is that if a court rules that the intent was to keep the bank from exercising its legitimate rights by hiding an important fact (the deed transfer), you can be accused of fraud (and you likely don't look good in orange). Telling the bank what you have done and being able to prove that you did so, kills any chance of accusations that you hid the transaction. No deception, no fraud.

Subject-Tos can be a most wonderful thing for some sellers, changing their life and saving their credit, but unfortunately, they can also do the opposite. Much of the paperwork that I see says, in effect, "Seller, you understand when you deed me your home that I am not guaranteeing anything!" To me, it is distinctly unethical to take someone's home without guaranteeing you can make the payment. Such so-called investors can and do get criminally prosecuted for this, and I completely agree with such prosecution. With this said, it is also very rare for anyone to have an issue with a Subject-To unless they don't pay the mortgage on time or completely took advantage of someone who didn't understand what they were doing.—Again, another reason to have the right paperwork when doing these types of transactions. These are not deals you want to just "wing".

A Subject-To can be a great way to buy property and to help many sellers who might not otherwise be able to find help. Most investors don't mean to hurt a seller, they just get in over their heads. They think that if a seller is willing to deed their home to them, it must be a good deal. Well, it might not be a good deal—check out Chapter 5 before you commit.

 Wendy's Ethics Advice

A Subject-To can really help a seller if done right, by helping improve their credit (assuming they were behind when you took it over). If done wrong, it can mess up their credit for a long time. Don't do a Subject-To if you can't commit to making the payments. Only do Subject-To's on what you can commit to, and then do what you say you will! Only do the deal if the deal is worth doing. If you are unlikely to make a profit, you are more likely to do the wrong thing and default on your solemn promise to the seller.

You might be asking yourself, what else can I do besides a Subject-To when I find a Subject-To type of seller? Well, you have three choices (the third is available only to licensed Realtors):

1.   You can buy the home outright. You must get the deed, but you don't have to do a Subject-To in order to get the deed. You *can* simply purchase the home, either for cash, seller financing, or by getting a mortgage.

2.   If the deal is very good, and you know it fits into a Subject-To and not a Lease Option, you can wholesale the deal to another investor. Wholesale means buying very low and selling low. You might sell it for a profit of $3,000 to $10,000 without ever having owned it. Normally I would choose the preceding option, but this one is a great choice for those who want quick cash. You can always find buyers for good deals at your local real estate meetings. Get a buyer's list together if you want to wholesale your leads. You can wholesale both Lease Option and Subject-To leads. Normally in a wholesale you sign a contract and then do an assignment of the contract. For example, I would tell an investor, "I have a lead, and for $XXX I will pass it on to you." I would sell the lead, rather than signing on a contract for the deal.

3.   You can also list the home for the seller and get a commission, if the seller has time for the selling process. This is a great reason to be licensed. Even if you don't ever want to list homes, being licensed allows you to refer the listing to another licensed agent for a 25-30% referral fee. Then they do all the work. If you aren't licensed in your state and want to know more about it, please email me at info@wendypatton.com to get more information. Having a real estate license has provided so many other benefits to me over the years. I highly recommend it.

Lease Option Advantages

A Lease Option has at least seven advantages:

1. <u>Minimum or zero down.</u> Whether you are buying from owners directly or through Realtors, there is little, or no money required to buy using a Lease Option.

2. <u>Little or no risk.</u> If you're buying a house using a Lease Option, you also maintain the right *not* to buy it. This, to me, is the best benefit of Lease Options. If the market goes up you can buy; if it goes down, you don't have to buy. It's your choice. If you *own* the home, you don't have this choice. You can't just give it back to the bank. And with a *Subject-To* you can't just change your mind later, because you *own* it.

3. <u>Monthly payment amount</u> (rent paid to owner) is usually significantly less than a mortgage payment would be. Typically, I like to get a rental payment for 0.5 to 0.6 percent of the value of the home per month. On a $200,000 home, that's $1,000 to $1,200 per month. If you can get that deal structured, you can get cash flow almost anywhere in the country. Now if you got a mortgage yourself on a home, and you put a lot of money down (10-20%), with non–owner occupied mortgage rates you will be closer to 1 percent per month for the same property (depending on mortgage programs and rates at the time). Example: 1 percent of $200,000 would be a payment of $2,000 per month vs the above of $1,000 or $1,200 per month. This is a huge difference!

   For instance, on a Lease Option the owner might owe $100,000 on a home that they Lease Optioned to me for $200,000, and their payment might only be $800 for principal, interest, taxes, and insurance (PITI). On a Subject-To deal, it would not be nearly that low. The seller would not normally deed the home over if they only owed $100,000. In most cases they would owe more and the payment would be higher; therefore, the investor would also be paying a higher monthly payment with a Subject-To than a Lease Option and not receiving as much cash flow.

4. <u>No qualifying.</u> In most cases you will never have anyone ask you for your income or credit information. This is done by building rapport with the seller (discussed in Chapter 6). With Realtors, however, there is a much higher chance they will want a full credit report or some kind of proof you are financially solid. This benefit is the same for a Subject-To.

5. <u>Great return on investment.</u> The return on investment should be infinite in most cases, because in most cases you would be putting little or nothing down and getting cash flow and a profit.

6. <u>You can buy them with your IRA</u>. You can buy Lease Options and Subject-Tos in your IRA. You must have a company that knows how to legally and properly invest and self-direct real estate through your IRA. I use Equity Trust, out of Ohio, but

there are other ones out there. Ask around your local REIA.

 Come See Wendy!

I am the founder of the Michigan Real Estate Investors of Southeast Michigan. If you are in Michigan, I'd love to see you! If you're able to make it, make sure to come and introduce yourself! Outside of Michigan, you can check for your local NREIA chapter at NationalREIA.org.

7. <u>The seller will love/appreciate you.</u> The seller will be thrilled that you helped them with their situation. They won't be able to thank you enough if you came up with a solution that was a win-win.

Lease Option Risks and How to Avoid Them

The biggest risk for a Lease Option is the possibility of the seller having a problem financially. Although in the beginning we only Lease Option from financially strong sellers, there are things that could go wrong in a seller's life. A Lease Option is control without ownership. Because the owner still holds the deed or title to the property, if they incur a financial problem, there is a chance the title/deed could have a lien placed on it. When certain procedures are followed, a lien can be placed on a piece of real estate if a person owes someone money. This may make it difficult for the seller to sell the home, which would be bad not only for you, the investor, but also for your Tenant-Buyer. Fortunately, there are several things you can do to assist in preventing the repercussions of these risks on you as the buyer.

First, make sure the seller is solid when doing a Lease Option with them. If they want to check your credit, ask to check theirs too. I have never checked any of my sellers' credit, but it is not a bad idea. You can also have a private investigator check them out if you aren't sure. Almost all our personal and financial information is public and easy for a PI to obtain. Find out where they are moving. Is it a better home? More expensive? Then you will know if they are moving up or down. Did they get a new mortgage? If yes, then their credit must be solid (at least at the time they received the mortgage).

Second, make sure you record a Memorandum of Option. This is a document that gives the world notice that you have an interest in the property. Then the seller can't refinance the home or sell it to someone else. See Chapter 7 for more information about the memorandum. Finally, focus on and pursue primarily the sellers with equity. If a seller has a lot of equity in their home, then even if something bad did happen to them, they will have some cushion to fall on.

Let's look at three scenarios:

1. The seller has $50,000 of equity and has a $30,000 lien placed on their home by the IRS. No problem—the sale will close fine. The IRS will take $30,000 and the seller will get the remaining $20,000 of equity.

2. The seller has $50,000 of equity and the IRS has a $70,000 lien placed on the home. Again, the sale will close fine. The IRS will take the entire $50,000 and the seller will still owe the IRS $20,000. The IRS does not want to stop a closing, but it will take what it is owed. You will probably have to coordinate with a title company or attorney, whoever does the closings in your state, to coordinate the payoff on the lien.

3. The seller has $30,000 of equity and has $45,000 of liens placed on them by five different individuals or companies. This one may be a problem if those five companies will not cooperate by taking a smaller amount to close out this home. In other words, most lien holders will take something now to get a partial payoff rather than nothing at all. If they are owed $10,000 on a lien, they might take $7,000 now as a full payoff, or they might be willing to take partial now with the remaining still owed by the seller. When these types of liens pop-up they usually can be resolved but it will take more work on the seller's part or, more likely on your part, to get these lien holders to cooperate. (Because of emotional tensions between the seller and the lien holders, the seller may not be the best one to negotiate with them to take a little less to make the deal close.) You might even be able to get them to take less as a full payoff—in other words, take $7,000 as full payoff for the $10,000. Either way, I have never heard of a deal where it could not work out. However, this is the risk for a Lease Option.

The worst thing I have ever had happen on a Lease Option deal was delinquent property taxes, which I knew about. There was plenty of money to pay for those at closing, and the sellers were not far enough behind to go into foreclosure over the taxes. Had they been in danger of going into foreclosure for back property taxes, I would have paid them myself or the seller would have paid them. Paying these is covered in my paperwork/contracts for Lease Options. I have provisions in my contracts for situations like these.

 Wendy's Advice on Lease Options

Only buy Lease Options from financially strong sellers. They are less likely to have financial problems down the road. Sellers with equity are the best choice because if financial problems do arise, they have some cushion to cover the problems.

Matching Motivated Sellers with Lease Options

As discussed previously, Subject-To sellers may be, though aren't always, motivated by bad debt and a desperation to restore their credit. Conversely, Lease Option sellers have debt. The sellers that would even consider a Lease Option fall into two categories:

1. Sellers who don't need their cash out of the home to move on.

2. Sellers who have no equity in their home—they are financed 100 percent (owe it all).

I prefer a seller in the first category. Why? This seller has some cushion financially if problems arise later. The second category of seller does not have a cushion, and therefore if they get into financial trouble, they're more likely to botch up the deal—either permanently or for a period until things can be resolved.

Here are five types of motivated sellers with good debt.

1. *Long-time home owners.* They usually have very low payments, if any, and usually have saved money elsewhere, which enables them to purchase another home without selling the current one. These types of sellers also have the cushion of their home equity, which will mitigate any bad luck on their part. When a seller has a low payment, it creates a good opportunity for the investor to get a lower payment also. This will be good for creating strong cash flow.

2. *Inherited property owners.* Sellers who have inherited properties also have a potential for a Lease Option sale. If there are many heirs, say five or six, for instance, it is less likely to work out as an investment or rental property because in large families there seems to always be one heir who is broke and needs the cash out. Also, when they divide the rent by five or six, the split of the money on the rental seems too inconsequential to bother with. This is why on inherited properties, I have found that cashing out the sellers (i.e., outright purchasing) is the best way with *many* heirs, whereas Lease Optioning is a possibility with a *small number* of heirs. I had one Lease Option property that the seller (one heir) had asked me several times not to pay off. My price to her had not changed. She liked the cash flow each month and didn't have to worry about maintenance or bounced checks when working with me. If the Tenant-Buyer in the home had been able to buy, then she would have cashed out. But because the Tenant-Buyer in the home couldn't get a mortgage yet, it worked out perfectly for all.

3. *New home builders.* The sellers have built or bought their new home and their old home hasn't sold yet. These sellers can afford both homes—they qualified for both—but why would they want to pay for two homes when one is vacant? As time goes on and the old home still has not sold, the seller's motivation becomes higher. This does not mean the seller *must* sell, but that they really *want* to sell or get rid of that old payment. They did not need their cash to buy the new home, and therefore are a good candidate for an option.

4. *Newly married/New move in.* The seller has recently gotten married or moved in with someone who owns a home. This seller would not need their cash out to buy a new

home, because they are living with someone who *has* a home. Since this seller could afford to pay the home payment *before* they moved in with their partner, they can certainly afford it *after* they moved in with someone. Most people don't want to pay for a home that is sitting vacant.

5. *Job transfer.* The seller has been transferred out of state. This type of seller will not necessarily need their cash out of their home (equity) because they may not be sure how long they will be in the new location, whether the job will work out, or even where they would want to live.

Subject-To and Lease Option Pros and Cons: An Overview

Let's examine the comparative pros and cons of Subject-Tos versus Lease Options.

Subject-To Pros	Subject-To Cons
Title is in your name – full ownership.	You own it and have ethical responsibility to the seller if the market changes or you can't sell the home. No changing your mind on this one.
Some sellers will pay you to take the deed.	Possible due-on-sale clause being called – therefore you might have to refinance or sell the property.
Easier to prove "seasoning of title" when you are the title holder, easer to refinance. (cont. from above)	In some states, mortgage brokers and Realtors could be fined and/or subject to revocation of their license. It could be against their code of ethics to assist a person violating a clause in contract.
If you are on the title, you will have long-term gains versus short term gains. if you hold the home for longer than 12 months. (or use a	Sellers with lots of equity will be hesitant or completely against relinquishing the deed.

Performance Mortgage)	

Lease Option Pros	Lease Option Cons
You don't have to buy later if the market drops or there is something wrong with the home. You can get out.	Title is not in your name, so you are vulnerable to seller error. You must be careful to screen the seller. Only Lease Option from strong sellers, not those in trouble or headed for trouble (unless you put the deed in a Land Trust).
More sellers will do a Lease Option rather than give up a deed – especially on nicer homes.	You will have short-term capital gains versus long-term if you are not on the title. This can be avoided if you finance it within 12 months of payments (see the pros column) – Get on the title and hold it for 12 months before closing with your Tenant-Buyer. This solution takes a *minimum* of 24-months.
After 12 months of payments, some lenders may treat a Lease Option as a refinance – as if you were on the deed. Lenders would treat it like a Land Contract refinance.	Some sellers might feel a Lease Option is not closure on their home. Alternatively, some will feel better with a deed being transferred or a Lease *Purchase* (which is a guarantee vs. an option).
Seasoning of title starts when you file a Memorandum of Option or lien of interest. Most lenders consider this adequate and similar to recording a deed (except for FHA).	
Sellers with lots of equity are	Sellers with lots of equity

more likely to give you the right to buy the home than they are to give you the deed to their home.	usually want to close and get their equity out quickly.

Putting the Techniques into Practice

Now let's see how you would apply these techniques in different situations.

An Example Where You Must Get the Deed

A seller calls you on the phone and says he is two months behind on payments. Do *not* Lease Option this home! This seller is in trouble financially and is not a good risk for a Lease Option. Anyone in a bad financial situation is usually not a good seller for a Lease Option. This is the type of seller that you must get off the title (with a deed) so that his financial situation will not affect the title to the property in the future.

Not every seller who is in financial trouble will tell you so, which is why you *always* need to do research on the title and get a current mortgage statement before you get the deed or do a Lease Option. In the case of overdue payments, you will need to bring the seller's mortgage current. You can bring their mortgage current by finding out from their lender what they owe and where/how to pay it. Before you do, you want to make sure that he is the owner of the property and that there are no other liens on the property unknown to you.

A seller calls you who owes $235,000 on his home, which is worth $235,000. Since he has no equity at all, this type of seller might be willing to give you the deed. And if there is high appreciation or a very low payment (i.e., low interest rate), you might be able to make a profit even though there's no equity. That being said, I am not a huge fan of zero equity and relying solely on appreciation or cash flow to make a deal solid, however, each deal should be evaluated on its own.

On the other hand, if the seller's payment is too high or the market is slow, you might need to have the seller *pay you* to take the deed. Yes, there are sellers who will pay you to take the deed to their home. Think about it: If this seller sells conventionally—that is, through a Realtor—he would have to pay up to $14,100 in commission to sell his home. Plus, he'll have closing costs, title fees, and will probably pay points or fees on behalf of the buyer. If he's willing to pay all this money to an agent to sell the property—and wait 90 to 120 days to sell, too—why shouldn't he just pay *you* to take over his payments *now*?

If the seller doesn't have the cash to give you, a Lease Option would be your best strategy. This way, the seller can pay you the $14,100 over time, or you could arrange for the seller to pay part of the monthly payment during the option period. This way, if he stops paying his portion of the payments, you have the choice of surrendering your Lease Option and simply giving the property back to him. If you do a Subject-To on this, you can have them pay part of the mortgage payment for a few months/years, etc.

Wendy's Tip

Just because a seller is willing to give you the deed doesn't make it a good deal. Double check the numbers and only take a deed when it is a good deal for you.

An Example Where You Should Lease Option or Lease Purchase

A doctor has a new home built for himself. His old home is worth $300,000 and he owes $225,000 (He has $75,000 of equity). He is not behind on payments and did not need the $75,000 cash-out to buy his new home. His old home is sitting vacant and is listed with a Realtor, but it's not pending/sold yet. He qualified for both house payments to purchase the new home. He can technically afford both payments, but who wants to make an extra house payment? The longer a home sits vacant and the longer the homeowner is in their new home, the higher their motivation for selling will be.

Although he is motivated to sell because he's paying out of pocket every month to own a vacant property, this type of seller is not going to simply give you the deed and let you take over the mortgage. It's unlikely he is going to give up all of his $75,000 in equity, and unlikely you are going to pay $75,000 cash out of pocket to Lease Option it.

When you Lease Option this house, he gets most of his equity back—although it won't happen until *you* sell the property (which is when you also purchase it, if you do). The deal might work like this: You Lease Option the property for $295,000 and make payments to the seller that equal his total mortgage payments. You then Lease Option the property to a Tenant-Buyer for 18 months for $329,900. You receive cash flow plus $34,900 in profit ($329,900-$295,000) when your Tenant-Buyer buys the property. The seller gets his payments taken care of and the bulk of his equity out. In the meantime, he doesn't have to worry about management, vandals, frozen pipes, or any of the other things that owners of vacant houses must deal with.

An Example Where You Could Lease Option OR Lease Purchase

The seller just inherited a property worth $220,000 from her parents' estate. It is owned free and clear, and she doesn't need the cash from a sale, though she would love some cash flow on this asset. This seller is not going to give you the deed. Let's say you can Lease Option this property for $1200 per month with $500 per month going to the purchase—or the Lease Option credit. Your real payment in this case is only $700. You also could do seller financing on this property (like a Land Contract/Contract for Deed or a mortgage with the seller).

Especially when a property is owned free and clear and the seller doesn't need their cash out, there are many options.

Conclusion

Subject-Tos and Lease Options are great techniques to help sellers in situations that might not otherwise have solutions. If you do your research on the seller and the market, and apply the right technique to the right situation, you will make a profit for yourself and at the same time help a seller who really needs you. Make it a win-win.

CHAPTER 5

Evaluating the Profitability of the Deal

Winner: Stupidest Moves Award

My investors group, from the 90s, used to give away an award called the "Stupidest Moves Award" for the person who made the most ridiculous real estate move during the year. I didn't even know this award existed until I received it one year. The *reason* I received it was because I was chatting away about my deals to other investors, and yes, I did deserve it. I received a mechanical shark, mounted on a plaque, that was devouring a large Monopoly® denomination, to depict the eating away of huge profits.

It was the early 1990s and one of my earliest deals with a Realtor. I was presented with a great deal for a $300,000 lakefront home. I felt I could rent it easily because of its price range and because it was lakefront property. Therefore, I quickly committed to start my Lease Option on October 1, whether or not I had secured a Tenant-Buyer. My rent commitment was $1,400 per month, and of course I planned to charge more in order to make cash flow. October turned into November, November into December, December into January, and January into February. Apparently, in Michigan, lakefront properties are not very desirable in the middle of winter. I finally rented it in March. In total I lost more than $7,000 plus utilities for the winter. I was paying more for a house I wasn't living in than for my own mortgage!

I could have avoided winning the "Stupidest" award by either (1) making my contract contingent on securing a tenant, or (2) waiting until spring to start the Lease Option. Lakefronts rent the best in the spring and summer in my area. People aren't crazy about moving into a property with a frozen piece of water in their backyard unless they're hockey players. I was too eager and didn't think it all the way through. Not only did I lose over $7,000 of my profit, but it was also $7,000 of cash that I paid out of pocket. Although I eventually made well over $25,000, it should have been $32,000 with much less stress. And that's how I earned the "Stupidest Moves Award" in my investment group. It's not the kind of award you want to get more than once, but everyone has a story like that in their investment portfolio. It's just part of the learning process. Hopefully this book will provide many ideas and tips for you to avoid this type of mistake. In my *Buying with Lease Options* course, I have the following paragraph in my rental agreement to prevent this from happening to you also.

Eagerness to start a deal should never outweigh the need for thoughtful preparation in evaluation of an offer. There are many sellers willing to sell on a Lease Option and Subject-To, but they must be profitable for you!

Keep an Eye on Local Real Estate Timing

Know your climate. People don't like to move in the winter in a colder climate. So, if you live in a place with bone-chilling winters, structure your deals, if possible, to start and end in the spring or summer. Also, try to work around holiday months, especially mid-November and December everywhere in the country.

Creating the Offer

Now that you've considered which technique to use, a Lease Option or Subject-To, you need to step back and take the time to work out the profitability of the deal. Normally you should not throw out numbers to the seller in the excitement of the moment. Even if you feel pressured, tell them you need to go back to your office and crunch the numbers. In the excitement of the moment, you may voice a dollar figure that doesn't include all the things you need to consider. In the quiet of your office, you will have the time to go through your own profitability worksheet, discussed later in this chapter, and make sure the numbers work for you. Negotiations and offers are an art form. Take the time to do them well. Only when you are dealing with distressed sellers who are calling every investor, do you need to move quickly on an offer.

There may, however, be situations where you'll need to respond immediately, such as in the case of a Subject-To offer on a pre-foreclosure or other competitive bidding situation. Lease Option offers, by their nature, rarely require an on-the-spot response. Therefore, you can respond according to your seller's situation.

Calculating Your Profit Requirement

As an investor, you must decide your profit requirement for any given deal. It may vary depending on the type of investment. For instance, I will accept less profit for a rehab than a Lease Option because I can be in and out of a rehab within a few months, while Lease Option transactions typically require 12 to 18 months or more. Do you require $25,000 profit, $50,000 – how much? Each of us must decide what our own bottom line is, however with this said, I would recommend you choose at least $25,000. What you think you might make in the beginning of a deal, doesn't always end up that way. Unexpected expenses or changes in the market can always affect profit. Once you determine your profit requirement, that becomes the bottom-line number that must be reachable in order to take on a property. For example, if your required profit is $20,000 and an opportunity comes along that will earn you only $18,000, then you'll need to either negotiate the terms of the deal to meet your $20,000 requirement or pass on the deal. It will not be a win-win situation for the seller *and* you if you don't follow your standards. Learn to walk away from deals that don't work for you. Alternatively, you might be able to wholesale the deal to someone else who has a bottom line that is lower than yours. I call this a *Cooperative Lease Option*, where you get out of the Lease Option deal either to an investor, or an end Tenant-Buyer. Basically, you keep the Tenant-Buyer Lease Option fee and then step out of the deal. These also work well when you have no interest in being a landlord in between. Unfortunately, this book will not cover the Cooperative Lease Option technique in detail, but you can visit my website to find out more. I have a course covering this strategy and some articles. Visit www.WendyPatton.com to find out more.

There are times when a seller will do only X, Y, and Z in terms of price, payment, and length of time. You can input those numbers into the spreadsheet in this chapter to determine if the deal meets your profit requirement. When it doesn't meet your requirements, you can negotiate a little further, as discussed in Chapter 6. Often the seller is not firmly set on X, Y, *and* Z, just X and Y; therefore, you can negotiate the Z. Chapter 6 will help you think of creative ways to help bring deals together. However, there will be some deals where you will need to just walk away. Some sellers are simply not willing to do what you need to make it a win-win; Some are not motivated enough or can't go down far enough on price because they owe too much. Wasted time is money to you, so learn to move on quickly and look for a real motivated seller.

 Is it a deal?

It is better to move on if there is no deal there. Try to negotiate to make it work but when you realize you can't make your required profit it's time to say NO or NEXT. Just because a seller says they will do a Lease Option or Subject-To doesn't mean it's a good deal. Evaluate each deal and make sure it's good for you! Many of my students have been so excited to get a "deal" that they end up being on the motivated side of the transaction. Make sure the seller is the motivated party in the deal, not you.

Profitability for Lease Options

The first thing we will do is create a worksheet for profitability for a Lease Option. We will cover Subject-To transactions later in this chapter.

Appreciation can't be predicted exactly, so you will need to estimate it. The Internet is a reliable source for the appreciation rates in your area or ask a few local Realtors. When calculating your option premium, use 5 percent in areas that are very consistent—condos, or in neighborhoods where all the homes are almost identical in size or model. If the neighborhood is very diverse, then you may use up to 10 percent, as the list of comparable properties should be there for the appraiser when you go to sell the home. By diverse, I mean acreage, water fronts, and other unique features.

Option Fee	What the Tenant-Buyer puts down to get the right and privilege to purchase the home in the future. <u>Right and privilege being the key piece of a Lease Option.</u>
Option Premium	The amount the seller can get above retail pricing because they offer terms. People, including investors, will pay a higher price when they can buy with terms. Anyone asking for seller financing will understand they don't get to negotiate price much.

You also need to determine Cash flow or rental values. You can do rental comparables just like you do sales comparables. Here are three ways to find the rental comparables:

1. Check with local Realtors/Property Managers. Check all the local rentals. Those are your "comps," or comparables when it comes to rentals.

2. Check with people in your local landlords' group. Many rentals are not on the MLS.

3. Not enough data from the first two sources? Run a test ad. Too many calls? Your price might be too low. Too few? Your price might be too high. It's a little like fishing—change the bait and see what happens.

Now let's use this worksheet to calculate profitability on three example deals.

Profitability Worksheet Lease Option		
Purchase Costs		
Purchase price		
Transactional funding fee (optional)		
Total purchase costs		
Income Sources		
Current value		
Value of Lease Option premium (5–10%)		
Expected appreciation.		
Expected sale price.		
Expected monthly cash flow.		
Total other income		
Option credits from Seller		
Expected Profit		

Example 1

Seller will sell you their home for $185,000. It is currently worth $190,000. The appreciation rate is 5 percent per year. It will be sold on an 18-month Lease Option, which will result in 7.5 percent appreciation (5 percent × 1.5 = 7.5 percent, eighteen months is 1.5 years). That gives us $14,250 ($190,000 × 7.5 percent) of appreciation value during the 18 months. You pay the owner $1,300 in rent. You can rent it out for $1,600, for a cash flow of $300 per month. I usually rent a home for $1,595 versus $1,600 ($1,595 sounds a lot better even though it's only $5 difference, making it appealing to potential Tenant-Buyers). I wrote $1,600 above because it's easier to show even numbers for each of the examples.

The homes in this neighborhood are diverse and unique. Prices range from $170,000 to $285,000. This allows us to build in a higher Lease Option premium of 10 percent, or $19,000. The $19,000 Lease Option premium and the $14,250 appreciation add $33,250 to the retail value of the home. What is your estimated profit in 18 months? Let's view how to figure out the profit of this deal:

Profitability Worksheet Lease Option	Example 1	
Purchase Costs		
Purchase price	$(185,000)	
Transactional funding fee (optional)		
Total purchase costs	$(185,000)	$(185,000)
Income Sources		
Current value ($5,000 above purchase price) Value of Lease Option premium (10%) Expected appreciation (5% annually, 7.5% over 18 months)	$190,000 $ 19,000 $ 14,250	
Expected sale price	$223,250	$ 223,250
Expected monthly cash flow ($300 per month for 18 months)	$ 5,400	
Total other income	$ 5,400	$ 5,400
Option credits from Seller ($500 x 18 months)	$ 9,000	$ 9,000
Expected Profit		$ 52,650

The resulting profit from this deal, if all payments are made during this Lease Option period and it goes the full 18 months, would be approximately $43,650, less deed transfer fees (if any), title insurance, closing costs, etc. Also, we haven't really discussed this in detail yet, but I like to get Lease Option credits each month from the seller. Example: Out of the $1,300-month rental payment, I would ask to get *up to* $1,300, but settle for less. In this example, if you were to get the seller to agree to $500 a month, then you would have 18 months X $500 = $9,000 credit off of your price with the seller. This line can be added to your worksheet for future deals. It adds $9,000 right to the bottom line. In this case the profit would be $43,650 + $9,000 = $52,650! This really affects the bottom-line profit! I LOVE asking for Lease Option credits from the seller. Does this meet your required profit? If so, then move forward with these terms in your offer or proposal to the seller. If you can't get the numbers to work, you continue negotiations on the deal or pass it up.

Example 2

Seller will sell you their home for $145,000 on a 12-month option. It is worth $145,000. The appreciation rate is 3 percent per year, which will result in an additional $4,350 ($145,000 × 3 percent) after one year. This home is in an area where all the homes are similar and range in price from $140,000 to $152,000. This results in a more modest option premium of only 5 percent, or $7,250 ($145,000 × 5 percent). The appreciation and the option premium total $11,600 ($4,350 + $7,250). Let's say you pay the owner $1,000 in rent and will in turn rent it out for $1,200. The seller is also willing to give you $200 a month credit off the purchase price.

Option credit toward buying this home. Let's look at your estimated 12-month profit:

Profitability Worksheet Lease Option	Example 2	
Purchase Costs		
Purchase price	$(145,000)	
Transactional funding fee (optional)		
Total purchase costs	$(145,000)	$(145,000)
Income Sources		
Current value	$145,000	
Value of Lease Option premium (5%)	$ 7,250	
Expected appreciation (5% annually, 7.5% over 18 months)	$ 4,350	
Expected sale price	$156,600	$ 156,600
Expected monthly cash flow ($200 per month for 12 months)	$ 2,400	
Option credits from seller ($200/month x 12 months)	$ 2,400	
Total other income	$ 4,800	$ 4,800
Expected Profit		$ 16,400

This deal would not be nearly as profitable for an investor as the one above. It would only generate $16,400 before closing costs, not leaving much room for dealing with potential problems/issues. This opportunity does not meet my minimum profit requirement. However, there are ways to renegotiate the deal with the seller. With the appreciation this low, it might be more of a buyer's market. You should be able to negotiate price and terms. Ask for a better price and for additional monthly credit towards the purchase.

You can also ask for the equity buy-down of the mortgage during the Lease Option period. Equity buy-down is what gets paid down on the mortgage during the Lease Option time period. For example, if the seller owes $100,000 on the home at the start of this option and at the end, they only owe $90,000, then you would receive the $10,000 of credit that was paid on the mortgage balance during the option period, because, in effect, you had been paying that mortgage payment during the option period. This doesn't work as well when the mortgage is new and you sell the home within 12-24 months (less going to principal), however if you have it for a longer time, I recommend adding this to your agreement. Example: if you are using Lease Options to build a portfolio then you would certainly ask the seller for an equity buy-down in the agreement (worded in my contracts the way you need it). This also works really well when the seller has had their mortgage for quite a few years (when a lot more is going towards principal).

If the seller does not agree to the additional terms, let it sit until their motivation increases enough for them to agree to terms that would make this transaction meet your profit requirement, otherwise walk away. It must meet your bottom-line number and result in a win for both you and the seller.

Example 3

Seller has a home worth $235,000 and they will sell it to you for $225,000 on an 18-month option. The appreciation rate is 5 percent per year (or 7.5 percent over 18 months), which would generate an additional $17,625. This home is in a very diverse area out in the country. The homes vary widely in square footage and acreage, and prices range from $150,000 to $450,000. These factors let us establish the option premium at 10 percent, or $23,500. The rent you pay the owner is $1,200, and the market rent you expect to receive is $1,450. The seller owes $150,000 on the mortgage and agrees to take $75,000, less closing costs, at the time of closing ($225,000 sales price less $150,000 current mortgage balance). This allows you to get the mortgage equity during the option period. The equity from the principal pay-down during this option period is estimated at about $200 per month or $3,600. What is your estimated profit in 18 months?

Profitability Worksheet Lease Option	Example 3	
Purchase Costs		
Purchase price	$(225,000)	
Transactional funding fee (optional)		
Total purchase costs	$(225,000)	$(225,000)
Income Sources		
Current value (10k above purchase)	$235,000	
Value of Lease Option premium (10%)	$ 23,500	
Expected appreciation (5% annually, 7.5% over 18 months)	$ 17,625	
Expected sale price	$276,125	$276,125
Expected monthly cash flow ($250/month for 18 months)	$ 4,500	
Option credits from seller ($200/month x 18 months)	$ 3,600	
Total other income	$ 8,100	$ 8,100
Expected Profit		$ 59,225

Note that no commissions are paid to Realtors in these examples. Working with Realtors is discussed in Chapters 10 and 11. However, if you are paying any Realtor commission or option fee up front to your seller, you will have some out-of-pocket costs. This will not affect your bottom-line profitability, as option fees are applied to the purchase price at closing, but it *will* affect your up-front cash out-of-pocket expenses.

Which of the three scenarios will get you to financial freedom? The answer is that they all can, if you do them correctly. The second one would probably require changes from the seller to make it work better for you.

The primary profit source is the back end—the difference between the purchase price and your selling price, which is realized at closing at the end of the Lease Option period. When you're first starting out, you might deal with smaller back ends. That's fine—those deals help you learn the business. As you become more skilled in working with options you will find more ways of improving the numbers to get you higher returns that are still a win-win. Obviously, the higher the back end, the easier it will be to begin working your way towards your financial goals.

Wendy's Tip

There are always unexpected costs in any deal. Therefore, I like to make sure that I have extra profit built into any real estate transaction. Always plan for something that could go wrong—someone who won't pay rent, a furnace that goes out, a roof that leaks, a septic field that fails, etc. Plan for the worst and you will be safe.

Profitability for Subject-Tos

Subject-To transactions are like Lease Options except you will be taking *over* a loan balance and possibly other liens or back taxes. Once you complete a Subject-To negotiation, you will be done with the seller. You'll have the deed to the property, and you won't close with the seller the way you do with a Lease Option. The worksheets seem more complex and there are more numbers to fill in, but they are essentially not much different than Lease Options.

As with a Lease Option deal, you will need to determine whether a Subject-To deal is profitable enough to consider. You must run the numbers. Here is an example of a profitability spreadsheet for a Subject-To deal.

Profitability Worksheet Subject-To		Totals
Purchase Costs		
Balance owed on first mortgage	$	
Balance owed on second mortgage	$	
Back payments and liens (Up-front cash requirement)	$	
Transactional funding fee (optional)	$	$
Total debt owed on property	$	$
Income Sources		
Current value	$	
Value of Lease Option premium (5–10%)	$	
Expected appreciation	$	
Expected sale price	$	$
Expected monthly cash flow	$	
Additional principal from mortgage Payments during option period	$	
Escrow balance	$	
Total other income	$	$
Expected Profit		$

In addition to the elements of the Lease Option worksheet, this worksheet asks for information about the balances on the loans, other liens, principal of the mortgage during the option period, and escrow balance. The principal on the loan is negotiable on a Lease Option deal, but it is a given on a Subject-To deal because you are now the owner. You will get the principal for as long as it is optioned to a buyer (or you own the home). The exit strategy (potentially selling it on a Lease Option) will be figured out the same way for a Subject-To as in the previous Lease Option examples. When you purchase it on a Subject-To, you can rent it, Lease Option it, Wrap it with seller financing or Flip it. In this book we will be mostly discussing how to Lease Option it, however, Subject-Tos might be a way to build your portfolio of rentals.

Any back payments due on a mortgage are part of the current balance due reflected on a mortgage. In other words, if the lender shows that the balance is $145,500 and the amount currently due is $3,200, then the balance will be reduced after the $3,200 payment is made. Make sure you show that in your calculations and adjustments. The escrow balance is the amount in the escrow account at the time of the Subject-To assumption. The escrow account contains funds set aside to pay the taxes and insurance that will be due in the future. Keep the relationship good with the seller, and make sure your documents and contracts have the remaining escrow coming to *you* at the payoff of the seller's mortgage. Note: Try to get the escrow applied to the mortgage payoff at the time of closing. With the proper paperwork this will happen in many cases. Sometimes, the lender will not allow that, and the check gets mailed with the seller's name on it. If you have a good relationship with the seller, then they will happily sign it over to you when you receive it. You can also have your limited power of attorney give you the authority to sign the final escrow check over to you.

Note: Escrow numbers vary monthly. The numbers in these examples are simplified. Also, the cash flow and principal payments have been rounded to even numbers to make the spreadsheet figuring easy to calculate. This is also how I do it for my deals. Tracking numbers down to the penny unnecessarily complicates your analysis. If I am close to my $40,000 profit that is good for me.

Example 1

The seller owes $140,000 on their first mortgage and $23,500 on their second. They are behind $3,300 between the two mortgages. Their property taxes and insurance are current, and they have no other liens on the home. The home is currently worth $175,000, and it is in a market that is appreciating at 6 percent a year. The neighborhood is diverse and has many comparables. It is comprised of homes ranging from $150,000 to $250,000. We will set the option premium at 10 percent to sell this home to our Tenant-Buyer.

The payments between the first and the second mortgage are rather steep: $1,050 for the first, which includes taxes and insurance, and $150 for the second mortgage, for a total of $1,200. This home will only rent for $1,100 a month, so you have a negative cash flow situation. It is not uncommon to have negative cash flow on a Subject-To for two reasons: (1) Some sellers have two mortgages, which results in higher payments; and (2) some sellers have higher interest rates, which also results in higher payments.

The principal portions of both mortgage payments during the option period are approximately $250/month, or $3,000 for the 12 months ($250 × 12). The escrow balance received from the seller when the home was purchased was approximately $1,750.

Profitability Worksheet Subject-To		
	Example 1	
Purchase Costs		
Balance owed on first mortgage	$(140,000)	
Balance owed on second mortgage	$ (23,500)	
Back payments and liens	$ (3,300)	
(Up-front cash requirement)	$	$
Transactional funding fee (optional)		
Total debt owed on property	$(166,800)	$(166,800)
Income Sources		
Current value ($10,000 above purchase price)	$ 175,000	
Value of Lease Option premium (10%)	$ 17,500	
Expected appreciation (6% annually)	$ 10,500	
Expected sale price	$ 203,000	$ 203,000
Expected monthly cash flow (−$100 per month for 12 months)	$ (1,200)	
Additional principal from mortgage Payments during option period	$ 3,000	
Escrow balance	$ 1,750	
Total other income	$ 3,750	$ 3,750
Expected Profit		$ 39,950

Would you do a Subject-To deal for $39,950? If so, this is a good deal for you. The numbers do not include the deed transfer fees, title insurance, closing fees, etc. You need to keep in mind the up-front funds required to do this deal. It requires $3,300 cash when you take the deed and a negative monthly cash flow of $100. Personally, I try to steer away from any negative cash flow deals, however, if the deal is strong enough and you can afford the negative, then it is not a huge deal. Also note, you don't have to sell the Subject-To on a Lease Option right away. You can hold it as a rental for years. Then you benefit from the mortgage buy-down along with appreciation. If the deal is valuable, then consider holding it for your rental portfolio. Unlike Lease Optioning from the seller, you don't have to sell these properties right away, or at all.

Example 2

The seller owes $322,000 on the first mortgage and does not have a second mortgage. They are current on their mortgage payments of $1,900 per month PITI (Principle, Interest, Taxes & Insurance) They have no other liens owed on the home. This seller is not in financial trouble but is willing to give you the deed on the home, which is worth approximately $340,000. The neighborhood is consistent with comparables, so only a 5 percent option premium is available on the resale side. Most of the homes range from $340,000 to $350,000 and are similar in size and square footage.

The real estate market in this area is appreciating slowly at 2 percent and the rental rate is $2,000 per month. You can sell it on an 18-month Lease Option. There is a $2,200 escrow balance available, and the mortgage payments have approximately $200 per month going toward principal.

Although I am using examples of a low amount per month going towards the principal, it could be much higher. Check the seller's amortization schedule to know for sure. The higher the interest rate the LESS goes towards principal. The lower the interest rate the MORE goes towards principal. It's a weird mathematical phenomena.

Profitability Worksheet Subject-To	Example 2	
Purchase Costs		
Balance owed on first mortgage	$(322,000)	
Balance owed on second mortgage	$ —	
Back payments and liens	$ —	
(Up-front cash requirement)	$	$
Transactional funding fee (optional)		
Total debt owed on property	$(322,000)	$(322,000)
Income Sources		
Current value ($10,000 above purchase price)	$ 340,000	
Value of Lease Option premium (5%)	$ 17,000	
Expected appreciation (2% annually)	$ 6,800	
Expected sale price	$ 363,800	$ 363,800
Expected monthly cash flow ($100 per month for 18 months)	$ 1,800	
Additional principal from mortgage Payments during option period	$ 3,600	
Escrow balance	$ 2,200	
Other income	$ 7,600	$ 7,600
Expected Profit		$ 49,400

Why is the profit on this deal better than the prior scenario, when the appreciation rate and option premium are lower here?—This one comes out better because of the higher value of the home. The appreciation and option premiums are based on a larger value. Also, there was more equity to begin with. This one would be riskier if you couldn't rent it for $2,000 a month, in which case you might want to rent it for less and take the negative cash flow for a few months until you can refinance it with a better rate loan. If the mortgage rates are low enough, you might be able to get a lower payment and make this home generate a positive cash flow. This will all depend on the mortgage market at the time you purchase it. There are many low interest rate loans on the market at the time this book was written. Those are the ones that I would go after and would be desirable. Over time this could be a completely different scenario. Figure out what works for your current situation.

Example 3

The seller owes $110,000 on a first mortgage and $22,000 on a second mortgage. The payments are $870 for the first mortgage and $150 for the second. The taxes and insurance are an additional $210 per month. The total of all payments is $1,230 (principal and interest for both mortgages, along with taxes and insurance - PITI).

The seller is behind two years in taxes for $4,200 (including penalties) and three months of payments on the first mortgage for $2,610. The home is valued at approximately $135,000. Homes in the area are very similar and the option premium would be only 5 percent. The appreciation in the area has been steady at approximately 4 percent per year. You can do a 12-month Lease Option and rent this home at the market rate of approximately $900 per month. This would put you in a negative cash flow situation. The payments on the mortgages are going toward principal at approximately $300 per month, and there is no escrow balance on this loan.

Profitability Worksheet Subject-To	Example 3	
Purchase Costs		
Balance owed on first mortgage	$(110,000)	
Balance owed on second mortgage Back payments and liens	$ (22,000)	
Back payments $2,610		
Taxes owed $4,200 (Up-front cash requirement)	$	$
Total debt owed on property	$(132,000)	$(132,000)
Income Sources		
Current value ($10,000 above purchase price)	$ 135,000	
Value of Lease Option premium (5%)	$ 6,750	
Expected appreciation (4% annually)	$ 5,400	
Expected sale price	$ 147,150	$ 147,150
Expected monthly cash flow (−$330 per month for 12 months)	$ (3,960)	
Additional principal from mortgage	$ 3,600	
Payments during option period		
Escrow balance	$ —	
Other income	$ (360)	$ (360)
Expected Profit		$ 14,790

This deal does not look good at all. You will only make $14,790, less deed transfer fees, title insurance, closing fees, etc. This also assumes nothing else goes wrong with the deal. Along with the low profit margin, you would need to pay $6,810 out of your pocket and endure 12 months of negative cash flow.

What can you do?—You must negotiate more with the seller. Chapter 6 discusses in more detail how to negotiate with the seller, but in this example one thing you can do is ask the seller to pay the $6,810 that is behind or make payments on it to you. You can also ask the seller to continue to make payments on their second mortgage while you make payments on the first mortgage only. Some sellers will even pay you to take the deed to their home so they can move on with their lives. Adjust some things around to see if anything can be done with the seller to make this deal work. But you may just need to say, "Next."

CHAPTER 6

Negotiating the Deal: Steps to Buying on Lease Options and Subject-Tos

Build Rapport and Make a Deal!

In one house I visited for a potential purchase, the woman had a lot of birdcages in her garage, and all of them had price tags. This home was listed with a Realtor, and I suggested to the Realtor that the seller did not need to leave during my viewing (something I love to suggest as it gives me time to build rapport with the seller to determine what their situation was). The seller was either about to have a garage sale, or she had already had an unsuccessful one. I didn't know anything about birds, but I suddenly had a crazy thought that I could get a parrot and teach it to say, "Hi, welcome to Keller Williams Realty", when people came through the office doors. I dropped the idea quickly when she told me that birds pick up almost everything, they hear you say—I could just imagine the bird repeating things my team says when they hang up the phone from tenant calls: "That tenant is lying"; "Liar, liar"; "Yeah, I bet your Grandma died again!" Nevertheless, I continued to chat with the seller about different types of birds while looking around at the house. I was asking a lot of questions.

This is an example of how to build rapport with a seller. People like to talk about what is important to them. It makes them feel more comfortable with you. As it turned out that day, one of the cages was marked $20 and I decided to buy it, thinking maybe one day I'd get a bird. I couldn't fit the large cage into my car, so I told her that I'd send some of my work crew back that evening to pick it up in their truck.

At this time, we were in a strong seller's market, and I already had a Tenant-Buyer who wanted to buy this home, so I was going to try to purchase the home outright. Our market was *very* hot!

I made an offer through the Realtor the very first day. She called me that evening and said, "Well, we have a few other offers on this home."

Of course, in this type of market multiple offers would be common. That home had just come on the market that morning, and homes don't stay on the market long in a hot market, especially in that price range.

She continued: "But let me tell you the dumbest thing I've ever heard."

I said, "What is that?" The Realtor said, somewhat frustrated, "She accepted your offer." I asked, "Why is that so dumb?" "Because the other offers were $5,000 more than yours with the same terms, and that's just dumb to me, Wendy. Do you know why she accepted yours? She liked you."

Did the birdcage discussion save me $5,000, or did it get me the house? I think it did both. I didn't buy the cage to get the house, but everything you can do to make a prospective seller feel comfortable with you will ultimately be worth it. I always tell my students that if they are not comfortable building rapport with sellers, they should send someone else, because it is *such* a crucial element to succeeding in this business. That seller was not able to just give away $5,000, yet it was important enough for her to sell her home to someone she felt good about that she took $5,000 off her price. Make it a point to establish rapport and you will almost always get a better deal.

How to Build Rapport with a Seller

If you were trying to sell your house, who would you give a better price to? The buyer who came in saying, "I don't like your carpet color. Are you going to replace it? The walls won't match my furniture. This kitchen is just not my style", or the potential buyer who said, "Your home is quite nice. I like the _____ and the _____? (of course, don't lie but tell them something you *do* like about their home—maybe it's the backyard or the kitchen layout. Well, you would choose the second person, of course, because they made you feel good about your home. You would instinctively want to work with them over the first person.

Building rapport with the seller is key to making a deal. If the seller doesn't like you, the deal will probably never happen. Therefore, if meeting people and being reasonably conversational and interested in their home isn't your strength, take someone with you who is warm and friendly and can bridge that gap for you. The reason this is so important is because, for either Lease Option or Subject-To transactions, you're asking someone to give you control of their house with little or no money down. They must feel comfortable with you and more importantly, trust you.

 Wendy's Tip

When you're in the seller's house; tell them what you like about it, not what you don't like. For example, perhaps you'll see something unusual, like older woodwork or a nice fireplace. Ask the seller about it. If you see that the seller likes golf, talk about golf; whether you like golf or not. Always focus on the positives, the interesting things. People like to know that you like their home, which builds immediate rapport.

In a rehab situation, while it's still important to establish rapport, it's also appropriate to point out problems in the property. You want the seller to be prepared for your lower offer when it comes. Buying at a low price is more critical for your profitability when doing a rehab and sale than when taking control of a property and holding via a Lease Option or Subject-To. In a Lease Option or Subject-To, emphasize the positive—you will want the seller on your side. This doesn't mean never point out something that's wrong or could be wrong, though, just do it in a kinder/gentler way.

Start out with rapport-building questions. As you enter the house, take a quick look around for items connected to children or pets, or something of significance, like a hobby or a collection—something to talk about that would interest them other than the house itself. Then ask about those items. You're seeking to get everyone to lighten up, and talking about something significant in their life will do that. NOTE: With this said though, you need to read the people. If they are *talkers*, ask more questions. If they are not engaging much, then likely they're the type of people who want to get to the point. With these types there isn't as much chit chat. Read the people to know where to steer the conversation and questions.

Then ask something like, "What is it that you're trying to accomplish with the house (*not* "your home"—I want to separate out the emotional element) as a result of my help?" Then, I shut up and listen to their reply, using my facial expressions and body language to acknowledge that I understand. I want them to see that I honestly care about them and their situation (and I do—if the deal isn't right for them, I won't do it). This will pay off huge returns when we start talking about the terms of the deal. They don't care that I've been in real estate for over 35 years, and they don't care that I've done hundreds of deals. What they care about is whether I can help them with the problem that's in front of them.

Some sellers like to feel they're dealing with an individual rather than a company, while others like to be reassured that there is a company behind the person. Each seller is different, and you need to learn how to read them and accommodate them. The more personal you can be with a seller, the better they will feel about making the deal. Of course, when the paperwork comes through, it will have my company name, but when I'm talking with the seller it's just between them and me.

Books have been written about negotiations with sellers. Read them to get more details on the psychology of negotiating. Some of them have really helped me understand people and why negotiating itself is so important to completing a deal. Also, there are many videos you can find online to help with these skills. This chapter offers ideas specifically on building rapport with *sellers*, presenting informal proposals to them, negotiating terms, and handling their questions and objections for Lease Options and Subject-Tos.

Putting Together the Proposal/Offer to the Seller

I tell my students to follow three basic steps in writing a proposal or offer to the seller:

1. Keep it simple.
2. Do your homework.
3. Determine your offer. Know your bottom-line profit.

Keep It Simple

Sometimes we get too formal. We want to make sure we have the proper letterhead and business cards and look official up front. We feel this gives us the legitimacy a seller expects. However, counterintuitively, there are times when too much polish may in fact be detrimental to us because the seller finds it impersonal. Save the formal documents for after the deal is negotiated, when it needs to be drawn up in detail (see Chapters 7 and 8). For preliminary proposals it's best to outline several scenarios, even handwritten. (Refer to the proposal in Chapter 11 used with Realtors. You can use the same format with a seller—less any commission or Realtor information.) Many deals are made on bar napkins, and they are legitimate and legal if they are signed and contain the details required for a real estate contract. It's all about personal relationships, not just professionalism. The seller needs to like *you*, not your business card. During the last 35+ years I have never given a seller my business card for purchasing their home, unless I end up giving them my Keller Williams business card (which I do when referred by another Realtor). This allows me to get them my information but also to disclose that I am licensed. My approach tends to be casual and personable.

Putting out an offer is a lot like fishing. We're trying to find out what's important to the seller—where they are financially, whether they need their cash out, and what terms will work for them. If the seller is not sure, use the proposal format in Chapter 11 and give them a few scenarios in writing to help them evaluate different alternatives. Many times, they will know what areas are most important to them. For instance, price might be the most important area to a seller. You then can work around price by negotiating the other areas of terms to make the deal work for *you*. You will have to tweak the other areas of the Lease Option or Subject-To in order to get your profit requirements, but at least you know where the seller is starting—where they are firm and what is important to them. Then use the profitability worksheets in Chapter 5 and make sure the numbers will work for you.

When you agree on the terms with the seller, then you should formalize the contracts. When I think there is going to be a meeting of the minds, or if the Realtor says they want everything in writing, or if the seller says, "I want to see every piece of the contract before I agree," then I put everything together. I try to make my offer in the way the individual seller prefers it. Some like to just discuss it and others want it in writing. Occasionally, timing is critical, and negotiations must be done quickly, and contracts are also drafted immediately.

Do Your Homework

You can't put together a proposal without first doing some research, especially if you are in an area of town that is new to you. You can't base your offer purely on what you think the home is worth; you must incorporate the comparables as well. Find out what similar homes in the area are worth, by checking the MLS. The MLS is protected by Realtors in most areas of the country; however, it is available to the public in some parts. Ask investors in your local real estate investor club the status of the MLS in your area. If you have a relationship with a Realtor, you can ask them what the comparables (comparable market values) are in a certain neighborhood.

Understanding the current economy is essential to making offers on Lease Options and Subject-Tos work and work effectively. For instance, are you in a strong buyer's or seller's market? Understanding the differences and how they affect the sellers is key to successful negotiations. The techniques I teach will work in either a buyer's or seller's market; however, it is important to know which market you are in so you can establish your offer correctly. (See Chapter 3 for more about buyer's and seller's markets.)

Strong Seller's Market

In a seller's market you are likely going to buy at a higher price. When homes are appreciating in a seller's market, I have no problem paying closer to retail for a property. There are times when you could even pay higher than retail and still be profitable based on favorable appreciation and other terms (like large option credits from the seller). You must work the numbers yourself. Your value in the property is going to come from not only the appreciation but also from the Lease Option when you sell. Just don't count on appreciation as the only profit area. With a Lease Option, there is less risk—you may choose not to buy it. However, with a Subject-To you do buy it, therefore, don't count on appreciation at all. Any appreciation is just a bonus, especially with a Subject-To.

Strong Buyer's Market

The opposite is true in a buyer's market. The economy will be slow, probably with higher unemployment rates. Real estate listings aren't moving, in which case you need to buy *low*—meaning below the retail value—because you can't count on appreciation. When it is really slow, you might have to account for *depreciation*. When the market is slow, the buyers have less money and are less able to take on more debt. The *advantage* of the buyer's market is that you can cherry-pick your deals.

Remember this in negotiating with your sellers. If your sellers are unwilling to give, you must move on, because they are not the motivated sellers that we discussed in Chapter 3. The slower the market, the more you can negotiate. As more properties are languishing on the market, there is a large pool of motivated sellers from which to choose. You can be selective to find deals that work out for both you and the seller.

How to Determine Your Offer

The following are potential areas of negotiation for a Subject-To:

- Price.

- Seller paying part of payment forever or a certain time frame.

- Seller paying you up front to take the deed to their home.

- Length of term, but I request the full remaining length of the mortgage.

- The time when the agreement starts.

With Lease Options, there are many variations to discuss in detail, so I will mention only the key areas available for negotiation. When structuring your Lease Option with the seller it is important to understand which of these criteria are most important for them:

- Price.

- Length of Lease Option contract.

- Monthly payment amount.

- Option credits.

- Mortgage buy-down—the principal adjustment.

In addition to these criteria for Lease Options, I usually include terms that will limit my risk. One approach is to include a clause that says my Lease Option can be terminated within 60 days with written notice to the owner. This provides an agreeable exit to problematic transactions. Another method that I use even more frequently is to make the start of the Lease Option contract subject to (not Subject-To ☺) finding a Tenant-Buyer. This significantly reduces your overall risk and avoids having to begin funding monthly payments before you have your own funding source in place.

Multiple Offers

Sometimes you will need to create multiple offers on the same property. This is usually for a Lease Option, but it may also apply to some Subject-To offers. For example, let's say you make an offer of three years at $225,000 and pay the seller $1,000 per month. The seller then looks at appreciation rates and says they don't want to lose out on all the appreciation that you will profit from in the next three years. You then structure a second offer where you might offer to go five years and give them a little more on the sales price as well as a little more each month, but they must agree to all five years. You might also want to do a Step approach based on appreciation with a lower percentage than the market appreciation, so that you aren't giving away the entire profit. For example, one time I purchased a home from a seller who wanted part of the appreciation, which at that time was 10 percent per year. I asked him how much he was expecting. He responded with 2 percent per year, which I felt was fair, and we settled on him receiving part of the appreciation and me receiving most of it. You can give away part of the profit and still make it a win-win.

When objections arise, put yourself in the seller's shoes and reflect on what they say. Always try to come up with creative solutions to keep the discussion going. Find out what their concern is, and if you can fix it, say, "If I could do that for you, would you do the deal this way?" Find the seller's key issues so that you know what terms are more flexible for them. Whenever you give up something, negotiate something back in return. With a seller, usually the first question they ask tells you what their most important issue is. If they mention two or three different issues, find out which is the *most* important.

Find the Seller's Sticking Point

Sellers will have something that means more to them than anything else. Find out what this is so that you can structure a deal that makes them happy while simultaneously meeting your requirements for profitability. For instance, the price of the home may be more important to some sellers than when they will receive it. Other sellers might want a very specific monthly payment, but their overall price may be negotiable. Work with each seller to understand what makes them tick, so that you can tailor an offer to suit them best.

Handling Rejection

When you make your proposals, sometimes the sellers will accept, and other times they will shake their head and walk away. It's best to soft-pedal their rejection with a comment such as, "Well, things might change for you, so please give me a call if they do. I will likely still be interested. Just keep my phone number somewhere in case anything does change for you." Some sellers do come back to me many months or even years later. Asking them to keep your phone number is a good idea. Sometimes people don't want to act immediately because it's not a win-win for them, but a few months down the road they might be feeling much more motivated. When motivation increases, what was *not* a win/win could become one. Always handle all sellers graciously and be accessible. You never know when they might call back and say, "Okay, now we want to accept the proposal that you presented to us a while back."

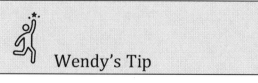

Wendy's Tip

Time always increases motivation. Sometimes if it's not a win-win for the seller now, it may be in a month or two.

Overcoming Sellers' Objections

If you have properly built rapport and trust with the seller first, their objections should be minimal and can be handled confidently and easily. Too many seller objections usually mean that you have a seller who is not as motivated as you thought; however, they may just have questions that need to be answered. Learn to *love* objections. Objections are what we call 'buying signals'. The seller is indicating that they need more information before they can make a buying decision (selling in this case)—In other words, when they have objections, they *want* more information. I have gotten to the end of my presentation and the homeowner had no objections, and I didn't get to buy the home. They weren't interested.

Obviously, I either missed asking the correct question or I didn't pick up on the homeowner's hot button. Most likely they weren't motivated enough to consider a unique solution. Once you have overcome a particular objection, it becomes part of your knowledge for future use. One technique that I like to use is to feed their question back to them, especially if I need time to understand the question or to assemble my response. Many times, we think we understand the question when the intent was something else. For example, if a seller says, "Your offer isn't enough!" I reply, "My offer isn't enough? What part isn't enough?", and then look at them and don't say another word. What I'm trying to do is see if the question is a smoke screen or if there is another objection. It could be that my offer isn't enough money *up front*; it could be that my offer is for too many *years*. By feeding it back, I put the ball in their court and get more information, so that I can give them a correct answer and avoid bringing up another objection they hadn't thought of.

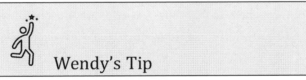

Wendy's Tip

Learn to love objections! They are buying signals. If they aren't interested, they will just say "No!".

There are, however, some common objections and questions that you need to be prepared to handle.

Lease Option Questions and Objections

Here are my recommendations on how to handle each of these objections and questions.

I Don't Want Tenants in My Home.

Answer: "I want you to know that I really screen my Tenant-Buyers and they are hand-selected by me. I'm also not going to put just any tenant into your home—I'm putting a future home buyer in your home. These types of Tenant-Buyers take better care of a home, because they're planning to purchase it. What else concerns you about a Tenant-Buyer?" Let the seller know that you understand their concern. They need to understand that future home buyers are people who want a home to take care of.

What If You Don't Make My Mortgage Payment?

When I am doing a Lease Option, I always want to make sure their mortgage payment is made each month (how do you think I learned this one?). Because of this type of set-up, they sometimes have a concern. There are at least three ways you can answer this question. Use the one most comfortable, fitting, and true for your situation.

1. "I understand your concern. I've been in this business a long time and can give you references from other sellers like yourself, if that might make you more comfortable."

2. "I understand your concern. What would make you more comfortable and yet protect us both?" If they want to make their own mortgage payment and have you make your payments to *them* instead of to the bank, you need to protect yourself. They should provide proof to you of their payment, and/or you will want to have bank authorization to check this out yourself. This is a document signed by the seller along with all of the other contracts for the Lease Option. There should also be a signed agreement that if they don't pay on time, you would have the right to switch your payments from the seller to the mortgage company. Better yet, if they want to make their own payments, write the check to the mortgage company with the mortgage loan number on it and mail it to seller. That way they can mail it onward to the lender and can't cash it. I normally like to have mine automatically pulled by the mortgage company vs. a check. Do people still use checks?

3. "I understand your concern. I could make your payments to the mortgage company and then email the receipt to you. This way I'm protected and so are you. Would this work for you?" This is really my favorite approach. Having monthly electronic withdrawals from my bank is my preferred method of protection for me.

Why Won't You Put More Down on the Option?

Answer: "If I were to put a lot more down, I wouldn't be able to buy more homes, and I'd like to help more sellers and invest in more properties. I'm sure you understand that, right? There's also more risk to me because I will not *own* your home during the option time period." Most of the time, I don't need to use the second part of the response at all. Also, I rarely put anything down with a homeowner. Usually, it's a little more when I work with Realtors.

What If You Don't Buy?

Answer: "If for any reason I didn't purchase your home, you would get the home back in equal or better condition." Reassure the seller that if the Lease Option doesn't get exercised, then the home reverts to the owner in equal or better condition. Agree to give reasonable notice of 30 days or more. The notice can also be discussed during this question (if it comes up) so they can plan if you choose not to purchase.

What Happens If You Die?

Answer: "The contract has provisions that if I die or you die, the contract still binds our heirs to continue on, but let's hope that one doesn't happen for either of us." Try to add a little humor on this one at the end with a smile.

How Long Will It Take for You to Buy my Home?

Answer: "Most likely I will close within 24-36 months, however it could be sooner." Be honest... Most Tenant-Buyers can exercise and purchase within 12-18 months, therefore, I will tell the seller this, however there may be more than one Tenant-Buyer before one exercises and purchases their home. We hold the buyer's hand all the way, walk them through the mortgage process, and do everything we can to make the purchase occur. We are not; however, mortgage brokers and we *offer no mortgage advice*. Also, note about 50% of people who Lease Option the home from you will purchase the home. Take that into consideration when answering the Lease Option seller's question.

Why Do You Need X Years to Buy This Home?

Answer: "I need time to find the right Tenant-Buyer and get them through the mortgage process. Approximately half of my tenants end up purchasing, which of course means half don't. It's very important to have enough time to make it work, and with each new Tenant-Buyer it takes at least a year for them to prepare and qualify for a mortgage."

How Do I Change the Insurance on the Purchase Agreement/Sales Contract?

Answer: "You will need to contact your insurance agent to make sure they know you are doing a Lease Option and that the policy needs to be a non-owner-occupied policy which names me (or your, the investor's company name) as additional insured." This doesn't affect the rates much (if any) but it gives the seller the proper coverage. Be willing to do a three-way call with the seller and the seller's insurance agent to make sure they get the right coverage. You want to have them to put you on as an additional insured, because you have an additional interest in the property. Being an additional insured gives you some liability protection in case there's a lawsuit from your tenant or anyone else regarding the property. You should *also* be an additional insured on your *Tenant-Buyer's renter policy,* so you have more liability protection. As an additional insured, you will get notice if the policy ever lapses. If their insurance does run out, you have the right to go buy insurance and then bill the seller for it. At least in my contracts you can do that.

What Kind of People Are Going to Rent My Home?

Answer: "The best kind. I am going to put someone in your home who wants to purchase it also." Some sellers want to discriminate regarding the types of tenants that move in, but I must tell them that by law I can't discriminate. If discrimination issues are important to the seller, I tell them I'm not the right person to buy their home. On the other hand, I *am* going to take care of their property and put someone qualified into their home.

What If the Tenants Trash My Home?

Answer: Naturally, this is a major concern to any seller. This question could mean the kitchen was entirely removed or it might be just a small stain on the carpet—It depends on the seller. I always clarify this question first. "When you think of a tenant trashing your home, what exactly would that look like or mean to you?" Because if it is truly a fully trashed home, then the insurance company might cover it as vandalism. However normally it's something much less. You can answer, "I can understand why this would be a concern to you, but I want to assure you that I really do screen my Tenant-Buyers carefully. I'm putting not just any tenant in your home, but a future home buyer in your home. If anyone does damage your home, I would take care of it. I am fully responsible for your home." If they need further assurance, you can let them know that their home is also *your investment*, so you're looking out for it very carefully.

Can My Attorney Review the Contracts?

A simple answer here: "By all means. I recommend it! Do you have an attorney you have in mind for this?" Then see how long it will take them to get it reviewed.

Can I List My Home with a Realtor Since You're Not Ready to Commit Yet?

Answer: "Absolutely, go ahead and list it, but please make sure you list my name with the Realtor as an 'exclusion to the listing contract', because if I do buy your home during the listing period, you won't have to pay a commission on my purchase." Note: purchase here means Lease Option. Also, make sure they really understand they must get that in writing with the Realtor for the entire listing period, otherwise, it will end up costing you more money. When the seller has to pay more, they will need to charge you more.

Can I Come Look at the Property During the Lease Period?

Answer: "Sure you can if you really want to check out your house. However, you need to coordinate ANY viewings through me." They can look at the property during the lease period, and it says so in the contract, but they need to go through you to do it. They can't stop by unexpectedly or drop in on the tenants, because that would violate the tenants' rights. They need to call you to coordinate their visit.

Subject-To Questions and Objections

Potential sellers in a Subject-To deal have their own set of objections.

This Isn't Enough Money!

Answer: "What were *you* thinking?" Sometimes a question back helps to see where they are if you don't already know. *Most* likely you aren't making a blind offer without first knowing where they stand or what they're thinking. However, this is typically the biggest objection for Subject-To sellers.

If you need to: A great way to field this objection is to get a full understanding of the question and then do a cost analysis *together*. Get out a sheet of paper and give them the calculator. Hand them the comps and ask what the average sales price of the house is. They will calculate it and give you the figure. Then ask them what commission a Realtor gets in their area. Deduct the commission, then ask them what repairs need to be done to the house (and the cost) to bring the property up to current market standards. Then deduct those costs. Ask how long they think it will take to sell the house and then how long before the house closes. Add up the mortgage payments for that period and deduct those. Then deduct all the closing costs. Try to get them to put down anything else that will reduce the value more and help them be more realistic—for instance, what is their *time* worth? As they do this themselves on the calculator it becomes harder for them to then argue about the value of their home. You are now working on something as *partners*, not adversaries.

You can consider asking them, "What would work for you?" You might only be a little bit apart and it could work for you, or you can split the difference with your response.

Why Should I Give You the Deed and Control of the Property When I'm Left on the Hook for the Mortgage(s)?

Answer: "This solution doesn't work for everyone, and I understand your concerns. Would you rather list it with a Realtor?" This is a legitimate question and one *I* would certainly be asking if the roles were reversed. It demonstrates why it is so important to build rapport with the seller and make them feel comfortable with what you're suggesting. Remember, this will not work for everyone. To answer this objection, you might want to offer references or testimonials from other sellers. Here is how Lyle Reichenbach from Phoenix would reply to this question. It's a little long but use the parts that work for you. I always say KISS – keep it super simple:

"I can understand your concern, and I would probably feel the same way if I were in your shoes. All I can tell you is this: The bank will not let me assume your mortgage, and for me to make a fair return on this deal, I can offer you $_. I'll be glad to buy it right now at the price I've quoted, but then how would you cover the difference to pay off your current loan? You are being very savvy and getting top dollar for the property by letting me take over your payments; we both save all the costs that we'd incur—commissions, closing costs, and so on—if I were to just buy it from you. The minute you okay this paperwork, I kick into owner mode. I will be doing everything possible to sell this house as quickly as I can, using my expertise. I've spent thousands of dollars on training to do this business, legally and morally. It would be futile for me to let this property go back to the bank just because I didn't make the payments."

I Must Get the Price I'm Asking or I'm Not Selling.

Probably one of the most common challenges is getting the seller from "La-La Land" to see reality. A reminder here—If the seller isn't motivated enough, you need to walk away. You need to get a deal that works for *you* first. Remember to use the profitability worksheet. Here are some ideas on how to overcome the price objection:

Sellers usually think rigidly about price—they have a specific figure in their head. They tend not to think outside the box. But, if a deal is properly structured, with the right terms, I *can* afford to pay full asking price.

First, we must verify that their asking price is within true market value. I usually accomplish this in one of two ways. The easiest is to provide comparable sales in their area; sometimes you might want to delete the most expensive one from the list and recalculate. I've found often that the highest-priced houses in the neighborhood are usually in A+ condition, having new carpet, paint, and so on *before* they sold. The second way is to get the seller to buy an appraisal, which they would ultimately need even if they were able to sell retail as a FSBO. If you have an appraiser, you usually work with, simply let him know that, contrary to normal, this time you're looking for as low an appraisal as possible. I've never had a seller balk at using a price that was in writing from an appraiser as a starting point for negotiations. Unfortunately, appraisals can be misleading and bumped up in value, especially when done directly for a refinance or for a homeowner, so a bit of caution on this: An appraisal is not a true indication of value.

Your explanation to the seller might go something like this:

"I understand that you feel the property is worth $XXX but let me show you what's happening right here in your neighborhood. This house at 123 Main Street is 1,480 square feet with a pool and it sold for $XXX; all the homes on this list are within a few blocks of your house. Remember, these prices are what houses have sold for, not what someone is trying to get for a property. Based on these comparables, the program has calculated your house to be worth $XXX. I could be generous and pay you the

price you want, but for it to make sense for me, *I must get the following terms."*

Then spell out the terms you require. Remind the seller of the risk you are taking in assuming responsibility for the property, making payments, and waiting to make your profit at some future time.

I Want to Have My Attorney Look Over This Agreement.

Answer: "Sure, do you have an attorney in mind yet?" Many times, if the seller is in financial trouble, they won't want to pay to have the contract reviewed, but I'm always positive if they want to. Most attorneys will tell them not to do a Subject-To. And this is for good reasons. Remember, they are on the hook for the mortgage, but giving up their ownership. Even with some of my sellers reviewing it with an attorney and the attorney telling them no, they still decided to do the deal with me. This is a reasonably common concern/question—normally just a way for the seller to stall before they make a final decision. Ask if there is something they don't understand and offer to go over it again to clarify things. Sometimes they just want to talk about it a little bit more and then they will sign the contract. Your goal is to get the seller to decide and get off ground zero. But they can always go to an attorney. Never discourage that.

I'm Thinking of Just Listing It with a Realtor.

This is usually another stalling tactic. You can reply: "If you'd like to list your home with a Realtor, that's fine. But if you'd like to sell it now, then you have a buyer here in your home and you won't have to pay any commission. This is going to save you $XXX." If they insist on listing it now, then make sure they put you as an "exclusion to the listing contract." This will keep the Realtor from getting any commission on the home if the seller ends up selling it to *you. However,* don't suggest this immediately, or the seller will see it as a risk-free trial offer to list it with a Realtor. Rather, the exclusion will be a last-ditch effort to save the seller a commission if they choose to list it with a Realtor anyway. Also, Realtors might not understand Subject-Tos and would likely convince the seller to avoid doing one.

Lyle specializes in Subject-Tos. He recommends the following to help:

> *At the onset, there are two critical things to do.*

> 1. *When the seller answers the door, I confidently reach out with a handshake and say, "Hi, I'm Lyle, I'm the Buyer you've been praying for!"*
> 2. *Typically, the seller will want to give you a tour of their house. I politely but firmly say, "I appreciate your kind offer, but after looking at so many houses through the years, I prefer to just wander through by myself. If I have any questions, I'll ask them in a few minutes. In the meantime, please sit down and look through my Seller's Information Manual." This is my credibility kit. On the front is a full-color photo with a banner stating, "It Is Finished" and a giant "SOLD!" sign stamped across the front cover.*

Now for me, I *do* like the seller to walk through their home with me. It gives me a chance to ask questions and observe their responses. Also, I feel it might make a seller feel uncomfortable if they aren't with me. For me this is a rapport building time. You will find what works best and is most comfortable for you. There is certainly more than one way to do this business.

Other Negotiation Points

Here are a few more things you can work with in negotiating your deal.

Seller Paying Part of the Payment

Many times, you will find it necessary to ask the seller to make some of the payment for the deal to make financial sense. Usually this happens when a seller has taken all or most of their equity out through a second mortgage. These normally have higher interest rates and therefore higher monthly payments. I've asked sellers to continue to pay that second mortgage for some predetermined time, until either I can get the property resold or appreciation catches up. Bear in mind that the seller has either done some debt consolidation or spent that money on other things; in other words, they have already spent their equity. I use a form of promissory note from the seller to try to influence them to continue the payments. Obviously once you solve a seller's dilemma, they can relax a little, and not *all* sellers will keep their word about making these payments on a house they no longer own. I've had a couple occasions where the seller did not make the payments as promised, but I kept the deal anyway because I was still in good shape. If you use the following approach, or something similar, it makes sense to the seller to continue these payments. Note also, it depends on the interest rate on their mortgage(s).

> *"I see you have two mortgages on the property. Why did you feel it necessary to take out a second mortgage?" Wait for their reply. "Well, I can certainly empathize with you, but since you've already spent your equity for this reason, not only do you have no equity left, but for this deal to make financial sense to me, I'm going to need you to continue to pay only the second mortgage for the next two years. I'll take care of the first, but as you already know, there's no way I can rent the property for the amount needed to cover both these payments. I won't even have enough to pay any management fees. If you were in my shoes, would you want to take all this risk for a negative cash flow? If I were in your shoes, I wouldn't like to have to do this either. But look at it this way: Isn't it going to be more financially feasible for you to pay just $244 per month instead of the whole $1,179 you're paying now? If you step in and do your part, I'm willing and able to help you by taking the other $935 burden off your back. Together we've created what will be a win-win situation now, don't you agree?"*

That is a lot in one breath, so make sure you spread it out a little and wait here and there for some replies from the seller. Use only the parts that make sense based on the conversation. Pausing for them to reply or nod during this, or any other discussion will be important.

Seller Paying You to Take Over Payments

If there is not enough room for profit in a deal, you may need to ask the seller to give you a sum of money to take over the deed. It may sound crazy, but depending on the situation, this might be a huge blessing for the seller.

Length of Term

I usually make sure, and my paperwork spells out the same, that the term could conceivably last the entire length of the note—although that will probably rarely happen. Most of the time you will have *sold* the home before the loan is paid off.

The Point at Which the Agreement Locks In

This is a negotiable point. You can have the seller make several more payments until you take them over. If you don't feel you can or want to take the risk of carrying those payments until you find a tenant, or Tenant-Buyer, then put this type of provision in the contract.

Understanding some of the many ways to approach Lease Option or Subject-To negotiations will equip you to creatively solve sellers' problems. There are so many times when one area of negotiation is so important to a seller, like sales price, that we forget to negotiate the rest of the deal. Investors might walk away based on price alone when many times, we can end up with the same bottom line by negotiating the *rest* of the terms with the seller—If we just *take the time* to work out the details. It is up to you and the rapport you've built with the seller to make it all a win-win situation!

CHAPTER 7

Getting the Paperwork Ready for a
Lease Option Deal

Now that you've *found a motivated seller* who is perfect for a Lease Option, you've *determined the technique*, you *know the profitability*, and you've *negotiated the deal*, you will need to *get the paperwork ready* to be signed by the seller. For a Lease Option deal there are several contracts and forms that need to be signed: There are also more steps that need to be taken to complete and organize the deal. I use a checklist so that I don't forget any step during the process and to ensure that all items are completed. A checklist is crucial when you are new at this or when you have many properties going at one time. With more experience you will know what needs to be done and likely not forget much, but when you are working on many properties at one time, there are things you can't keep straight in your head, things that may slip through the cracks. A checklist will help you keep things straight on each of your properties. There are checklists in every one of my courses.

I have a checklist form for each of my properties that I review every day, or every other day to see what needs to be completed for each one. A task doesn't get checked off the list until it is completed.

Let's look at the checklist I use for Lease Options.

Buying With Lease Option—Checklist

```
Address:_____ Contact:_____
Phone:_____
Projected starting date:  _____
```

- Use this checklist after your proposal with the seller, either written or verbal, is agreed upon.
- Create your Owner Folder for this home (I use a green folder, legal size with tab on the right) - or digital
- Draft and get seller to sign all documents: *Rental Agreement, Sales Contract/Offer to Purchase, Lease Option Agreement, Memorandum of Option, Affidavit of Liens, Bank/Mortgage Authorization*
- Get Seller to fill out a *Lead Based Paint and Seller's Disclosure*
- Advertise the home.
- Inspect the home if you want a professional home inspection or with a builder.
- Order pre-title work – this may cost up to $200. You can also do the *title search* on your own at your county building.
- Check the *property taxes* to confirm they are paid and up to date.
- Check whether the *mortgage* is up to date (this may not be caught in a title search)
- *Get a key* or access so you're able to show the property.
- *Set up utilities* if they are not on – make sure seller has them in their name until you take over on your Rental Agreement
- Water Softener (if well /rental?)
- *Get insurance* (liability) – it might be like a property manager policy.
- *Make sure Owner puts you on their insurance as additional insured.*
- *Review title work* to confirm it is free of liens.
- Record the *Memorandum of Option* once you find a Tenant-Buyer and are 100% moving forward with this transaction.
- *Set up auto-payments* if you are paying mortgage payment directly and in full.
- If you don't purchase the home and have recorded a Memorandum of Option, you need to record a *Quit Claim Deed* to remove your memorandum.
- *Maintenance*/Work to Be Completed:
  _____
  _____

Using the Option Checklist

If you have several properties, keep them filed in order of which ones are projected to start first. I would focus my attention on those and would also advertise them more heavily.

Fill out the information at the top of the checklist: the address of the property, owner's name and phone numbers (how you will reach them—if there are several numbers, put them all down), and when the Lease Option is projected to start.

Now let's go through the items on the checklist.

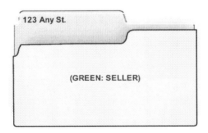 **Download My Buying on a Lease Option Checklist FREE!**

As a bonus for you reading this book, I have included the Buying on a Lease Option Checklist. You can download this checklist by going to: www.WendyPatton.com/Bonus

Create Owner Folder for This Home

For a manual setup:

I use a left-tabbed green folder (think green for money!). I set up an owner folder for each property that I buy on a Lease Option, outright, Subject-To, etc. (I use right-tabbed *red* folders when I sell on a Lease Option later, to hold all the *Tenant-Buyer* information.) All contracts, memos, notes, surveys, title work, or anything regarding the home will go into this folder. This is strictly for the information that involves the seller and you—nothing concerning the Tenant-Buyer will go into this folder. (Note: The folder itself doesn't have to be green (or red), though it's more noticeable than just the tab part or the address.)

123 Any St.

(GREEN: SELLER)

For digital setup via Dropbox / Google Drive:

With the ease of access that websites like Dropbox and Google Drive provide us, it only makes sense to keep these files digitally if possible. This way, you can reference the documents on the property at any time. Once you've created an account on Dropbox, Google Drive or a similar service; you will create a folder for the property. Inside that folder, you will create two additional folders: 1. Owner Documents, and 2. Tenant-Buyer Documents. The Owner Documents folder will include all contracts, memos, notes, surveys, title work, or anything regarding the home. In Google Drive, you can change the color of the folders to differentiate.

Be sure to label all documents by name in both folders for them to be searchable. This way, you can find anything that you're looking for quickly. You will also be able to send any file needed with ease.

Draft All the Documents

To make a Lease Option work, three main agreements are needed. It is possible to roll all three into one or two contracts, but I like to keep them separate to make it clean and clear. It is especially important to keep them separate when you sell on a Lease Option (see Chapter 13).

1. *The Option Agreement.* On the selling side, the option agreement turns control of the property over to the optionee *without ownership*. When I am doing a Lease Option, I sign an option with the seller and they give me control for a specified amount of time (usually 2 to 5 years), during which I will be trying to secure a Tenant-Buyer to close on their home.
2. *The Rental Agreement.* The rental agreement specifies how long I will rent their home and how much I will pay them each month for the rental. The rental payment will always go first to their mortgage company, if any mortgage is due on the home, and then to the owner if any rent is remaining. For example, if my rent is $1,200 per month and the mortgage payment is $1,300, the mortgage company will get $1,200 from me and $100 from the owner. If the mortgage payment is $1,200, then the mortgage company will get one check or electronic payment from me for $1,200. If the mortgage payment is $1,100, then I will write one check to the mortgage company for $1,100 and one to the seller for $100. The check to the mortgage company must have the mortgage account number on it so that it gets applied to the correct mortgage. (The owner could have two mortgages with the same mortgage company.) Protect this mortgage and make sure that it is getting paid.

Wendy Patton's, LLC
3676 Clarkston Rd
Suite A
Clarkston, MI 48348

www.WendyPatton.com

1025

DATE

PAY TO THE
ORDER OF **BANK ONE** $ 1,100.00

Eleven-Hundred and 00/100------------------------------- DOLLARS

Wendy Patton

MEMO **Loan # 123456**

⑆000000000⑆ ⑆000000000⑆ ⑈1025

3. *The Purchase Agreement.* This agreement sets the terms of the final sale. Again, there are two of these—one for my deal with the seller, and one for my deal with the Tenant-Buyer. The deal with the seller has a set sale price, which remains constant regardless of appreciation or even depreciation. However, it is always negotiable up front. For example, you could agree that the price is $150,000 if purchased within two years and $155,000 if purchased between years two and five.

There are five other forms that the seller will need to sign.

1. *Memorandum of Option.* This is the document that gets recorded against the title of the property. It does two things. First, it gives the world notice that you have an interest in the property by "clouding" the title. When you cloud a title, the seller can't refinance or sell the home to someone else and give clear title. A reputable title insurance company would not insure it with this memorandum on the title. This document protects your interest in the property, and it is *very* important that it gets recorded. Having it signed and notarized does you no good; *recording it* is a necessary step.

2. *Affidavit of Liens.* This is a sworn statement, signed by the seller, that discloses all the liens on the home. It also asks about liens that are not yet recorded but known about; for example, if the roof was replaced last month but the roofer has not yet been paid for, this could become a lien. The seller must disclose it or be guilty of fraud.

3. *Bank Authorization.* This document gives you authorization to get information about the mortgage. You can find out at any time the status of the mortgage, balance, payment history, payoff amount, etc. It gives you authority to find out information from the mortgage company as if it was your own mortgage. Because all payments made in the future should be made directly to the mortgage company and not to the seller, you will want access to the seller's mortgage information. This will protect you from having this home go into foreclosure.

4. *Seller's Disclosure/Property Disclosure.* This is a statement the seller fills out that discloses the condition of the home. The seller must disclose any problems with the home. Each

state has different Seller's Disclosure statements. Ask a local Realtor for a blank Seller's Disclosure statement for your state. There are several names for this disclosure depending on which state you live in.

5. *Lead-Based Paint Disclosure.* This disclosure is a federal requirement in the sale or rental of any home. Prior to 1978, lead was a component of paint products used in residential homes. Lead poisoning has caused many problems for people, primarily permanent brain damage in children. The Department of Housing and Urban Development (HUD) passed a law requiring sellers and landlords to have the lead-based paint disclosure signed, and to give the pamphlet called "Protect Your Family from Lead in Your Home" to all potential buyers and tenants. If this step is not completed, the fines are significant. If lead-based paint is present in your home and you don't do this step, you can be sued if a child is later found to have suffered brain damage from your negligence. Some states require that you completely remove lead-based paint from your rental homes. Check out your state's lead abatement requirements. You may want to avoid those homes or confirm abatement has been completed prior to your taking it over.

Advertise the Home

Get the home advertised as soon as you know it has passed your inspection, or even before. You want the period of vacancy to be minimal. Advertise it online, with local employers, on a web site, etc. Advertise anywhere you might find a buyer. (See Chapter 12 for more detailed tips on advertising.)

Order Pre-Title Work

Sometimes called a "Commitment for Title", this is not to be confused with Title Insurance. Normally you can't get title insurance on property you don't own, but you *do* need to *research* the title to see what's on it and whether there are liens. If you order a title search from a title company, it can take 7 to 10 days, maybe fewer if you have a relationship with the title company. You can do it yourself if you're knowledgeable in your own state and county about what you need to research and where to look. This is where you verify that the title is clear of judgments and liens. If you are in an attorney state (vs. title company state), an attorney will do the title search for you.

Check not only the title liens but the state and IRS tax liens that might go against the *person* on title. A title company will pull the information from all relevant sources to give you a complete picture. If there are liens other than the seller's mortgage, this would indicate the seller is not likely a good candidate for a Lease Option but rather a Subject-To, because this would be considered *bad debt* on the property.

The title work will also show all owners of the property. It is very important that you purchase the property from *all* its owners. Sometimes I've looked at title work and seen, "Joe and Sally" on the title when Joe said *he* owned the property. Joe forgot to mention he had divorced Sally. The problem with this situation is that Sally is still on the deed/title of the home. Sally must get off the title by deeding her interest to Joe or agree to all the terms of the Lease Option and sign the paperwork. Whoever is on the deed/title *must* sign. I also recommend that married people have their spouses sign the documents also, even if they're not showing on the title.

Check IRS/State Tax Liens

The pre-title work will usually show these liens. Talk to the title company or attorney to see if those would show up on the pre-title work.

Check whether Property Taxes are Paid

You can call your local county or state building and get proof that taxes are paid. Find out how to confirm that *all* property taxes are current on a home in your state or area. Call your local city assessor's office and ask them about the home. In some states any back taxes might be paid by the county, and the city might not know whether the taxes are paid, so confirm with the assessor, and possibly other real estate investors in your area as to how you will know if they are paid fully up to date. You can also ask the seller to provide proof by showing you a recently paid tax bill— though that won't mean that a tax bill from two years ago was paid. Find out for sure and protect yourself.

Check if Mortgage is Up to Date

The best information source for the mortgage is the seller. Many mortgage companies will give their seller a statement each month to show what has been paid, what is still owed, and whether any payments are late. If the seller does not have a current account statement, they will have to order one. If taxes and insurance are escrowed in their monthly payment, then you will also know that those are current—a mortgage company would not let those go unpaid or be delinquent. (An escrowed payment is a payment that includes the taxes and insurance as part of the monthly payment.).

Get a Key to the Home

Make sure that you have a key or accessibility to the home. If the home is listed through a Realtor, you may be able to get the lockbox combination and have access to show the home anytime, if it is vacant. If the seller is still living in the home, which is often the case for me, I make sure that I either can call the seller and make an appointment for a showing, or that the seller gives me a key and I give them a courtesy call to let them know when I'm going to be showing it. If the seller gives you a key, consider keeping it in a lockbox at the house. You can purchase one at most hardware stores or Home Depot.

Set Up the Utilities

Do this when you are about to take possession of the property. For example, if it's April 28 and I'm taking the property on May 1, I will go ahead and turn on the utilities in my name (electricity, water, gas, etc.). Turn on anything that is required to be in your name and out of the seller's name. Be especially careful about winter months in cold parts of the country—you don't want any days to go by without heat! I have discovered ice skating rinks in a few of my homes over the years because the heat was not turned on.

Water Reading

In some cities and municipalities, a water bill can be a lien against the home if not paid, so get a final reading to make sure it's current and paid from the day that you take possession from the seller. Also, have the water bill mailed directly to you. This way you can either pay it and bill the tenant or forward the bill to the tenant and know that it is getting paid. (This is specifically for states/cities that allow an unpaid water bill to be a lien against the home).

Water Softener

If there is a water softener on the property, make sure you are taking care of it. If it's a rental softener unit, change that contract over to your name. I have a water softener company that I work with, and I will set up a lease-to-own on the softener equipment. The tenant pays the bill, and if they end up not exercising their option; at the end of their lease the water softener belongs to me. Having a water softener is critical if you have hard water. Most properties with city water will not need a water softener, but some do. This was a big deal when I wrote this book originally in 2004/2005. I am not sure that water softener rentals are a big deal anymore.

Get Liability Insurance

Since you don't own the home, you can't insure it. However, you have a liability issue just by being the landlord of the home. As far as the *tenant* is concerned, *you* are the *landlord*, and as far as the *owner* is concerned, you are the *tenant*. You have both tenant and landlord roles without even owning the property. I recommend purchasing some type of *commercial general liability policy* that would cover you for properties you don't own. This is not going to be a make-or-break on your first deal or two if you don't do this step on the checklist, but it's something you should consider if you're going to stay in this business. Talk to an insurance agent to get educated—get several opinions and quotes. Some will try to sell you more insurance than you need.

Owner's Proof of Insurance

Make sure the owner has insurance on the home itself. If they have a mortgage, the mortgage company will require it, but if they own it free and clear they may not have insurance. Also make sure that on the insurance policy they name you as an *additional insured*. Some insurance companies will not want to put you on their policy without you being an actual lien holder (like a mortgage holder—see the "Performance Mortgage" section in Chapter 9 for a way to accomplish this). Push hard for this with their insurance provider if you need to. You do have an interest in the property with a Lease Option and therefore should be able to be added as an additional insured. This will help you with much of your liability exposure. My *rental agreement* and my *offer to purchase* require my owners to list me as an additional insured on their homeowner's policy. They might have to switch insurance companies to find a company that will do this. There are several benefits of being an additional insured: (1) You get liability protection; and (2) you should get notified if the seller cancels their insurance policy for any reason, even nonpayment. Being an additional insured is a great thing, but it should not usually be a deal breaker.

Review the Title Work When It Comes Back

Check for liens and for ownership; make sure the title is clean and clear. You want no surprises. Do understand, however, that some things can show up on the title work in error. I have had several titles show up with old mortgages on them, where it appears that the owner has two mortgages. Don't assume the owner is hiding something from you—ask them about the mortgages showing up on the title work. Many times, the owner had refinanced the home and the old mortgage didn't get discharged properly. Don't be alarmed, just get the old one cleared up. The title company can help you with all of this.

Make Sure All Documents Are Signed by the Seller and by You

Have two complete, signed sets: one for them and one for you. This is if you do a physical copy. At the writing of the first edition of this book it was the only way we did real estate deals. Now most of our contracts are done electronically. The main one that still can't be e-signed is the Memorandum of Option as it must be notarized to be recorded. There are experiments right now with e-signing of these types of documents, but they are still not mainstream.

Wendy's Tip

It never hurts to have a witness when signing your documents, however it is not necessary. Only the Memorandum of Option needs to be notarized so that it can be recorded.

Record the Memorandum of Option

This is usually done at the county building, or better yet with a title company. Once you are certain that you are going to move forward with the deal—if you've got a start date coming up or if you've got a buyer for the property, then you want to record the Memorandum of Option. This will get recorded against the title. It then shows the world that you have a claim against the property and that you have the right to buy it on an option.

Wendy's Tip

Make certain that you leave a 2.5-inch blank margin at the top of your Memorandum of Option, or it will not be able to be recorded. Check your state/county recording requirements prior to completion of this form as these standards will likely change over time.

Set Up the Payments with the Seller

You can set up an automatic payment with the seller's mortgage company that goes directly out of your bank account. I use QuickBooks for my bookkeeping. *Memorizing this automatic transaction in QuickBooks* will keep your balance straight. This eliminates the risk of forgetting to write the checks out in a timely fashion. Plus, not many people write checks anymore.

A List of Maintenance or Work to Be Completed before I Take Possession

This is a list that either you or the seller is responsible for, depending on what deal you've made with the seller—things like replacing linoleum, repainting trim, replacing the mailbox. All repairs are to be done by my contractors (so I can control the quality) unless otherwise specified. All repairs, both major and minor, are the responsibility of the tenant except during the first 60 days of the agreement—I leave that first 60 days of responsibility to the owner. For instance, if the furnace went out two days after I took possession, I don't want to be responsible for that. Everything is negotiable, and while 60 days is my standard, it's completely flexible. You can make it longer; you can also make the seller responsible for all repairs for anything *over* $500, and the Tenant-Buyer for anything *under* $500. Structure it the way you want and what works for the seller.

Wendy's Tip

When juggling between the receiving of the rent from the tenant and the payment of the mortgage to the owner, you might want to stagger them a few days to give the tenant's payment time to clear before you make a payment to the owner.

Some of My Favorite Clauses

Each state may require slightly different information for your rental agreements and purchase agreements/sales contracts. I offer contracts on my website that are generic and can be used in all states, but these should always be checked by a local attorney, because each state has its own unique laws. There will always be various clauses that are required in some cities or states for your sales contracts or rental agreements. Attorneys can be very expensive but can tell you what clauses are required.

Legal Shield provides great legal services for a very reasonable price. Check out www.GotLegalPlans.com to find out what's available in your state. Example: in my state we pay under $30/month. Now don't expect them to do everything for that fee, but most of their attorneys will review your contracts and give you feedback for free. They won't draft documents for free, but they *will review* most. All of the contracts for Lease Options and Subject-Tos are on my website and available to purchase www.WendyPatton.com. These contracts will save you a lot of money if you seriously want to get into these two techniques.

Legal Shield has been great for me since 1998, though they usually aren't experts in these creative types of strategies. Someone in your local REIA might be able to help you with the required clauses for your additions to my contracts. Legal Shield is some extra protection for you from being sued and for other matters that come up for real estate investors.

Here are a few examples of things I've used with my sellers—some of the clauses that have been my favorites over the years in my contracts to buy with Lease Options:

The Option Agreement

- There shall be an additional option consideration of $___ per month given by Optionor (seller) to Optionee (buyer) as credit towards purchasing the home. (This is what we call option credits. I only ask for them from the seller, but due to some issues with Dodd Frank, I don't give any to my Tenant-Buyer)
- Optionee (buyer) has the right to multiple list (MLS), advertise, or resale this

property before, or anytime during the option period.

- Should the property become uninhabitable at any point during the lease period, the tenant will be released from all rent liabilities until the property is habitable and is re-let. The period that the home is uninhabitable will be added to the Option Agreement and the Rental Agreement and Offer to Purchase signed this same day.

The Rental Agreement (Lease)

- Tenant will have access to the home on xx/xx/xxxx to show the property to prospective Tenant-Buyers and contractors.
- Tenant will be sub-letting this home to another party but is still responsible to the owner per this agreement.
- Landlord agrees to use their homeowner's insurance to cover any items/repairs/damage that would be covered under their policy (i.e., storm damage, fire, etc.) because the tenant can't utilize the landlord's insurance for these types of repairs.

The Purchase Agreement (Offer to Purchase)/Sales Contract

- Purchaser will put $___ down on this property. Check will be written directly to (realty company of listing office) upon execution of the attached rental agreement. This amount will be applied directly to the purchase price at closing as a credit to purchaser, and to any listing commission owing. The remaining commission, if any, will be paid at closing out of seller's proceeds to the appropriate offices. (This, if you are working with a *Realtor* on the Lease Option)

- Seller agrees to change their homeowner's insurance policy to a non–owner occupied policy and to name the purchaser as an additional insured within three days of purchaser taking possession of the home.

The paperwork is vital to your successful ability to make a Lease Option deal, so don't skip any steps. Make sure all sections of the checklist are covered. You will modify and add your own favorite steps and clauses over the years as you do Lease Options and develop new ideas.

CHAPTER 8

Getting the Paperwork Ready for a Subject-To Deal

The contracts and forms for a Subject-To are very different from those for a Lease Option. Again, I use a checklist so that I don't forget any step during the process, and I make sure that all items are completed. You should have a separate checklist for each Subject-To property.

 Wendy's Tip for Paperwork

Keep a specific digital folder with *blank* master copies of the different documents you will need for each property/deal as well as your checklist. Add your checklist to each folder to easily reference and fill online. You may end up additionally *printing* your checklist to have it visible on your desk. Each time you get a new Subject-To property, you can duplicate or copy the *master folder* and rename it with the property name. That way, all the documents needed are ready to be filled and signed. The sooner that you create this system, the smoother your job will be.

Buying on a Subject-To—Checklist

- Use this checklist after your proposal with the seller, either written or verbal, is agreed upon.
- Create Owner Folder for this home - Physical or Digital

- Check status of mortgage(s) - current or anything overdue

- Prep and get signed: Offer to Purchase/Standard Sales Contract, Seller's Acknowledgments, Seller's (Real Estate) Disclosure, Lead Based Paint Disclosure

- Order Pre-Title Work

    - Check for paid taxes.

    - Check IRS/state tax liens.

- Get a Key or Access for inspection and showings.

- Water Reading (if City H2O - MI only)

- Water Softener (if well / rental?)

- Set up Insurance Policy

    - Name Lender(s) and old owner as additional insured

- Review Title Work

- Home Inspection, water, septic, pests, radon, etc.

- Advertise the home: flyers, REI club, Buyers list, Internet. (before or after closing)

- Prepare the following for the title company for the closing - make sure they are part of the closing documents:

    - Limited Power of Attorney and Notice to Mortgage Company Change of Ownership

- Bring Mortgage(s) current prior to, or at the closing.

- Set up utilities if applicable.

- Close with title company or attorney (depending on state)

    - Get copy of seller's Driver's License and date of birth if you don't have those.

Address:_____
Contact:_____
Phone:_____
Mortgage company name: _____
Mortgage company phone:_____
First mortgage $_____
Loan #_____
Mortgage company name—second:
Mortgage company phone:_____
Second mortgage $ _____
Loan #_____
Projected starting date: _____

- Have seller cancel old insurance policy and confirm new one in place.

- Get docs signed listed above that were provided to the title company.

- Set up auto-payments if paying mortgage payment.

- Close with Title Company.

- Change locks.

- Maintenance / Work to Be Completed:

Using the Subject-To Checklist

If you have several properties, keep them filed in order of which ones are projected to close with the owner *first*. These are the ones I would focus my attention on initially. I'd also advertise them more heavily.

Fill out the information at the top of the checklist: The address of the property, current owner's name and phone numbers (how you will reach them—if there are multiple numbers, put them *all* down), *when* you are projected to start the Subject-To, and all of the *lender information*. There might be two mortgage companies. You will want to put all information on each of them down; contact numbers, loan balance, and loan/account numbers.

Download My Buying on a Subject-To Checklist FREE!

As an added bonus for you reading my book, I have included the Buying on a Subject-To Checklist. You can download this checklist at:

www.WendyPatton.com/Bonus

Create Owner Folder for This Home

This is a green folder, in contrast to the *red* tenant's folder.

For a manual setup:

I use a left-tabbed green folder (think green for money!). I set up an owner folder for each property that I buy, on an option, outright, Subject-To, etc. I use right-tabbed red folders when I sell on an option later, to hold all the Tenant-Buyer information. All contracts, memos, notes, surveys, title work, or anything regarding the home will go into this folder. This is strictly for the information that involves the seller and you—nothing concerning the Tenant-Buyer will go into this folder. (Note: The folder doesn't have to be green—just the tab part or the address.)

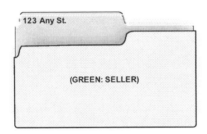

For digital setup via Dropbox / Google Drive:

With the ease of access that websites like Dropbox and Google Drive provide us, it only makes sense to keep these files digitally if possible. This way, you can reference the documents on the property at any time. Once you've created an account on Dropbox, Google Drive or a similar service; you will create a folder for the property. Inside that folder, you will create two additional folders: Owner Documents and Tenant-Buyer Documents. The Owner Documents folder will include all contracts, memos, notes, surveys, title work, or anything regarding the home. In Google Drive, you can change the color of the folders to differentiate. Be sure to label all documents in both folders for them to be searchable. This way, you can find anything that you are looking for quickly. You will also be able to easily send any file you might later need.

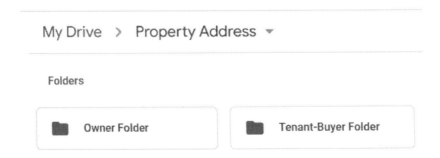

Check Status of the Mortgage(s)

Require that the seller get proof from their mortgage company(s) concerning the status of the mortgage(s). Don't go by their word. Get it in writing or on the phone directly from the mortgage company(s). Even though you should be getting title insurance on your Subject-To deals, they won't get any mortgage information, because you are buying the home Subject-To the underlying mortgage. The mortgage will be an exception to their title policy, so they won't check that out for you. You will want to know exactly how much they are behind, if at all, and how much they owe. Some sellers are not behind at all on a Subject-To or have only one mortgage, but you want to make sure. Confirm all the information they give you. A recent mortgage payment statement might show the exact information, but some mortgage companies don't mail statements. Because you will be the owner on a Subject-To once the seller signs the deed, it is more important to be careful you don't miss any steps.

Draft All Documents

1. *Offer to Purchase/Purchase Agreement/Sales Contract.* As in Chapter 7, this is a full contract describing the terms of the purchase.

2. *Warranty Deed.* This puts your name on the title of the home.

3. *Seller's Acknowledgment.* With this document the seller acknowledges important things about the sale of their home. This way they can't come back later and say they didn't understand what they were doing or didn't realize they were really deeding their home to you. In my Subject-To course, there are twenty-five seller acknowledgments they must agree to.

4. *Affidavit of Liens.* This is a sworn statement in which the seller discloses all of the liens on the home, whether recorded or unrecorded.

5. *Bill of Sale.* This document lists all of the personal property to be included in the sale, such as appliances, window coverings, and anything else you want to ask the seller to include in the sale of the home.

6. *Limited Power of Attorney.* This gives the investor power to act on the owner's behalf as it pertains to the home, but it does not give the investor power to act on the owner's behalf on any other matters. An example of this document is shown in Chapter 9.

7. *Notice to Mortgage Company.* This informs them of the transfer of ownership of the home, if you are telling them outright. If not, you will still want to notify them of a change in address for mailing of mortgage payments, yearend interest, and so on.

8. *Bank Authorization.* This document gives you the right to call the bank or mortgage company and get any information on the mortgage, including loan balance, loan history, payoff information, payoff request, escrow balance, and the like.

9. *Seller's Disclosure*—described in Chapter 7.

10. *Lead-Based Paint Disclosure*—described in Chapter 7.

Order Pre-title Work

This can also be called a "commitment for title," but it is not to be confused with title insurance. You can get title insurance (and I recommend it highly) with a Subject-To unlike a Lease Option, however the title policy will have an exception on it with the mortgage that's not being paid off. You may need to rush this title work if you are doing this deal quickly. If you order it from a title company, it can take 5-7 days, maybe less if you have a relationship with a title company. Refer to the corresponding section in Chapter 7 for more information on pre-title work.

Check If Property Taxes Are Paid

You will want to confirm exactly where the taxes stand on a Subject-To deal. Sometimes you will be taking over back taxes, and sometimes there are none that are due. You need to know the exact numbers, so you know your bottom-line profit and out-of-pocket expenses. When getting title insurance, the title company or attorney will also handle this area for you.

Check IRS/State Tax Liens

As stated in Chapter 7, usually the pre-title work will show these liens, but if you are doing your own research, ask for help in checking both areas to help confirm that the seller does not have any IRS or state tax liens against them. If you are getting title insurance, your attorney or title company will do this part for you.

Get a Key or Access

This is described in Chapter 7; it works the same in a Subject-To as in a Lease Option.

Water Reading

Make sure you do a water reading (ask the city if they do it or if you have to do it) and check to make sure the water bill has been paid. In a few parts of the country, the water bill can become a lien on a home. You might not even know it is a lien until months after the seller has moved out of town. Again, if you are getting title insurance the title company will make sure there are no water liens on the home.

Water Softener

If there is a rental water softener unit, make sure the rental payments are current. If the seller owns it, make sure it is part of the Offer to Purchase/Sales Contract and listed with all of the other appliances in the home.

Set Up Your Insurance Policy

There must be an insurance policy on the home that matches the owner's name because you are the new owner. This is for your protection and is also a mortgage requirement. The seller will cancel their policy. You will also want to name the seller as additional insured on your policy. This will help the lender match up your policy with their mortgage. Make sure your insurance guy/gal also puts the seller's mortgage company information on your policy.

Review Title Work

Make sure the title work shows the owner of record and the liens that you expected.

Get an Inspection

Just like with a Lease Option or any other real estate purchase, you should complete a home inspection. Make your offer to purchase contingent upon a home inspection. This will allow you to get out of the deal if you find too many things wrong with the home or something that would be too expensive to fix. You can always go back and renegotiate if you find something wrong, but not if you don't have this clause in your contract.

Advertise the Home

Once you think this home is going to be purchased on a Subject-To, start to get it ready for a Lease Option to sell, or to rent. Put out an ad to get it rented to a tenant or Tenant-Buyer.

Prepare Closing Documents

Prepare a Limited Power of Attorney form for all closing purposes. You will also need to prepare a letter to the bank: Notice to Mortgage Company Change of Ownership. You can have a local attorney draft these forms or you can find them in my "Get the Deed: Subject-To" course on WendyPatton.com

Bring Mortgage(s) Current

Once the documents are signed and recorded, then you should bring the mortgage current, if necessary. If the seller is in pre-foreclosure, get the funds wired to the lender immediately. If they are just a month behind, you can send the payment by ordinary mail. Just make sure your check clears, or ACH/Wire, and you get a receipt and proof of the payment.

Set Up Utilities

Set up all utilities when the seller is out of the home. Make sure you know what utilities are used there—gas, oil, propane, electricity, trash removal, etc.

Sign All Documents

Get all documents signed. The title company will draft your warranty deed. You can provide them with anything else you want signed that you don't get pre-signed with the seller when you get your offer signed. Get the documents to sign to them early.

Record Warranty Deed

The title company will handle this for you. If you choose to do your own closing, then you can record this document. It is usually at your register or deeds at your county building.

Set Up Automatic Payments If Paying the Mortgage Payment

Do something to make sure you don't forget to make those payments on time each month.

Personally, I like to have the mortgage company take the payments right out of my account each month.

Maintenance/Work to Be Completed

Make a list of repairs and other work that needs to be done on the property.

Some of My Favorite Clauses

Seller's Acknowledgments (a few out of 25)

- We may be selling the property below market value, but because of our personal circumstances and the immediate need to sell, we are satisfied with the price and terms that we have negotiated.

- We understand that the loan on my home might be called 'due' and that the buyer is not guaranteeing that they will pay the loan off if this happens. The buyer has no intentions of defaulting on the loan nor harming the seller's credit in any way, however, they can't guarantee that the loan will not be called due when this transfer takes place. The buyer will, in good faith, assist the seller in trying to figure out a solution with the mortgage company if this situation arises.

- We understand that the purchaser is a real estate investor and intends to resell the property at some future date and expects to make a profit.

- We are not signing this contract under duress and have signed this agreement of our own free will, without undue financial pressure. The buyer has in no way pressured us into signing the agreement.

John Hyre, a tax attorney, is involved in many real estate transactions. He uses the following form for his Subject-To deals:

Summary of Our Deal

You are selling me your house. I now own it.
The mortgage to the house is staying in your name and on your credit report.
I do not intend to refinance the mortgage, though I may one day choose to do so.
If the bank calls the loan due, as is its right, I will not refinance the loan. As such, the bank could foreclose on the property if it calls the loan due. That would hurt your credit.
I will make the payments on your mortgage in full, on time, every time. That is the payment that I am giving you for the home.
I will pay arrearages on the mortgage in the amount of $_____.
I will also put $_____ of repairs into the house to make it rentable or saleable.
This deal is FINAL. You do not get the house back. The loan stays in your name until such time as I should see fit to pay it off at my sole discretion. You will NOT contact any tenants to whom I rent the house.

- *The Benefits to You:*
  - *A bad house that is going into foreclosure/costing you money/ruining your credit will be off of your hands. The financial bleeding stops right now.*
  - *Your credit will be helped over time by my on-time payments.*
- *The Risks to You:*
  - *The loan could be called due by the bank and foreclosed upon.*
  - *The presence of the loan on your credit report could limit your ability to take out future loans.*
- *The Benefits to Me:*
  - *Like you, I expect to be paid for my work. I intend to profit by selling or renting the house. I have purchased it at a favorable price and/or on favorable terms to make a profit.*
  - *The loan stays in your name, so I do not need to get one in my name, pay closing costs, etc.*
- *The Risks to Me:*
  - *Tenants could trash the house; in which case I'd have to pay for repairs.*

- *Tenants could skip out or the house could sit empty, but I still need to make the payments on your loan.*
- *The bank could call the loan due, and I could then lose whatever I put into the house.*
- *The house could sell or rent for less than I'd planned, but I'm still on the hook for the payments I promised to make.*
- *The repairs could cost more than I'd planned.*

The paperwork is vital to your successful ability to make a Subject-To deal work smoothly, so don't skip any steps. Make sure all areas of the checklist are covered. You will add your own favorites through your own experiences with Subject-Tos as you learn new ideas and master the strategy.

CHAPTER 9

Advanced Concepts and Strategies for Buying with Lease Options and Subject-Tos

While I have suggested strategies that you should start with, there are more advanced Lease Option and Subject-To strategies available to help you build your portfolio. These are things I have learned from other students, national experts, and my own experience. You can succeed with just the basic concepts, but these topics will broaden your capabilities and elevate your business. The strategies shared in this chapter include additional ways to protect yourself and additional methods to increase your profitability on each deal.

Remember that all your strategies must be negotiated before any paperwork is signed. You will need to determine which, if any, of these strategies make sense for each individual situation. Some of these techniques may be viewed by certain sellers as intimidating or overly complex. This will give you a reason to learn how to simplify what you're asking for with the seller. Therefore, you will need to know your seller and understand them by building the relationship, as discussed in Chapter 6.

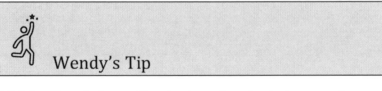

Wendy's Tip

K.I.S.S. - Keep It Super Simple. A confused mind says no!

Extra Ways to Protect Yourself in a Lease Option

As a Lease Option holder, you are dependent upon the good faith performance of the seller, who holds title to the property. In Chapter 7 we discussed protecting yourself by filing a Memorandum of Option. In this section I discuss some additional techniques to protect yourself and strengthen your position.

Place a Deed in Escrow

This approach can be used along *with* the filing of a Memorandum of Option. The seller would sign the deed at the same time that they sign all of the Lease Option contracts. However, the deed is not yet recorded on the title. Instead, it is *held in escrow* by an attorney or title company with instructions for its release. While this approach does not protect the title against the potential filing of liens, it tends to give sellers the feeling that they have deeded, or sold, their property, so they are much less likely to try to back out later from their Lease Option agreement. It can also allow the investor to close on the home without the seller being present.

The instructions included with the deed in escrow specify how and when the deed can be released and recorded. For example: "When Wendy Patton pays $155,000 in certified funds to Joe Smith, this deed can be released to her. These funds must be paid by (date)."

Performance Mortgage

This document called a Performance Mortgage would *replace* the filing of a Memorandum of Option. A Performance Mortgage strengthens your ability to ensure performance by the seller by having the seller pledge the property as collateral for the Lease Option agreement. It is recorded at the time the Lease Option agreement is made. Signing a Performance Mortgage also protects you from the seller selling to anyone else.

Like the Memorandum of Lease Option, it allows their insurance company to put you on the owner's policy, but likely as a lender vs. just an additional insured, and it shows you as a lien holder for any type of foreclosure, so you should be notified of any proceedings.

A huge benefit for the Performance Mortgage is when you sell. When you sell, the sale is treated as a long-term capital gain vs. short-term (ordinary income). This assumes the law doesn't change and that you have the performance mortgage recorded for more than 1 year.

While this is a good concept that strengthens your position, many sellers find signing it objectionable, so you may not be able to use it in every case.

You'll want the specific terminology to be reviewed by a local real estate attorney, but here are some of the key Performance Mortgage clauses:

- Whereas, the said Mortgagor has executed a certain Option Contract agreement dated under which Mortgagor is obligated to the said Mortgagee to deliver fee simple and clear marketable title to that certain parcel of real estate, legally described below, which obligation is attached hereto and by reference herein made a part hereof. . . . (don't you just love the hereto and herein? An attorney gave me these)

- To secure to the Mortgagee the compliance and performance of the Mortgagor in meeting both the letter and the spirit of the agreement evidenced by said Option Contract, (name of optionor) does hereby mortgage, grant and convey to Mortgagee the following described land, situated, lying and being in the County of_____, State of___, more particularly described as (legal description) _____.

- Unless Mortgagee and Mortgagor otherwise agree in writing, insurance proceeds shall be applied to restoration or repair of the property damaged. If the restoration or repair is not economically feasible or Mortgagee's security would be lessened, the insurance proceeds shall be applied to the sums secured by this Security Instrument with any excess paid to Mortgagor.

- The proceeds of any award or claim for damages, in connection with any condemnation or other taking of any part of the property, or for conveyance in lieu of condemnation, are hereby assigned and shall be paid to Mortgagee.

Extra Ways to Protect Yourself in a Subject-To

Chapter 8 suggested several ways of protecting yourself in a Subject-To deal, but there is another useful technique to consider: a Land Trust.

Land Trust

Note: I do not personally use Land Trusts, but many investors do. If you are using a Land Trust, make sure it is not to "hide anything from the bank". If so, this would be considered mortgage fraud, which is something I stay far away from. A Land Trust does not mean you are committing fraud. Fraud is the intention to hide something, in this case from the bank. If using a Land Trust is your normal way of doing real estate transactions, then it's likely fine. If you only use Land Trusts for Subject-Tos but you use LLCs for everything else, it will look questionable. I am sharing this information with you as it is an advanced technique and something you may consider or want to know more about.

A Land Trust device is used to minimize potential exposure to litigation, or other issues, by hiding true ownership. The actual owner or beneficiary of the trust is not recorded. Only the name of the trust is recorded in public property records. Thus, the extent of the beneficiary's property holdings is not apparent and not a magnet to potential litigants. While the document is somewhat lengthy, I've listed some key clauses of the trust agreement here:

- The Beneficiaries are about to convey or cause to be conveyed to the Trustee by deed, absolute in form, the property described in the attached Exhibit A, which said property shall be held by the Trustee, in trust, for the following uses and purposes, under the terms of this Agreement and shall be hereinafter referred to as the "Trust Property."
- The persons named in the attached Exhibit B are the Beneficiaries of this Trust and, as such, shall be entitled to all the earnings, avails, and proceeds of the Trust Property according to their interests set opposite their respective names.
- The interests of the Beneficiaries shall consist solely of the following rights respecting the Trust Property:
- The right to direct the Trustee to convey or otherwise deal with the title.
- The right to receive the proceeds from the rental, sale, mortgage, or other disposition of the Trust Property.

- The foregoing rights shall be deemed to be personal property and may be assigned and otherwise transferred as such. No Beneficiary shall have any legal or equitable right, title, or interest, **as realty,** in or to any real estate held in trust under this Agreement, or the right to require partition of that real estate but shall have only the rights as set out above, and the death of a Beneficiary shall not terminate this Trust or in any manner affect the powers of the Trustee.

- The interest of a Beneficiary, or any part of that interest, may be transferred only by a written assignment and delivered to the Trustee.

- Powers of Trustee including:

  With the consent of the Beneficiary, the Trustee shall have the authority to hold the legal title to all of the Trust Property, and shall have the exclusive management and control of the property as if he were the absolute owner thereof, and the Trustee is hereby given full power to do all things and perform all acts which in his judgment are necessary and proper for the protection of the Trust Property and for the interest of the Beneficiaries in the property of the Trust, Subject-To the restrictions, terms, and conditions herein set forth.

- This trust may be terminated at any time by the Beneficiaries, and with thirty (30) days written notice of termination delivered to the Trustee, the Trustee shall execute all documents necessary to vest fee simple marketable title to all Trust Property in Beneficiaries.

The trust document further defines the duties, compensation, liabilities, and other dealings with the Trustee. The document is then signed, witnessed, and notarized.

Additional Creative Ideas and Strategies

Here are some other strategies I have found useful. No doubt you will discover more as you gain experience using Lease Options and Subject-Tos.

Nursing Homes

It may sound morbid to you but consider this in the states where older people can keep their homes and still be on Medicaid. If the person on Medicaid were to sell their home, Medicaid would take the proceeds; however, if they keep their home until they pass away, then they can benefit from cash flow while they are alive. If the person *can* keep their home, this is a good possibility for a Lease Option on the seller side, but on the Tenant-Buyer side it can be no more than a rental situation since the owner is still living. In other words, you could not actually sell it to a Tenant-Buyer, you could only rent it until the owner passed away. In this case, your Lease Option agreement might be based on the death of the person.

This is a great way to make cash flow in the meantime because the owner would not get to keep rental proceeds either, or not much if they are on Medicaid—that would also go to the state. Therefore, you may be able to negotiate a great rental rate, as it does not really affect the owner. The owner is happy, the renter is happy, and you're happy with the cash flow. Someday you might be able to buy this home, and it could appreciate significantly during this time. The estate does not have to pay utilities or maintenance during the years of the Lease Option while their loved one is in the nursing home. Those responsibilities can be a huge financial and emotional stress on some families. The freedom of not having to worry about the monthly expenses and yearly taxes can be an immense relief for many families in this situation. This can truly be a win-win.

Limited Power of Attorney

In many states the transfer fees (the costs to record a deed) are extremely high and doing a simultaneous closing (discussed in Chapter 15) becomes expensive. In some states the fees can be as high as 3 percent of the sale price of the home. On a home priced at $400,000 this would take an extra $12,000 in profit right off the top of each deal for investors in those states. There are two ways around this:

1. You can have the seller sign a new purchase agreement with your buyer for a higher amount, and you pay the *difference in fees* for what you paid the seller versus what you sold it for to your buyer. For example, if you paid $350,000 to the seller and you sold it for $400,000, you would have the seller sign a new contract with your Tenant-Buyer for the $400,000 and you would pay the extra costs on the $50,000 increase in price. This is fine if you don't mind and the seller knowing what you are making on the deal. Sometimes it's fine, other times it causes bad feelings. The seller already knew you were making a profit, but to put it in front of their faces can diminish their joy in the deal that once was a definite win-win for them. You can also offer to give them a little bonus with this. For instance, let's say

they were going to receive $95,000 in cash at closing. If they sign this document, now you will give them $96,000 at closing. Then it becomes more of a win-win again. They get more money, and so do you. You only pay $1,000 for the first $250,000 in closing costs, and then your state's transfer fees and title insurance fees on the additional $50,000 on the raised price.

2. Another good reason to have the Tenant-Buyer sign directly with the seller might be the lender. The Tenant-Buyer's lender might require the Tenant-Buyer to buy directly from the seller who is on title due to the seasoning issues discussed previously in this book. You can then change the price to the new price and have the seller sign directly with the buyer. You can put a lien on the property to be paid at closing for your profit less their extra fees due to raising the price. They will have additional title insurance fees and maybe other fees in your state. The seller will receive a larger 1099 on the sale of their home, so they will need to be aware that it won't affect them taxwise. They can talk to a CPA, or their tax advisor, but they should be allowed to subtract the amount they are paying you to get to the exact same price as if they were selling to you with the original agreement.

Partner with the Seller for High-End or Hot Markets

There are some states and locations where property values are very high and might be cost-prohibitive or risky. Consider partnering on those homes with the seller, making the seller a *partner* in the profit of the sale. If a home is worth $700,000 and the rental rate is $3,000 per month, you may feel hesitant to take on this property; however, this home may also net $150,000 or more in profit. A seller of this home may also feel uncomfortable giving away all the profit for this type of property. This might become an objection for a seller in this price range or in a hot market that is appreciating rapidly. You can always *offer* to partner with this type of seller. A partnership doesn't *have* to be 50/50, but it can be. If *you* are doing all the work, the partner should cover all the risks. For instance, if the home is vacant, the seller should continue to cover the monthly mortgage payment, or if the Tenant-Buyer doesn't pay their rent, then the seller should cover the payment. If they want part of the reward, they need to cover the risk.

Ethics and Capital Gains

There are ethics issues you will need to deal with in the real estate investing business. Many times, we as investors will know about certain IRS or other regulations or laws relating to real estate that the seller may not understand or even consider when making a deal with us. It is important to deal with everyone fairly. The IRS rules are constantly changing, and you can't give tax advice unless you are a CPA, so have the seller check with their CPA or tax adviser, but you should be aware of the capital gains rules and how they can affect your sellers.

The Capital Gains Rule

If you have lived in a property as your primary residence for more than two years out of five and you sell it, you don't have to pay capital gains. The IRS has changed the capital gains on our personal residences to a rule that, in simplified terms, goes like this: Every two years you can sell your primary residence (yes, the one you *live* in, not your investment deals) and you can keep the profits of up to $250,000 if you are single and $500,000 if you are married, tax-free. Anything above that is taxable, and any time period different than that becomes more complex. Basically, if the seller lives in it for two out of five years, it qualifies for this tax-free gain. This allows the seller to rent the home for three years—but not one day longer. This rule may also change at any point in the future.

Wendy's Ethics Example – Capital Gains

Suppose you have a woman who has lived in a house for 30 years and she has over $200,000 worth of capital gains (yes, a real deal of mine). The IRS allows you to have up to $250,000 capital gains tax-free if you are an individual and $500,000 if you are a couple. If you buy her house within three years of initiating a Lease Option deal, she pays no capital gains, but if you go over this by even one day, she'll have to pay taxes on the $200,000 in capital gains—it would not be tax-free anymore. Your inability to close a deal within the three-year period could cost her tens of thousands of dollars. This would not be fair to her.

If you have done a five-year option with her, you have just erased the most recent two years she lived in the home and potentially exposed her to capital gains. Many sellers think the old law of "one sale over age 55 and no capital gains" still exists, but it doesn't, and if you're educated about that, you should be ethical and educate the seller as well. I care about the people who have been in their homes many years and who have a lot of capital gains—and therefore a lot to lose— especially since they probably don't understand the current tax laws. If your seller has a lot of capital gains, advise them to speak with their CPA and attorney if they really want to go for a five-year deal so that they understand the financial risks and liabilities.

If the sale somehow can't close in the right timeframe, see if the seller will do a short-term seller financing so they don't lose their capital gains. Think creatively and not at the last minute. However, if I know the seller has little to no gain in the home, I am far less concerned about their capital gains and may do a five- or ten-year option.

What to Do When Your Option Comes to an End

Time is running out on your contract—now what? Let's assume you had three years with the seller to purchase their home. The time is fast approaching, and you do not have a buyer who can purchase yet. First, make sure you don't end a contract with a potential buyer on the same day that your contract ends with the seller. I recommend leaving three to six months at the back end of a deal. For instance, if you have three years with the seller, you should give your Tenant-Buyer 12 to 18 months. If they don't exercise, then give the next Tenant-Buyer only 12 months, thereby leaving yourself six months at the end of your contract with the seller for other possibilities. This also gives you some wiggle room at the end of the contract to give a small extension to your Tenant-Buyer if they are able to close on the mortgage but need a short extension.

Let's say buyer number two doesn't want to exercise either. What are your choices? Surprisingly, there are many—I'll name six here. You can do any of the following, and in any order that you choose, but I recommend that you always try number 1 first:

1. *Ask the seller for an extension if you want one.* Most sellers will give you an extension if you ask. Many times, the sellers will just give it to you with no costs. Sometimes the extension might cost you more money—a little more *now* in the form of an option fee, in the *future* on the sales price, *or* more each month. If you can work it out with a win-win, do it. Make sure the extension is in writing—don't take their word for it. All real estate contracts *MUST* be in writing, or they are not enforceable.

2. *Buy it yourself.* You can get a mortgage with a lender and purchase the home yourself. You would want to consider this if you can afford to do it and there is enough profit in the deal. Don't give the home back to the seller unless it isn't worth the amount you agreed upon or there is something wrong with the market or the home (something that you or your tenant didn't create). Look around and talk to some lenders, but don't wait until 30 days before the end of your contract—talk to a mortgage broker months in advance. Sometimes these types of loans can *take* months—I found this out the hard way.

3. *Sell the home directly to another buyer.* You will have to sell the home to another buyer directly, not a Tenant-Buyer. It may be someone referred by a Realtor, or someone you found via an ad.

4. *Partner with someone if you can't do the mortgage yourself.* If the home has some equity and you can't refinance it, you can't sell it, and the seller won't extend, then bring in a money partner who can get a mortgage or pay cash. Give them a part of the equity or a fixed amount for doing the financing/cash. This will give you more time to resell it on the market or to Lease Option it again. You can find money partners in your local real estate investing group.

5. *Don't exercise your option.* Tell the seller you don't want to purchase, and then you can walk away from the deal. Remember that an option with the seller gives you the

right/privilege, not the obligation, to purchase. You must return the home in equal or better condition, less any normal wear and tear. You can't return the home with damage.

6. *Assign the deal to another investor*. You can wholesale this Lease Option to another investor for a fee, and then *they* can do one of the above five choices.

PART 3

HOW TO GET REALTORS
TO HELP YOU
DO LEASE OPTIONS

CHAPTER 10

Building Rapport and Sharing Lease Options with Realtors

Why Work with Realtors?

Approximately 80 to 90 percent of the nice homes on the market are listed with Realtors. The percentage varies from city to city and area to area, but they certainly control most of what's being sold in the market. They have access to the sellers that we need to get to in order to buy those homes. They will not participate in Subject-To deals because of the risk to their sellers, so I will not talk about that acquisition technique in these next two chapters on dealing with Realtors.

Working with Realtors will change your investment strategy forever. Thanks to Realtors, I get more deal offers than I can go look at, so I don't chase them anymore. Once you get the Realtor system working for you, you will only need to decide which deals you want to pursue. The Realtor system is getting Realtors bringing you deals. This is why I put together a course just on this topic called **"Working with Realtors, Getting Realtors Begging You to Buy Their Listings".**

Many investors believe that real estate agents don't have the best deals, or that the deals have already been picked over by the time they hit the market. In many cases, this is true—there are deals that never even hit the market because they are very good. Realtors have clients who buy the best deals before they ever list them on the MLS (Multiple Listing Service). There are also deals that never get to a *Realtor*—foreclosures, traditional for-sale-by-owners, the homes investors find by driving by, etc. But I believe some of the sweetest deals are sitting on the market, listed with a Realtor—deals that no one even sees because they are looking for traditional or wholesale investment homes (meaning paying cash or getting a mortgage on the home) and not a Lease Option.

When an investor considers traditional financing or buying with cash, they must be able to purchase the home for a much lower price. However, when they can buy the home on a Lease Option (terms), they can pay a higher price, therefore enlarging their choices. When working with Realtors, it is less possible to lowball a home and get the deal through. Realtors typically don't like investors for that reason.

Since most of *my* Lease Option deals come from Realtors, it is important to me that I understand their perspective. Most of them have been trained to sell real estate for a living—traditionally, from beginning to end—in these ways:

Six Steps a Realtor Goes Through on a Traditional Sale

1. List a home for sale.
2. Find a buyer.
3. Get a contract signed.
4. Have the buyer get a mortgage.
5. Close on the home.
6. Get the commission.

Most Realtor deals are done this way—But what about the times when their listings don't sell? Or when they don't sell quickly enough for the seller to feel comfortable? Most Realtors are not taught to bring creative alternatives to the table for their sellers.

In a strong seller's market, Realtors typically don't need to consider anything creative, because homes sell very quickly. However, even in a seller's market there are some homes that won't sell quickly for whatever reason. These are the homes that Realtors will need to consider being creative with.

In a buyer's market it is much easier to pursue Lease Options with Realtors and sellers. They will be more creative and open to different ways to sell their listings. In a buyer's market the Realtors won't get any commission if the home doesn't sell, or if the listing expires and the seller lists the home with another Realtor. Also, in a buyer's market, sellers tend to put more pressure on their Realtors to sell their home, which pushes the Realtor to be more open-minded to new ideas and to pursue other alternatives for their sellers. They really do want to sell their customers' homes, to help both their sellers and their own business. That's where you come in. You can teach Realtors about the alternatives you offer and how you can help *them* help their seller.

Finding the Right Realtor

The Realtors you will need to find for Lease Options will be sellers' agents, what are called *listing agents*, the ones that list the homes of sellers. A listing agent is the one who works with the seller and has their name on a sign in the seller's yard. If you want to buy in a certain neighborhood, you can usually find the strong listing agents by driving through and seeing whose names appear on the real estate signs in the yards.

Buyers' agents, on the other hand, represent and work for buyers. A buyer's agent looks out for the best interests of the buyer, whereas a seller's agent (listing agent) looks out for the best interests of the seller. You want a buyer's agent when you're purchasing your own home, but a listing agent is the one to work with when buying Lease Options or Lease Purchases—with my strategy.

Realtors have a relationship with their sellers that is unique. Sellers tell their Realtors almost everything about their personal lives. Realtors therefore know who is motivated and why. They know: who is getting divorced, in trouble financially, if their builder is almost done with their new home, who has custody issues, who is worried about double house payments, how many grandchildren they have—as well as the name of their dog who died last year and what Uncle Ned did at the family reunion. Realtors sometimes want to say, "That's really more about your personal life than I ever wanted to know," but they don't. They stay as interested as possible to build rapport.

Because the Realtor is providing a very necessary service to the homeowner in helping them sell their house, and because the homeowner so freely tells the agent *everything*, the homeowner is not shy about calling the Realtor and saying the four-letter word after the home has been sitting on the market awhile: "Realtor, if you don't sell my home soon, I am going to have to **RENT** it!" This word makes a Realtor cringe. The only thing you can say to a Realtor that's worse is, "Take my home off the market." If the home doesn't sell soon, the Realtor won't get any commission and has lost countless hours in showing the home as well as the expense of advertising and marketing. Although the Realtor is licensed to rent it for the seller, most Realtors won't want to and/or don't know how. The commission for renting a home is small, it is generally not worth their time, unless they're in a property management company and do a large volume of rentals. Many real estate companies don't handle rental properties at all because the rental business is so different and carries more liability for lawsuits.

In my area, when a Realtor hears the four-letter word, **RENT**—my phone rings. I have spent years developing rapport with the many real estate offices in my area, as well as with individual Realtors. They know what I am looking for, and they know how to pique my interest in ways that might get me to drive by the house and see if I'm interested. Why? Because when they work with me to give me leads on potential Lease Options, they know they can get their commission paid—AND paid much more quickly than on a traditional rental deal. Although I don't pay it myself, technically—the seller always pays that—I am willing to *front* the commission. This creates a win-win-win between the Realtor, seller, and myself: The Realtor sells the listing, the seller sells their home, and I buy another investment home. We all win!

Networking with Realtors

You only need to work with two to four strong listing agents per year to make a comfortable living. You can find listing agents by asking other Realtors who the top listers in their office are. When I was at the height of buying Lease Options through Realtors, I had one Realtor in my area who gave me at least one deal a year, and I made at least $30,000 on each deal. I stayed in touch with her every few months just to keep my name fresh and to keep the relationship at the top of mind.

Realtors know lots of other Realtors, so if you have one contact, you can network through *that* one to access others. Call the local real estate board to find out when they have local functions and *go mingle*. Exchange business cards at the functions. If you don't have cards, get some printed. It's more important at this point for you to have their cards than for them to have yours, but having a card to exchange is more professional. You want them to know who you are and how to get in contact with you.

Rent a conference room and invite Realtors to a wine and cheese party; then give them a presentation about Lease Options or Lease Purchases. Draw them in by focusing on what's important to *them*: "Would you like to sell more listings and make more money this year? I can teach you for free!" Do something to advertise it that grabs their attention without giving away all the details. Don't be alarmed if only a few show up, because those few are very interested in creative solutions. You might even put on your invitations: "Would you like to be more creative than your competition? Would you like to know things that your competition doesn't know? I can teach you some creative ways to sell your listings that your competition hasn't even thought of."

If you aren't sure who to call to get started, talk to the people in your local investing group, since there will be some Realtors in your group. These are not the Realtors you will be working with, as these are investors themselves and not traditional listing agents (normally), but they should be able to tell you who the listing agents are in their office. The top listing agents from the companies are also listed on their website (sometimes). It's worth starting a database or spreadsheet to keep up with who is where and what they do, especially with the people you begin to contact and with whom you develop relationships.

Your local real estate investors group can also be a great resource for brainstorming more ideas on drawing people in. Not only will they be interested in giving you feedback, but you may even find a money or managing partner there who is also keen on investing in the Lease Option strategy. You can then go in as a team and make a presentation.

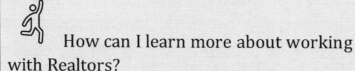

How can I learn more about working with Realtors?

As you can see, working with real estate agents can provide great benefits. I am an agent myself who has worked with many other agents. I have compiled what I've learned to be the best practices in my Course, "Working with Realtors." All my courses have the contracts you will need, audio training, step-by-step instructions on how to use the technique, filled out example contracts, and much more. You can find all my courses on: www.WendyPatton.com

Sharing the Realtor System and Targeting Realtors

"Working with Realtors" is a multistep process. Building a relationship with a Realtor does not happen overnight. Just as you need to build rapport with your sellers, you also need to build rapport and credibility with Realtors. Here are some tools to get the process moving forward.

Becoming an Agent Yourself

Becoming a real estate agent is something I highly recommend. When you are a real estate agent you are, "one of them". When I first started investing, I was not licensed, but soon realized I didn't like waiting on someone else's timeline to see a home or write an offer. There are so many benefits to getting a real estate license. If you do decide to become an agent, email me at Info@WendyPatton.com. I'll help you find an investor friendly office near you and potentially free real estate school!

 How do I become a Real Estate Agent?

If you want to learn the process step-by-step, including what you need to know and how to find the right brokerage then get my **FREE** eBook *Becoming a Real Estate Agent*. You can find this eBook and all of my courses on: WendyPatton.com.

Letters

I have a couple of letters that I use to contact Realtors, primarily those with homes that have been listed over 60-90+ days on the market. One letter is for use during a buyer's market (Lease Options) and the other for use during a seller's market (Lease Purchase). The letters both explain when a Realtor should consider me and how Lease Options and Lease Purchases can help them and their sellers. It is *very* important that a Realtor understands how you will help their seller. Their first obligation, by contract and fiduciary duty, is to the seller. Next, they are concerned about themselves. My letter explains how I will help their seller *and* pay *them*.

Phone Calls

I will also *call* Realtors and present the same information as in my letters. You might want to catch them after hours so you can get all your thoughts out on their *voice mail* without flubbing it up, or if your time is limited. If you do leave a message, make it brief and to the point—Get to the bottom line of how you will help both them and their sellers. Then they can listen to it more than once and call you back with any questions. Also, after hours voice mail doesn't tie you up in a thirty-minute call where there may be no interest.

Basically, my message will sound something like this:

Hi Sally, this is Wendy Patton with Keller Williams Realty. I am calling about your listing at 123 XYZ Street. I am wondering if it is still available? I noticed it has been on the market for a while and I wonder if your sellers would consider something a little creative? Something like a Lease Option? If your sellers don't need their cash out now but would like their monthly payment made and you would like to sell their home, and get paid your full commission, please give me a call. Sally, if it won't work for this seller, but if any of your other sellers have said to you that if their home doesn't sell soon, they might have to consider renting it, please give me a call. I buy homes when sellers can consider terms like this. Don't lose your commission with sellers who want to rent. Please call me. Thanks, Sally, for considering this. My number is . . . Again, my number is . . . and my name is Wendy Patton. Thanks, Sally.

This might be what I would say in a buyer's market. If it was a seller's market, I might change the wording to a Lease *Purchase*. I would add that it's a guaranteed sell for the seller and that the Realtor's commission is paid up front. This makes it a much stronger call, which is more acceptable in a strong market. If you don't want to ever guarantee the purchase, then you will not use the Lease Purchase wording. See Chapter 11 for the letter I use in the seller's market, with wording that makes it appealing to the Realtor.

Getting Your Foot in the Real Estate Office Door

Real estate offices get many requests to host speakers and salespeople, so it can be hard to get an appointment. The best way to start is to go to a real estate office where they know you and can recommend you. If you know someone who is a Realtor, ask them if they can assist you in getting into their company meeting agenda so that you can do your presentation. If you don't have a contact, then call the office directly and speak to the office manager or broker and use an introductory letter. Of course, if you become a Realtor, then you can work this strategy in your own office. My office in MI has 300+ agents and my office in AZ has 150+ agents. Why would I need to go anywhere else? However, if you aren't licensed, tell them a little about yourself, keep it brief, and ask if you can present your ideas to their agents. They get bombarded daily by mortgage companies, title companies, and many others trying to get their business, so they don't like a lot of salespeople and they like to keep it short and sweet. However, keep in mind that the Lease Option or Lease Purchase system offers something unique and different. The real key is to show them how this system will help them to sell more of their listings. As for getting into their offices, it will be much more likely during a buyer's market. During a seller's market, the agents might not think they need something creative to sell their listings, and they could be right.

I like to send a letter to **the broker/manager** that grabs their attention. That means I leave out stuff about me, my background, and my credentials, because when it comes down to it, I'm trying to sell a concept more than I'm trying to sell me.

Your letter should be on letterhead and might sound something like this:

Dear (broker's name),

Would you like to assist your agents in learning new ways to sell their listings? I buy real estate in this area and have some ideas for your agents on how to sell more of their listings. When you and your agents have availability, I have a professional presentation that I would like to show you. I understand you get bombarded with salespeople trying to speak to your agents. What I offer is unique and is something every real estate agent should know about. This costs your Realtors nothing but will help them sell more listings especially listings that aren't moving very fast.

My goal is to show your team some creative ideas that might help you sell some of your office listings; not to sell anything. My presentation is only 10 to 15 minutes, so it will not take up much time.

We have many references from clients like yours and from other real estate agents, including (agent 1, agent 2, agent 3). Please talk to them to find out how easy it is to sell a home to (your company name). Please call me to set up a time when I can meet with you and share the information that I would like to present to your real estate agents. My phone number is (222) 333-2222.

Sincerely,
Wendy Patton

I also have letters that target specific Realtors and their listings, and I send them out constantly. It is part of my **"Working with Realtors"** course.

Educating Realtors

Realtors are not trained to be creative when selling, and sometimes investors think they are not very sharp because they don't know how to do unique deals. That's one of the biggest stumbling blocks for investors trying to work creatively and effectively with Realtors—investors expect something from Realtors they are not trained to do. As an investor, you will need to teach a Realtor if you want them to be able to work effectively with you. This doesn't mean teaching them how to invest, but what key words they should listen for and how it will help their seller and themselves.

When someone gets a real estate license, they are trained mostly on the law—seller contracts, lead-based paint, legal issues, fair housing, and things that are required by the state to make a real estate transaction go professionally from start to finish. Realtors are not taught things like, "What if the house doesn't sell?" or, "What if the seller says that four-letter word?" It is your job to teach a Realtor what to listen for and how to help their seller, you and themselves in these types of situations.

Most of us know at least one Realtor, or we know someone who knows a Realtor. Practice your presentation on Lease Options or Lease Purchases with a Realtor, and ask for feedback: "Did I present the Lease Option concept clearly?" "Was my presentation too long? too short?" "Is there a better way for me to communicate this idea to Realtors?" "May I set up an appointment to present this at your office?" The last question is especially good if your practice presentation has gone well, and you are ready for the next step.

You will then want to go to the Realtor's office meeting. Call their broker or have the Realtor set it up for you to come to one of their meetings.

What to Bring to a Meeting

You must have a presentation prepared before going into a meeting. Don't ever think that you know enough to just wing it. Here's a list of what to bring:

- When you attend a meeting, it is customary to bring donuts or bagels, so call first and ask the office manager or broker what the agents would like.
- Have all your materials organized neatly and accessibly. You don't want to be fumbling for information and making them wait on you. Time is money- chop chop- they will want you to be in and out quickly.
- Handouts of your presentation for everyone who attends the meeting and for the absentee agents—Call first and get a head count. Always have more than necessary in case they ask for extra copies. You won't need to give them a copy of each slide you present, but you can give them a one-page overview of how Lease Options will help them and their clients.
- Extra business cards (stapled to your handout).
- Make sure all handouts have your name and contact number on them.

Begin Your Presentation

Realtors will be open to the idea of Lease Options or Lease Purchases if you help them understand how they work and when they are appropriate for their sellers. Lease Options are not the right thing for most sellers. The presentation needs to be educational about the benefits of Lease Options to *them* and to *their sellers*. I give a PowerPoint presentation going over the program step by step, and then open it up for questions and answers afterwards. If you don't have a computer to bring with a PowerPoint presentation, then just use a white board to talk through the slides. I have the customizable Realtor presentations in my **"Working with Realtors"** course.

Your presentation might start off something like this: "Thank you for allowing me to come to your meeting today." Always remember to thank them for their time. "I am here to share with you some very exciting concepts that I've discovered that work for Realtors and their clients. Specifically, creative options for Realtors—things that you may not have thought about before or may not have considered for your clients. Let's get started."

Here is an outline of what I cover in my 10-minute presentation.

1. Introduction of myself and the name of my company.
2. My agenda: Discuss creative and innovative options for Realtors.
   a. Why I'm not a competitor but a partner (especially as an agent myself).
   b. How to help them sell more of their listings.
   c. Unconventional versus traditional sales approaches.
3. What to look for in a seller who might need my services.
4. What to look for in a buyer whom the Realtors can't help.
5. The Lease Purchase or Lease Option
   a. How it works.
   b. How you front part or all of their commission.
   c. Benefits to the seller:
      - You take over payments.
      - You take over maintenance (if you do this).
      - No rental headaches.
   d. Benefits to the listing agent:
      - Quick sale—saves time and money.
      - Commission paid up front (or part if in a buyer's market).
6. What types of homes you'll consider
7. What price range you'll consider.
8. Referral fees.
9. Final statements.
10. Q&A

This agenda looks long but should be short and sweet – 10 minutes to share this information. I don't stay very long once I'm done. Usually the questions are brief, and I'll stay as long as they continue to ask for more information. But Realtors generally don't have a lot of free time in the office, so they're looking to get as much information from me in as short a time as possible. Many times, after my presentation, they realize how I can help their sellers. Then they start to write down addresses on the back of their business cards for me. I often walk out of presentations with lots of cards and leads to pursue. If you take leads of homes from the meeting, make sure you follow up quickly with those agents. The last thing you want is to lose your reputation because you don't follow up on what was given to you.

Making the Realtor Part of Your Team

If you're new at this business you might feel like a very little fish in a big pond, but when you have established a relationship with a Realtor, they become a part of your team whether they realize it or not. Now you're going to start to work together on finding solutions for the "*rent*" problem. You will also be able to help them during a buyer's market when things are slow by cherry-picking their motivated seller deals as investments.

Building Rapport: The Follow-Up

Because they are a part of your team, you will want to build that relationship above and beyond just what they can do for you and what you can do for them. How about sending a thank-you gift every time a deal goes through that you did together? These little rewards go a long way in keeping the rapport top-notch and ensuring even more leads in the future!

Follow up monthly with Realtors who might be strong listing agents or who work with lots of sellers. Remind them what you're looking for. Remember, if they are successful, they are busy, and they might not always remember you. You might have to remind them of what you do and how you can help them in their business.

I don't like to call Realtors during the day and interrupt them or interrupt my own day. I prefer to call their offices late at night and leave a voice message. That way they can listen to it first thing in the morning—they start their day off with me reminding them of a creative way to do business. If they don't have an office phone, then texting occasionally or emails might be the best way to remind them of what you do.   A reminder message for them might sound something like this:

> *Hi Kathleen, this is Wendy Patton. I wanted to say hi and let you know I'm looking for another home that I can buy on a Lease Option. Do you have any sellers right now that might be able to consider this type of solution? If so, please give me a call. My number is 248-394-0767. Thank you, Kathleen, and I hope to talk to you soon.*

If I haven't done business with them yet but I have been trying to start the relationship with the first deal, I would say something else:

> *Hi Kathleen, this is Wendy Patton. I am still looking for a home and I was wondering if any of your sellers have said that they might consider renting their homes if their home doesn't sell soon? I know most of your sellers do want to sell their home outright, but if you do ever hear one of your sellers say they might rent it, Kathleen, please do call me. I will make sure you get your commission in full. I can be reached at 248-394-0767.*

If you aren't a licensed Realtor, you can add:

> *Also, Kathleen, you will get to double-dip on the commission and receive the full buyer agent portion, too, when it closes on the back end. I will write up the offer, but you*

can have the entire commission. If your sellers rent out their home, they might not sell it, and neither one of you would really get what you want. I would love to do a lease with an option and make sure you both get paid in full. Please keep me in mind if this type of situation comes up. This usually works well for any type of seller that does not need their cash out at closing to move on to their next home. Thanks so much, Kathleen. Feel free to call me with any questions. My number is 248-394-0767 Again, that is 248-394-0767.

Once I received my license, I started to receive the buyer side of the commission and the agent *didn't* double dip (meaning getting both listing and buyer side of the commission). Giving up my commission is something I don't do except in rare circumstances. Example: a flip or rehab before it hits the MLS that is brought to me. I would usually let an agent double dip these type of situations. It is not a Lease Option that has been sitting on the market for a long time. Those I do take my commission on.

Follow-up is key with Realtors. However, don't be a pest. I would recommend a reminder call no more than *once a month*, maybe even every other month, especially after you have the relationship established. And you don't want to say the same thing each time you call. Try another way to explain how options or creative deals work. Here's another example:

Hi Kathleen, this is Wendy Patton. Just checking in to see if you have any sellers who might not need their cash out of their home at closing or who might be financed near 100 percent? If so, my type of solution might work well for them. Give me a call on any listings you have like that so I can set up a time to go and see them. I hope to talk to you soon on one of your listings. Kathleen, thanks for the opportunity to work with you. My number is 248-394-0767.

Wendy's Tip

Get "Working with Realtors" and start to share these ideas with Realtors. **"Working with Realtors"** is a great course on my website to help you. The sooner you do this, the sooner you will get Realtors begging you to buy their listings!

Ethics with Realtors

Honesty and integrity with Realtors will be the key to successful relationships with them. If the relationship with a Realtor isn't good, it's going to affect your reputation and damage the business for other investors. Real estate is a small world, and word gets around if you stiff a seller or walk away from a contract and tell them, "Go ahead and sue me!" Realtors find out, and as previously mentioned, they control 80 to 90 percent of the homes on the market. Even if your own ethics are good, if Realtors hear horror stories about deals gone bad because of *investors* who reneged on their Lease Options or Lease Purchases, it hurts the market for the rest of us.

If you've committed to something with a Realtor, get back with them and do it. There's nothing worse than going to a group of Realtors with a presentation, getting 10 leads, and then never getting back to them regarding what happened with those leads. The Realtors will wonder what the point of helping you with leads is if you don't follow up. It's the surest way to kill the rapport you have worked to establish. Did you look at the properties? What did you think? Are you interested? Are you going to pursue? Follow up and let the Realtors know! Even if you don't have time to look at the properties, or they weren't what you wanted, communicate *that*. Keep the lines of communication open so they will continue to provide you with leads. The relationship must be a two-way street. And the more *you* give, the more *they* are willing to give.

Sometimes a Realtor will call me about a dumpy property. I look at it and know it is overpriced. Now I'm faced with a dilemma: I don't want to insult the Realtor, because I want to keep that relationship positive, however, they were the ones who called me about the property. The best strategy is to be honest with them. I would say something like this:

> *Sally, I looked at the home on 123 Main Street today. Boy, with what it needs, and what I think I can sell it for, and my carrying costs, the most I could offer would probably be an insult to the seller. I certainly don't want to affect your relationship with the seller. I think I will have to pass on this one, unless* you *want me to still write it up. I will leave this up to* you.

See how I keep the door open to them? I explained my reasons in terms that the Realtor can understand without being insulting to her or the property. Not only that, but I've left the lines of communication open in such a way that the Realtor will call me back one way or another regarding the house. This is what I want: I want them to continue to call me because they are my first relationship. Forget the house! Many times, they *know* it is overpriced and they just want an offer to show the seller. If they want me to write up an offer, I will. What often happens in this case is that the seller doesn't think their home is overpriced until they get an offer from me and are shocked into reality. Then the seller reduces the price, and the agent can finally sell the home. Thus, I have helped the Realtor make the sale. This might not help me as an investor today, but it will help me when the Realtor thinks of me for their next listing. For me, that one home is just a home. I want the *relationship*, so that they will bring me five more homes down the road.

Remember investing is a long-term strategy. Building rapport with Realtors is an essential part of the long-term big picture.

CHAPTER 11

Closing Deals with Realtors

Why Aren't Lease Options or Lease Purchases Appealing to Realtors?

When I first started doing Lease Options with Realtors back in the early 1990s, it was a strong market in Detroit, but I wasn't getting very many leads. This both puzzled and bothered me because I thought I had something great to offer them. I went to my best friend, Debbie, who is and was a local Realtor. I said, "Deb, look what I'm offering these Realtors—it's a great thing for their sellers! Why aren't they all coming to me with their deals?"

She looked at me and said, "Wendy, do you truly believe it's a great deal for the Realtors if they have to wait three to five years for their commission? They might not even be with the same real estate company when the house closes. This is a *hot* market—they can probably sell their listings to someone else and get paid before then. They're not motivated to work with you on these types of deals. Why should they wait for years for their commission when if they just wait for a couple more months, possibly weeks, on the MLS, they'll get their full commission now?" I replied, "So what should I do? She said, "You're creative—Think of something." I said, "You mean like pay their commission up front?" She responded, "That would be a really good start and I think that could work."

And that's when I started paying Realtors their commissions up front, and my ability to purchase completely turned around, especially in a seller's market.

Addressing the Commission Issue

Realtors are not greedy, but they do want to be paid for the services they are providing for their sellers.

By contract, Realtors are not entitled to their commission until the sale closes. There's not a good likelihood that a Realtor will want to wait for a closing that is several years down the road. As stated above, they may not even be with the same real estate company by then and the deal is with the company, not with the Realtor. In most states if a Realtor leaves one agency and goes to another, they may completely forfeit their commissions. This makes the **option** strategy unappealing for Realtors, primarily in a hot market.

The Realtor's job is to look out for their sellers' best interests, and many Realtors don't feel a Lease Option is a good solution for their sellers. If a Realtor is simply dead set against it, just move on. There are lots of Realtors who are creative enough to want to work on finding innovative solutions for their clients. You just have to help them understand when these solutions would apply. Likewise, if a seller adamantly won't do it, move on. Only spend your time on the people/sellers open to the idea.

Now the reason most Realtors don't consider these creative solutions and can't help their sellers move in that direction is because most sellers *can't* consider a Lease Option or purchase. Most sellers need their cash out in order to buy their next home. I estimate that only 5 to 10 percent of sellers can consider a Lease Option because these sellers *don't* need their equity out of their home to buy their next one. In my experience, sellers who can consider a Lease Option or Lease Purchase will usually do it for two to five years in a seller's market and three to ten years in a buyer's market. The seller's situation will determine the length of the Lease Option, the payments, the price, and other terms.

When a Lease Option is a viable solution for a seller, the next hurdle is to ensure that their Realtor will benefit from the deal as well. This chapter explains how to keep the Realtor in the win-win-win formula, and how to keep that positive rapport with the Realtor for future deals.

In a seller's market, my letter to the Realtor would look like this:

> *Dear Sally,*
>
> *Would you like to sell your listing at (address of property)?*
>
> *Maybe we can help. We buy homes . . . especially when your clients can accept terms like a Lease Purchase. As soon as your client says to you, "If my house doesn't sell soon, I might have to rent or lease it," this is a great indication that our services might help you sell the listing.*
>
> *When your client sells their home to (your company name) . . .*
>
> ***YOUR COMMISSION IS PAID UP FRONT!***
>
> *and it would be a guaranteed closing for your seller.*
>
> *When would a client be able to accept a Lease Purchase?*
>
> *Here are some situations:*
>
> 1. *They don't need their cash out yet but would like to either have cash flow or have their payment made.*
> 2. *They have very little equity (i.e., financed near 100 percent).*
>
> *We have many references from clients like yours and from other real estate agents, including (agent 1, agent 2, agent 3). Please talk to them to find out how easy it is to sell a home to (your company name). Give us a call if this type of solution might work for your client.*
>
> *Sincerely, Wendy Patton*

In a buyer's market I would use the words "Lease Option" and I would also say their commission is paid "in full" versus "up front." It is not as strong, but still very positive.

After I started to send out this type of letter, the deals started to come in. The commission was no longer a stumbling block issue for the Realtors—they didn't have to worry about waiting for years to be paid for the work they were doing then. Obviously, if you don't have Realtors you have worked with yet, you need to remove the list of names. Over time you will develop this list. I will always list the most well-known agents I've worked with in this letter.

In a weaker market or a buyer's market, I don't pay the entire commission up front—I might only pay part of it, likely 1 to 1.5 percent versus the 3 percent I would pay in a seller's market. They would then have to wait until closing for the remainder of their commission. In a weaker market they realize that they might not get paid at all if their listing doesn't sell. At the same time, I am getting less from my buyers in these markets. Remember, a slower market for sellers means a slower market for buyers; less money for sellers translates to less money for buyers. Realtors understand that when business is slow for them, it is slow for me, also.

Here's an example: I offer $200,000 in a seller's market and I pay 3 percent of the listing portion of the commission up front. This is $6,000. I would owe $194,000 when I pay off the seller (when I exercise my option). However, if I don't exercise my option, I would not get that money back. I am fronting the seller's expense for the real estate commission. The real estate agent would not have to return the commission if I don't purchase the home.

Structuring the Deal for the Realtor

Understanding the current economy is essential for making the offer work effectively. Know whether you are in a strong buyer's market or seller's market so that you can structure your offer appropriately.

Seller's Market

This is the market where things are selling quickly, appreciating strongly, and sometimes multiple offers are made on the same house on the same day. This is also a time when the economy is good, things are happening, there's a lot of new construction, and so on. When homes are selling quickly, Realtors are getting paid quickly and in full, so in the beginning of a Lease Purchase, I offer to front their commission *in full*. Realtors prefer a *Lease Purchase in a strong seller's market*. A Lease Purchase means you are guaranteeing you will buy that home, so don't do it unless it's a strong seller's market, with good appreciation, or you're positive you want that home for the deal agreed upon.

Buyer's Market

A strong buyer's market is the opposite: Business is slow, unemployment is higher, homes are sitting and sometimes going from one Realtor to another to sell, and there's little or no appreciation, sometimes even some depreciation. Net result: Realtors are not selling their listings. The result is Realtors are much more negotiable because they're likely to lose their listings, and the sellers know that the economy is slow, which is making them more anxious. This opens many opportunities for Lease Options. During this time, I only offer part of the commission up front, possibly part in 12 to 18 months, and the rest at closing. Keep in mind, however, the fee is really coming out of the option fees that the Tenant-Buyer pays to me and not out of my own pocket. When I assist the Realtor in getting paid, they are more likely to work with me again.

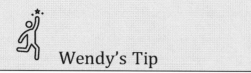

Wendy's Tip

The rule of thumb is: Weak market, weak offer; strong market, strong offer; but above all, always be fair.

Sequence of Events When Working with a Realtor

The Realtor gets paid when I put someone in the home—in other words, when I get money from someone else. The sequence of events is as follows:

Timeline of Working with a Realtor
1. The Realtor gets a listing.
2. The seller says the four-letter word, "rent" and the Realtor shares it with me.
3. Go look at the property.
4. Negotiate through a proposal.
5. Agree on the terms.
6. Write up a full offer.
7. The offer gets signed.
8. Find a Tenant-Buyer.
9. Pay the commission or a portion of the commission to the Realtor.
10. The Tenant-Buyer moves in.
11. Closing happens at a later date when Tenant-Buyer exercises their option.

Sometimes I say, "I'll commit but not until . . ." and I give them a future date because I need time to find a tenant or Tenant-Buyer. Even if my tenant doesn't move in by the start date, I am still responsible for paying the full commission on that date. It is a stronger offer to a Realtor and to the seller if you commit to starting on a certain date, regardless of whether you have a Tenant-Buyer. If there is no Tenant-Buyer, the commission will come out of your pocket—not exactly zero down for you the investor, but it is still a low-down payment on the deal. If you have a Tenant-Buyer, the commission you need to pay will come out of the option fees from your Tenant-Buyer. You'll have to decide what risk you can afford when you set the start date.

If a Realtor is working with a non-Realtor on a sale, the Realtor will be glad to wait for half of the commission up front, but they won't wait for all of it on the back end. They will wait for a double dip, however. A double dip is when the Realtor gets the portion from both the seller *and* the buyer. If you are not licensed, the Realtor would get both sides of the commission. Whenever I talk about paying the Realtor, I will always mean I am paying the brokerage firm the Realtor works for. *All real estate commissions go through the broker.*

Structuring the Deals—the Details

A proposal is used to put together a simplified offer to a Realtor that they can then present to the homeowner or seller. It will put down the overall terms in writing without the specifics.

This saves a lot of paperwork because you only fill out the entire offer *after* you have an agreement on the *proposal*.

Here is what a proposal can look like to a Realtor or a seller. This is a Lease Purchase example, but it could be modified in format for a Subject-To or Lease Option.

Wendy Patton's, LLC

Proposal

123 XYZ Street

Innovative Approaches to Leasing/Selling

Wendy Patton's, LLC
has 2 programs to offer you...

Please review the following options that we can offer you as a seller and consider which would serve you best!

Lease/Purchase to Wendy Patton's, LLC #1
Wendy Patton's, LLC can guarantee you a monthly fee of $1,100.00 for a lease term of 3 years. We would then guarantee the purchase of your home within the 3-year term at a price of
$250,000.00.

Lease Purchase to Wendy Patton's, LLC #2
Wendy Patton's, LLC can guarantee you a monthly fee of $1,150.00 for a lease term of 5 years. We would then guarantee the purchase of your home within the 5-year term at a price of
$255,900.00.

In options 1 and 2 we would pay the rental amount whether the home is vacant or rented. You would still need to carry your homeowner's insurance and pay your property taxes until the home is closed. We would be responsible for everything else from the date this agreement starts, including all maintenance (minor and major, except the first 60 days). We will do a home inspection prior to taking over the Lease Purchase agreement. We would like to have all the appliances left with the home. At the closing you would only pay the seller's title insurance, seller closing fees and transfer fees (if any). These are standard closing fees for a seller.

We will start this contract when we find someone to lease from us; however, in the meantime you have the right to leave the home on the market. If you sell the home before we lease it, then this offer would be declared null and void.

The purchaser will put $7,500 (3 percent) down, which will be paid directly to (realty company name) and applied toward the listing portion of the commission and the purchase price at closing. Any remaining commission due will be paid out of the seller's proceeds at closing, to (realty company name). Note: because I am a Realtor the buyer side of the commission would come to my company. (If you are not licensed it would go to the Listing agent's office or to your buyer's agent's office, if you used one.)

We have many references available upon request. Thank you for considering Wendy Patton's LLC!

Don't be anxious on the proposals—make it low pressure. When you're first starting out, you'll want more deals to go through because there's a great excitement in the newness of the business. You'll be revisiting your proposals, wanting a quick response, and thinking of ways to use the money you're going to get on the back end if everything goes as expected. Although I do try to come up with creative solutions for sellers, if I think there's a profit to be made, I don't spend time chasing my proposals to get a deal done. It's a bit like testing the doneness of spaghetti: You throw it against the wall, and if it sticks, it's done. If your deals stick, you're done. If they don't work out, hopefully you've got others in your hip pocket that you're working on. Don't get too wrapped up in a single deal, because a lot of them won't work out. Approximately 30 percent of my proposals work out—which means that 70 percent don't.

With some of the Realtors I know very well; I might even do a verbal proposal. For example, I might say, "See if your seller will consider $1,200 per month with a price of $255,000—for three years— If they do, then I'll put together a proposal." I'm just fishing a little bit to see if it's even worth sticking around in that spot or moving to another. If the seller goes for it, I hammer out a proposal, and if not, there are plenty of other deals out there!

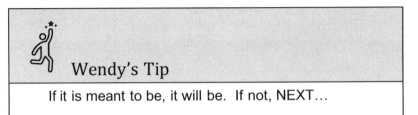

Wendy's Tip

If it is meant to be, it will be. If not, NEXT…

PART 4

STEPS TO SELLING PROPERTIES WITH LEASE OPTIONS

CHAPTER 12

Finding and Qualifying a Good Tenant-Buyer

Understanding how to screen and select Tenant-Buyers is the key to not only being a good landlord, but also to the business of selling and using the Lease Option technique.

A Story About Working with Buyers

A strange thing about prospective Tenant-Buyers is that you can't always tell who is going to exercise by how well things are going with their tenancy. Some people struggle to pay their rent but end up getting a mortgage on your home, while others pay perfectly and don't end up buying.

I had perfect tenants in an 18-month Lease Option, and everything was going so smoothly I was sure that they were going to exercise the option. Then in month 17, I received a call from the woman, who was crying. She said, "We have a problem. I can't pay my rent next month."

She was sobbing. She and her husband were getting a divorce and she didn't have the money for the rent. She was very embarrassed and wanted to work things out in any way possible. Thinking she wouldn't be able to stay, I asked if it would be possible to start showing the house right away, and she said, "No problem. By the way, I do have some *jewelry*. Would you take that in exchange for my rent?"

My ears perked up. "Jewelry? What kind?" I do like jewelry, but really, I was thinking I might never get paid, so perhaps I should *consider* accepting the jewelry.

The woman answered, "Diamonds and emeralds."

I said, "Really? When can I see them?"

She replied, "Well, how about Now?"

When I got to her home, I found out it was her

anniversary ring and wedding ring. I said, "I can't take those!"

"Really, I want you to have them. I can't pay the rent."

"But what if you reconcile?"

She answered, "We won't,"

and I replied, "You just don't know. I really hope you will."

Now this kind of thing tugs at your heart a bit, so I said, "Tell you what—I'll keep these for you. I'm a free pawn shop. I'll keep them a couple of years, for free. If you ever want them back, just pay that rent—no late fees, nothing. Just take them. I don't want your rings."

The woman responded, "Oh no, I'm not coming back for those."

I replied, "Well you never know. You might work it out. I want you to work it out."

She answered, "No, no, you don't understand. I've been divorced twice now—from *him*."

She never came back for the rings, and I still have them to this day. That was over 25 years ago.

Maybe one day I'll have them reset for one of my daughters or granddaughters. The point is that you just never know what you're going to end up with in this business!

Finding the Best Leads for Tenant-Buyers

Finding good Tenant-Buyers is the key to making the deal successful. There are many ways to find a good Tenant-Buyer for your home. One of the primary ways I use to market my houses is to advertise on the Internet. Use whatever sites are being used in your area. If you aren't sure, then Google a rental in an area you are interested in, and it will pull up the results. Then you know what sites might be good. Some will be free, and some will charge you a fee. Try a few *different* ads. If you get no response, make changes and try again.

I have a student who ran *this* ad, "Free pizza with this home". People would call her up and say, "What's this about free pizza?" and she would answer, "Every month that you pay your rent on time you get a free pizza delivered to your new home." It's amazing what people will do for a free pizza! You could make it "For the first year you get a free pizza...". It's just an idea. Get creative if you need to. Know your market. Know whether you're in a buyer's or seller's market.

How to Post a Successful Ad

When you run an ad, remember that "romance sells." Beautiful Sunsets, Bring your Canoe— think of something short and catchy for the ad, things that might reflect a holiday or time of the year. Or you can push on the credit issues, location, or special features of the property. There are many ways to reach Tenant-Buyers. Try different approaches to see what works for you. If one ad doesn't work, try another; if one website doesn't work, try another website.

> Rent with option to buy this 3 bdrm, 1 bath home in Xyz Town near Xxx Park. Large yard and sunset view of Blue Lake. $1995/month and $10,000 option fee gets you in. Bad credit OK. (248) 394-0767.

This is a very basic, generic ad. It should appeal to a broad range of potential Tenant-Buyers.

> Bad credit, no credit, poor credit? We can help. We have homes in this area to help you get your credit reestablished. Own a home soon! Small amount needed to get in. (248) 394-0767.

This ad will bring in the Tenant-Buyer with credit issues. We are trying to find someone with poor credit—not a *deadbeat*, just someone who needs another chance.

> Sunset views with a bottle of wine help you celebrate your new home. Low payments required $2250/month. Small option fee gets you a new start. Call today (248) 394-0767.

This is the romantic type of ad. Tenant-Buyers respond to different ads, just like the sellers.

> Buy your family a new home in 20XX! Start out fresh! Own a home now! 3bdrm 2ba in XYX Town with great schools. $1495 month and low amount required to get in. Call today. No bank qualifying. (248) 394-0767.

This ad is great to run at the end of the year or the beginning of a new year. It is perfect to work on people's New Year's resolutions.

> Stop Renting! Buy Now! We have several homes available with lease option terms. ABC and XYZ Counties. Start building your future today. Homes ranging from $1195 to $2495 per month. We can help YOU! (248) 394-0767. www.yourwebsite.com

This ad contains your company web site, which is always a good thing to include in an ad if you have one. Usually, you won't have one until you've accumulated more properties. Nothing looks worse than a website with zero or one property. Websites are one of the cheapest ways to advertise, as I discuss a little later in this chapter.

Note that if you are a Realtor, you must disclose that in your ads.

> Land Contract Wanted? We have a home available on terms. Call for a unique way to buy a home. 3bdrm home in XYZ Town. $1795 month. $4500 can move you in. (248) 394-0767. Seller is a licensed real estate agent.

This is a great ad for parts of the country where the words, "Land Contract" are used for seller financing. If your part of the country doesn't use this term, then substitute the words, "Seller

Financing", or "seller to hold the mortgage". This attracts people who don't feel they can get a mortgage. They know they will need the seller to assist them in their financing. We are not going to give them seller financing or a land contract, but these words will attract them. We will later discuss with them that we are doing a lease with an option to buy and that they can clean up their credit to get a mortgage during this time period. Or, depending on whether you own the home or how much they have to put down, you might consider doing a Land Contract or other type of financing.

Referrals from Realtors

You can also get Realtors to refer buyers to you. Realtors usually only work with buyers who are able to get a mortgage immediately. If the buyers don't have a preapproval letter, then they basically throw the buyer's name away. I created a letter with the heading, "A Piece of Garbage or $1,000?" The amount of money in this letter could be $500, or more than $1,000. The intention is to get Realtors to give you the names and numbers of the people who come through their doors that they can't help—people who can't buy a home traditionally through the Realtor. If they refer them to me and they buy a home using a lease with an option from me, then I will give the referring Realtor the amount stated in the letter when the buyer moves into one of my homes (not when they close). You can also entice Realtors by offering them more on the back end in the hopes that the person buys the home down the road. Realtors have leads on lots of these types of buyers. If you can't find them yourself, or if you need more, then consider offering to pay more upfront or something on the backend. Realtors get buyers who can't get a mortgage all the time. These are the very Realtors I work with when finding sellers. Now can you see how powerful it can be to work with Realtors? They can bring you sellers *and* they can bring you buyers. You might start with Realtors and their buyer leads but end up down the road with seller leads also. It is a process, and it takes time to build the relationship. Think of it as a long-term customer relationship. This type of relationship can pay you over and over again!

Websites

A website is not only one of the best ways to show your prospects the details of how Lease Options work, but also to show the specs and information on a particular home. And, if you have several homes to offer, you can show *those* properties on the site. It is an inexpensive way to advertise your homes. I am not a technical person, nor do I want to be one. You can buy a web address for a low annual fee and hire a high school or college kid to set up a website for you. Websites are not expensive, and they can provide viewers with a lot of information on your homes and services.

Signs

Post signs in front of your homes that say, "Lease to Own," "Rent Option," "Lease or Buy," and so on. Also, if you have a rental home that is on a busy street or on a corner lot, write into the lease with that tenant a clause that allows you to put a sign out front to draw in tenants for other homes during their lease. Signs in front of homes do bring in calls, for that home or for others.

Referrals from Tenants

Offer your current Tenant-Buyers a discount on rent if they refer a friend who Lease Options from you. Be careful if you offer option credits to purchase. The Dodd Frank act makes this type of incentive a little bit tricky.

There are many other ways to find Tenant-Buyers, so experiment and see what works best for you.

Types of Tenant-Buyers and Their Credit Situations

There are many types of credit situations. The four types we will discuss are:

(1) Good

(2) Deadbeats

(3) Bad with reason

(4) Unknown

When a person has perfect or <u>good</u> credit, they don't need to consider a Lease Option. This technique is not necessary for them to buy a home. People with good credit can work with a Realtor and buy any home in their price range. They can also find a home for sale by owner and work directly with a mortgage broker to get a loan. They have many choices, so they don't need this technique.

The opposite of good is <u>bad</u>. Deadbeats are those who have poor credit and no excuse for it. They earn enough, but they choose not to pay their bills on time, or at all. They tend to be poor money managers or are lazy and don't want to work to pay minimal bills. These are not the type of buyers you want in your home. They need to make habit and lifestyle changes, and you won't be the one to make those happen. Deadbeats are deadbeats—you don't want them!

Then there are the people who have poor credit <u>for a reason</u>. They are good people to whom something bad happened. Bad credit can be the result of many things, including loss of job, divorce, medical problems with no medical insurance, disability, being young and dumb, etc. These individuals have hit bottom financially and are on their way up again. They've improved their situation, but not enough to go and buy a home yet. These are the types of Tenant-Buyers you want to consider.

There are also people with *<u>unknown</u>* credit. This might mean they don't have any credit and they need to establish some prior to qualifying for a mortgage. Or they could be debt free and have a big savings account, but lenders don't like them because they don't know whether they can keep up on payments. Go figure, and don't get me started....

Bankruptcies are at an all-time high in our country and aren't likely to get better. When someone files for bankruptcy they won't be able to get a mortgage for several years after the discharge. People with collections or late pays on their credit reports need time to heal their situations. Many folks don't want to *wait* until they can qualify for a mortgage. We, as real estate investors have an opportunity to help people in these situations through Lease Optioning. People want to *buy* now but can't. They are willing to pay more for a home on a Lease Option and have it now rather than wait and save money. It's the common, "we want it now" mentality that floods our country.

There are two things many people ask themselves when buying a car: how much down and how much per month? If those two things fit in the budget, then they buy the car. Whether the price of the car is $68,000 or $28,000 is irrelevant. It's the same mindset with homes: The end price is not as important as the *terms*. Lease Options give terms to people with less than perfect credit.

 Wendy's Tip

Putting people in your homes who CAN get a mortgage if they do the right things will allow you sleep at night. Putting people in your homes who CAN'T get a mortgage should keep you awake. In other words, if they screw up, you should be fine with keeping their option fee.

Qualifying the Good Tenant-Buyer

When you run a credit check, you are looking for someone who had a blip on their credit and who is now on their way to financial stability. When you look at someone's credit record, see if they are on their way up or not. Notice what they have paid recently and what is still behind—this will show up on their credit report. Learn to read credit reports and get set up on a reporting system that works for you. If you don't know which system to use, talk to others in your real estate investors group or you can go to my website to see who I recommend. You can also work with a mortgage broker to run credit and do the Lease Option approvals.

Your Standards

It is a federal law requirement that landlords put their rental *standards* in writing. If you don't have your standards in writing (and, unfortunately, few landlords do), you are liable to end up in a pickle if someone accuses you of being in violation of this law. Your standards do not have to be complex but should be reproducible if someone at a local or federal agency, or anyone off the street requests a copy of them.

Written standards can be as simple as this:

Qualifications for Tenant Selection for Wendy Patton's, LLC
Lease Options

- No landlord tenant judgments unpaid.
- Ability to pay all outstanding judgments/collections.
- Good landlord reference.
- Gross monthly income equal to three times monthly rental rate or more.
- If any bankruptcy, it must be discharged.
- Option fee available or must be negotiated/financed.
- Prefer they have spoken with a mortgage representative.

In my Lease Option standards, I don't include a credit score requirement, but I do state that if they have a bankruptcy, it must be discharged. I also don't put length of employment, but you can. These are only my standards for *Lease Options*—my standards for my *regular rentals* are stricter. You must *establish* your standards and they must be in *writing*. Remember, whatever you make them, strict or less so, you must follow them for any applicant—You can't accept someone who doesn't qualify just because you like them.

Screening a Tenant-Buyer is extremely important, and yet some investors still go by instinct or illegal decisions.

"We liked them," some investors will say to me. We want to buy from sellers who "like" *us*, but we *can't* sell that way. There are too many good Tenant-Buyer liars in the world. You may feel you can read people, but relying on your gut will set you up for a rude awakening. Many of my worst situations arose from my own desire to believe in people. We should screen all people the same, strictly on the facts and not our opinions or prejudices.

Screen a tenant by reviewing their application thoroughly. Check it for accuracy (see below) and make sure they did not lie—If someone lies to me, they are denied immediately. Check their name—get a copy of their driver's license. Check their landlord history. The current landlord may want to get rid of them, but the previous landlord has nothing to hide. Call them both. Confirm they are the real landlord(s) in one of two ways: check it on county records or call the person and mention a different amount of rent than on the rental application stated.

> For example: "Hi, my name is Wendy, and I'm calling for a reference on your tenant named Joe Smith. Can you tell me how long he has rented from you? How does he keep your home? Has he been a good tenant? Would you rent to him again? Also, I see he pays you $1300 per month, right?" Actually, the application says $1000 or something else. If this is Joe's friend, he will say, "Yes, that's right, $1300 per month."

> If it is the real landlord, he will correct it: "No, Joe only pays $1000. Did he say he paid $1300?" Then I say, "Oh, no I see you are right. It does say $1000—I misread it. Does he pay the $1000 on time each month? Has he ever been late? (if so, check how late) Thanks so much for your time."

Check the applicant's employment also. I use the same technique when I verify their income as I do their rental amount. When I contact the employer I say, "Joe put on his application that he is making $36 per hour—is this correct?" when he put $29 per hour. If the person you reached is his employer and not his buddy, they will correct you on this one. On occasion I will also ask the applicant for recent pay stubs to put in the file. Sometimes it's hard to get the information without a signed release by the applicant.

All this information is also handy to have in case you ever have to garnish wages. Be sure to verify hours they work and time on the job as well. Also check their banking information—you might need it later.

Know What Are Reasonable and Unreasonable Expectations

Many of my tenants have pets, and many of them smoke. For this reason, I never say, "No smoking" and "No pets" because if I did, I wouldn't have many tenants. In my rental agreement it will not allow for smoking, of any kind, inside the home. They must smoke outside. Smoking and pets don't make people bad prospective Tenant-Buyers, however, here are some things to look for on their applications that are potential smoking guns for bad tenants:

- Why did they move? When prospective tenants say they had a "bad landlord" before, it puts up a red flag for me. I know there are bad landlords out there, but the red flag it raises is that they are blaming someone else for their problems/situations. I look further to see if there are other instances of blaming. If their business went into foreclosure, are they blaming their accountant? If they have tax liens, are they blaming the IRS? Be especially watchful for this blame game tendency. Having someone who takes responsibility for where they are financially is what I am looking for.

- How long have they had their current job, and how long did they have their previous jobs? What salary are they currently making? If they haven't been employed very long in their current situation, call their current employer to get an employment verification. Get the verification from an executive in the company or from the

CPA/accountant. *Do not get it from the receptionist!* Get the start date of employment as well as the current salary.

Finding and Qualifying a Good Tenant-Buyer

The Credit Report

Run a credit report and see what's going on with their debts. Some people may have medical issues that have caused their current financial difficulties, but most mortgage brokers will overlook these. What is more important are repossessions, foreclosures, bad credit card debt, judgments from landlords, etc. If they have a string of bad debts, you could be the next bead on that string.

The credit reports I receive have bad debts shaded and good debts in white. I like to see a lot of white on the page. Too much shading indicates a lot of current and potential future problems. Do they have frauds on their report? Do they have bankruptcies in their report?—This is not necessarily a deal breaker, as bankruptcies can happen to even the best people and can sometimes be out of their control. However, the important question is, what are they doing to repair the bankruptcy? How long ago was it? Has it been fully discharged? Are they paying their bills on time?

Criminal Background Check

I don't run criminal background checks, even when the tenant looks like what I would consider to be "a criminal". Don't deny this, you're thinking right now about what that looks like to you! If you run criminal checks for one applicant, you must run them for all applicants. Also, I am someone who believes in forgiveness and second chances. If they served their time, I want to give them the benefit of the doubt. The ones who don't serve time are the ones you might not even know about. Accepting or denying past criminals are something you will have to figure out for your own business. That said, criminals are one of the categories that are not protected with fair housing. You get to set your own standards with this topic. In order to comply with fair housing what you do for one person you must do for all.

I remember when one of the first homes I ever bought was up for rent. Two rough-looking guys on Harley Davidson motorcycles drove right up into the driveway and wanted me to show it to them. At the time, I was just 21 years old and feeling a little intimidated by these big, scary looking guys. Honestly, I thought when I went inside with them, I might not come back out alive.—Luckily, that home didn't have a basement. They wanted to fill out an application. Once I started to chat with them, I realized they seemed like really cool guys. They actually ended up renting the house. They paid their rent perfectly and on time every month, and they left the house better than when they rented it. This is precisely why we can't go on looks or a "feeling", but on the credit and criteria standards we set up before we even meet an applicant. You must turn a blind eye and only focus on applicant's qualifications. In that spirit, you should also be thoroughly versed in the current fair housing laws.

What You Should Know About Fair Housing Laws

Fair housing laws could be the subject of an entire seminar. Realtors around the country have half to full-day training sessions on this topic alone (and sometimes yearly), because fair housing rights, when violated, can cost the violators hundreds of thousands of dollars. This is not an area where you want to mess up.

The bottom line is this: Select a tenant based on their application alone and nothing else. There are federally protected categories and there may be some state ones also. This list is changing all the time with new categories being added. Your local real estate investors group can help point you in the right direction. The simplest way to be safe is to refrain from making decisions about anyone based on their looks, talk, religion, sexual orientation, sex, national origin, age, and several others. Therefore, I say that we should be blind and deaf when selecting a tenant. If we evaluate on the application process alone, we'll stay out of trouble. Make the selection based on facts, not on gut feelings. Stick with the law.

Some federal and state protected categories include (but may not be limited to):

- Religion
- Race
- Nationality
- Sex
- National origin
- Color
- Sexual preference
- Marital status
- Age
- Weight/height
- Familial status. While you can't ask potential tenants how many children they have, you *can* ask how many people total will be residing in the home. You don't have to rent your two-bedroom home to a family of nine.
- Mental and/or physical handicap
- And they have likely added a few more recently....

Be extremely careful in this area of federal and state law. Even an inadvertent misstep can haunt your career for a long time.

Rejecting a Rental Applicant

If you reject someone's application, you must let them know why you rejected them in writing, and there is no need to pussy foot around your reasons. Be honest but be kind. Let them know that if they can clean up some of their credit difficulties, you may be able to help them in the future. If you feel inclined, you might even suggest they talk to a lender or financial counselor about how they can get their credit report into a more favorable position.

Buyer's Objections

Although Tenant-Buyers will rarely have any objections to renting from you, there are a few that might come up. You will need to know some ways to handle these objections and what you can say to your Tenant-Buyers. Here are two of the most common:

1. *What happens to my option money if I don't buy this home?* Answer: "It's nonrefundable. I am committing to a price and timeframe and the house is going off the market during the option period. That is the fee for this service. If you're not sure you want to buy this home, you shouldn't put an option fee down—You should rent from someone else. We want to rent this home to someone who wants to purchase it in the future. You do want to buy one day, don't you?"

2. *What if I can't get a mortgage?* Answer: "Then you would lose your right to buy this home. We do have the right to *extend* or give you another chance to buy it, but at this point we're not guaranteeing anything. If the market goes up, we also might increase the price of the home. We're only fixing the price and terms during the period we have agreed on today. You should talk to a mortgage broker before you sign any contracts. It's usually a requirement of all lenders that the applicant pay off judgments, liens, and collections before they can qualify for a mortgage."

I don't want the potential Tenant-Buyer to delay deciding, so I always say that I have other people looking and that my ad is still running, so they need to decide what they're going to do and how interested they really are. After all, they are the ones in need, not me.

There are times when you will find the Tenant-Buyer does not have the full amount to put down for the option fee. Be creative with the option fees. I've taken two mobile homes in trade for option fees. I'm not in the mobile home business and actually don't like them, but it got the deal done! Or you could work on monthly payments with them. You could take an extra $200 per month toward the option fee until it's paid in full; however, you should always get more up front than what you would have received if you were getting a security deposit. Don't ever do less than what your security deposit would be.

Once you have your terms determined and your good Tenant-Buyer selected, you must get the paperwork ready and signed. Get them locked in and set for the move-in date!

CHAPTER 13

Getting the Paperwork Ready for the Tenant-Buyer

Approved!

Once you have approved a Tenant-Buyer for your Lease Option home; all you must do is draft the paperwork and have them sign. You don't need to give more than 12 to 18 months to the Tenant-Buyer on a Lease Option. This time frame is most often enough for a Tenant-Buyer to get a mortgage. For you, there is a benefit in keeping it short-term, especially in appreciating markets; or if you want them to cash you out. Whatever appreciation is written into the contract is what you must honor, regardless of whether the market goes higher. Additionally, appraisers have a 5 to 10 percent leeway on appraisal values. You could also structure a long-term Lease Option that says the sale price will be a starting value plus the appreciation during the Lease Option time period. You will just need that appreciation value to be defined. Where you will find that value to determine the price so that the value will be clear to both parties when it is time to close. Just make sure if you do this you state what source you will use for the appreciation. If you want an appraisal to determine the value instead, then you should state (in your agreement with the Tenant-Buyer) who will pay for the appraiser and who will hire them. If it's my appraiser, the Tenant-Buyer may feel taken advantage of, and if it's the Tenant-Buyer's appraiser, the appraisal might be too low. Keep the term short to avoid problems.

If at the end of the time period your buyer wants to extend, you can do so at your discretion. This can also be an opportunity to renegotiate. If the homes in that area have appreciated more than you expected, then you would want to extend, but increase the purchase price somewhat. You could also ask for another $500 to $3,000 option fee for the convenience of extending the Lease Option. Finally, you could raise the rent slightly. Sometimes I have given my Tenant-Buyers an extension for free, because of certain circumstances. There are also times when I've said no. It's totally up to you how you want to handle extending.

Options you have at the end of the Lease Option Period where your Tenant-Buyer doesn't, or can't, exercise their right to buy:
1. Renegotiate terms
2. Extend the contract for an additional option fee
3. Increase the rent
4. Increase the price
5. Keep everything the same and just give an extension.

You can't predict what the market will be like in the future, so getting further out than 12 to 18 months can be risky for you, and you might forfeit your ability to sell the property outright at the end of the Lease Option.

If it is more than a few days between the end of the option and the day they plan to move into the home, your best bet is to get a nonrefundable deposit from them to hold the home until the move-in date. This protects you from them changing their minds at the last minute. A personal check at this time is okay if it has time to clear before the move-in date, otherwise I would have them bring a cashier's check or send a wire. Make a photocopy of the check to get their bank account information. If they end up ditching the home and owing you money, you will know where to garnish their bank account (available in most states). Although their account information should be listed on their rental application, getting a check helps you verify it.

Have all the forms printed and ready to go. Get the tenant to sign early if possible. Depending on how busy you both are, try to get all the documents signed after they give you the deposit. You can also get them all signed electronically and in advance.

When you are working with the buyer, you are the landlord to them. You are also the seller, as far as they are concerned, because you have set the terms for the sale, including the option fee, the monthly payment, and the sale price. You need to use pro-seller forms. These are forms that specifically favor your end of the deal as the seller. These are the ones in my, **"Selling with Lease Options"** course.

At the beginning of this transaction, you have either optioned the home *from* the seller and optioned it *to* a Tenant-Buyer or you own the home outright. As with the purchase process, it's helpful to use a checklist to make sure you don't miss any steps.

Selling with a Lease Option Checklist

Address:_____

Move-in date: _____

Seller name: _____

Phone: _____

- Advertise home.
- Get application fee.
- Get application.
- Confirm applicant meets criteria.
- If not, send a rejection letter.
- Get nonrefundable deposit and Nonrefundable Deposit Form if Accepted.
- Cancel advertising.
- Create tenant folder.
- Draft contracts.
- Videotape home or take pictures and add them to your tenant folder.
- Get check-in/out list.
- Sign contracts.
- Sign lead-based paint disclosure.
- Sign seller's disclosure.
- Confirm utilities in their name: Water, Gas, Electric, Trash, Other.
- Confirm check-in/out returned.
- Confirm they have renter's insurance.
- Remove sign and lockbox.
- Make a copy of tenant's check for tenant file.

Some of the checklist items will be self-explanatory, but let's look at each of them.

Advertise the Home
This is discussed in Chapter 12.

Get Application Fee
You decide how much. I charge $40 per person over 18 years old.

Get Application
Make sure they fill out all areas of the application completely. My application requests information on each applicant over the age of 18, even if they are not working. It will be up to you to ask for the same or to have them pay/not pay for the credit report. It asks for their driver's license number, Social Security number, employment information, banking information, landlord or current address information, and previous landlord information. The more information you can gather, the better off you will be if you ever need it. It is not so much needed for your evaluation, because that is done to the standards you have set in Chapter 12, but if you ever have a problem with a tenant and need to collect from them you will want complete information on this application. Make sure it is filled out and signed by all parties.

Confirm Applicant Meets Criteria
See your standards from Chapter 12—this is a simple yes or no.

If Not, Send Rejection Letter
A rejection notice is required by law whenever anyone applies for credit or a place to live and is turned down. You must specify why someone is not accepted, whether it be landlord history, income status, credit issues, or anything else not federally protected by law. You must be specific.

Get Nonrefundable Deposit and Nonrefundable Deposit Form If Accepted
Once someone has decided they want to move into one of your homes, but they don't plan to move in for a couple of weeks, be sure to get a nonrefundable deposit. This is separate from an option fee, but it will be applied toward their option fee later. The nonrefundable deposit holds the property for them and demonstrates their intent to rent it. Later if they don't sign their contracts or move in, they would lose this deposit.

Create Tenant Folder
On the account you've created on Dropbox, Google Drive, or a similar service; you will create a tenant folder for the property. All information about the Tenant-Buyer (or tenant if only renting) and their contracts and correspondence will go into this folder. Be sure to label all

documents by name for them to be searchable. This way, you can find anything that you are looking for quickly. You will also be able to easily send any file you might need.

Draft Contracts

Draft the rental agreement, option agreement, offer to purchase, pet agreement (if applicable), lead-based paint disclosure, and seller's disclosure, and any other state required forms.

Videotape Home or Take Pictures

Do this *with* the Tenant-Buyer if possible. I suggest you take a video camera with you when you are doing the walkthrough for the Tenant-Buyer to move in. Say things on the video like "Marie, what do you think about the kitchen cabinets? What do you think about bathroom tiles? What do you think about the closet doors?", and have the date recorded on the video to prove everything. Then Marie can't come back later and say, "Those kitchen cabinets were trashed" when she said on the video that they were fine. Any pictures you take should be kept online in the Tenant-Buyer file for that house. After I take digital pictures of the home, inside and out, I put them in their file (online). Those pictures are to protect me later if they don't buy the home and have done damage to it.

Give Check-in/out List to Tenant-Buyer

The check-in/out list is a form the Tenant-Buyer can fill out to evaluate the condition of the home when they move in. This gives a baseline of the home and its condition. It is to protect you both if they don't purchase the home and they decide to move out. It will spell out the condition of the home at the time when they moved in. Each state has different requirements as to what judges will require and allow, but the more you can show on the condition, the better off you will be if you are trying to collect damages the tenant has done. Go overboard versus "underboard" on documentation and pictures. You hope you will never need them, but if you do, you will be glad you have them. Everything I do before and during the tenancy is to make sure I am prepared later if I need it. The *goal* of course is *not* to need anything I document.

Sign Contracts

The buyer must sign each of the contracts with you. If, however, they have already paid their nonrefundable deposit, I will allow them to take the contracts and review them. They must sign before they move in.

Sign the Lead-Based Paint Disclosure

See Chapter 7 for more detail. You can create a new one that is blank and says you don't know anything about lead in the home (if this is true) and sign it. You can attach the previous owner's lead-based paint disclosure and have the Tenant-Buyer initial it to acknowledge they have seen it. The lead-based paint disclosure is required by federal law.

Sign the Seller's Disclosure

If this is the first time you have rented this home, you may not know much about the home, so you can write on the seller's disclosure that you've never lived in the home and that the buyer should do their own inspection. Add that the home is being sold "as is". However, I also recommend that you attach a copy of the previous seller's disclosure to yours and have the Tenant-Buyer initial it. After all, you do know what the seller disclosed to you, and you need to disclose everything you know. Also, if you have had it awhile and the roof has leaked, you must disclose that, even if you fixed it. Don't skimp on this crucial step. Many lawsuits are filed because sellers *knew* about problems and didn't disclose them. If you had a leaking basement and fixed it, you need to put that on the seller's disclosure. It won't stop anyone from buying the home if it was fixed, but if it leaks later and they find out it wasn't disclosed, *you* will be fixing it again; If it *was* disclosed, *they* will be the ones fixing it.

Cancel Advertising

Cancel any advertising you have been doing for this home. Sounds simple, but it can be expensive. I have forgotten to do this, and it can cut into your profit if this is not on your checklist.

Confirm Utilities Are On

Once the tenant has moved in, make sure they have transferred the utilities into their name, including gas, water, electricity, and water softener (if applicable). Check all the utilities they need to turn on for your area.

Confirm Check-in/out Returned

Make sure you follow up and get this form returned from your Tenant-Buyer. If there is anything on the check-in/out list that needs to be addressed, take care of it. Personally, I prefer to walk through with them and have it signed, and returned when they move in—No form, no keys. We do it together with them filling it out and signing it.

Confirm They Have Renters Insurance

If not, continue to follow up in writing with them and put a copy of each request documented in their tenant folder. It probably won't be a make or break for you, but if something were to happen to their personal belongings, for instance, you will have all the proof you need that you tried and tried to protect them, but they failed to protect themselves.

1. Remove Sign and Lockbox.
2. Make a Copy of Tenant's Check for Tenant File, if applicable. You might need this later if you need to garnish their bank account—if they are a good Tenant-Buyer who turns bad.

Always Check Your Paperwork!

My partner, Debbie, and I purchased a property on Newman Street. The little house had 900 square feet with a walk-out basement to Paint Creek. The owner was an older woman who had split the lot, and a developer was going to build a home on the vacant part. The vacant lot was the same size as the one with the house. When we bought the property, I knew up front that the owner was going to sell the vacant part to a developer. We Lease Optioned the house to a couple who gave $5,000. As happens many times, everything was going perfectly, and it seemed like they were going to exercise the option. Sixteen months or so into the Lease Option, the couple called me and insisted, "You have to sell us the other property too."

When the couple first signed the Lease Option, I had physically walked the property with them and showed them what Debbie and I owned and what we didn't own, including the fact that we did not own the undeveloped part. They still said, "You have to sell it to us."

Standing firm, I reiterated that only the house and the property it sat on were included in the Lease Option, not the vacant split property.

At the end of their 18-month option they not only didn't exercise the option, but they stayed on an additional three weeks without paying and then moved out. I sued them for $900 for unpaid rent. They countersued for the refund of the Lease Option money, again insisting that it was their right to buy the entire property. It cost me $1,500 in legal fees but the judge awarded me their $900 in unpaid rent. The couple still refused to pay the rent and it ended up being scheduled with a mediator. Then the day before the mediation for $900, the couple called and paid it. End of story? No!

Two weeks later I got a call from the woman we bought the house from, who said, "We've got a problem. You own my vacant lot." It turns out that when we bought it from the seller through Century 21 and the title company, both parts of the property had been deeded to us, although the vacant part was not *supposed* to have been deeded. We actually *did* own both parts of the property, just as the wife had insisted, and if they had actually exercised their option, they would have owned both parts. We had copied what was on the deed when we purchased it onto the Lease Option agreement when we sold it. It turns out the wife worked for a mortgage company and had probably checked out the extra parcel and thus, understandably, thought I was lying about not owning the other part of the property. We honestly thought Debbie and I only owned the one half. I had taken the deed I received from closing, copied the legal description for the entire parcel, and put it right on my copy to her. After the case was settled, we deeded the vacant part back to the original owner. The moral of this story is to always check your paperwork, especially legal documents! The legal description can be slightly wrong from the title company or your mistake of typing. Really double check these before you sign to buy or sell.

What You Need to Know About the Three Essential Contracts

Each state may require slightly different information for rental and purchase agreements. My contracts are good enough to use everywhere, but they should still be reviewed by an attorney in your state. Each state also has its own landlord, tenant, and security deposit laws. Therefore, as recommended in Chapter 7, you should seek the advice of an attorney if you are using any generic contracts for your state to buy, sell, or lease real estate. I recommend Legal Shield attorneys at www.GotLegalPlans.com. They have plans starting at very reasonable rates per month to give you legal assistance. I have been a customer since 1998 and have saved thousands of dollars on legal questions, contract reviews, letters, and so on, for real estate matters and in multiple states. Each state has its own rules and regulations regarding rentals, lead-based paint abatement, evictions, and so forth. There are many more clauses when you are selling, especially the rental agreement. The option agreement and sales contract/offer-to-purchase might only have a few changes. When you are buying, the rental agreement is very short; when you are selling it is longer. Here are some of the items I consider in my contracts to sell with a Lease Option:

- *The option agreement:* On the buying side, the option agreement turns control of the property over to the optionee without ownership. When I am doing a Lease Option, I sign an option with the buyer. I control the property as if I owned it, but I am giving them the right to buy upon exercising the terms of the option, usually in 12 to 18 months.

- *The rental agreement:* The rental agreement specifies how long the tenant will rent the home and how much they will pay each month in rent to me. During the rental period they can purchase the home, unless otherwise specified. A rental agreement also comes in handy if you ever need to take your Tenant-Buyer to court. The rental agreement for the tenant is the main reason why I don't combine my contracts for selling with Lease Options. A judge could consider it like a Contract for Deed/Land Contract and make you go through foreclosure instead of an eviction if the tenant didn't pay you.

- *The purchase agreement:* This agreement sets the terms of the final sale. Again, there are two of these—one for my deal with the seller and one for my deal with the Tenant-Buyer. The deal with the Tenant-Buyer sets the sale price upon exercising the Lease Option. On the Tenant-Buyer side, the contract also has a specific sales price, and because you set the terms of the Lease Option, that price will be higher than the price you have with the seller.

Points to Consider for the Option Agreement

It is important to get the optionee (Tenant-Buyer) to be responsible for the maintenance and well-being of the house and property during the option period. The optionor is the owner. Here are some points in my option agreement:

- Optionee (Tenant-Buyer) agrees to accept the property in "as is" condition.

- Optionee agrees to make all repairs major and minor to the property. Usually I will ask the Tenant-Buyer to do anything under $500 and I will pay for anything over $500 (which really goes to the original seller).

- If the optionor (you the seller) must make any repairs to the property, the cost of the repairs will be added to the purchase price. (If someone's water heater or furnace goes out and the tenant can't afford to fix it, you should go ahead and pay for the repairs. In all states, that I know of, it is difficult to require tenants to do repairs. However, in the OPTION agreement you *can* put in verbiage that puts most, or all of the maintenance on the Tenant-Buyer.)

- If there is a pool, the optionee agrees to open and close the pool each year and to maintain the pool. (The opening and closing of the pool are essential if you live in a cold state.)

- The Option may become Void if the optionee pays their rental payment or any option payment more than 10 days late. (It is important to remind your tenants that their record of payments will have to be submitted to the mortgage company and may damage their ability to secure a mortgage. If they are serious about owning the home, they need to be serious about paying on time.)

- Optionee understands that optionor does not hold title (own) this property but is transferring their interest in the property. If optionor can't transfer title due to something out of their control (i.e., owner refuses to close or can't transfer clear title), optionor will reimburse optionee the entire option consideration plus an additional $500 for their inconvenience, as full and complete liquidated damages for optionor not being able to close on this property.

- Optionor has advised the optionee to seek the advice of a mortgage lender and attorney prior to signing this document. (The mortgage broker might look at their credit and their history and tell them that even with an 18-month option they will not be able to clean up their history enough to qualify for a mortgage. They should also always have a lawyer look over any type of document that commits them to an agreement. In my experience, most people talk to neither, but they sign the document saying that they have.)

Points to Consider for the Rental Agreement

The rental agreement gives the Tenant-Buyer the right to occupy the property during a specified period. It is like the rental agreement you signed with the owner/seller, except obviously your rental agreement with the Tenant-Buyer will be very pro-landlord (pro-you).

The rental agreement needs to be separate only for selling on an option. The reason is that if the tenant doesn't pay, or the deal goes south, you will want to be able to evict them as quickly as your state allows. If you have all three agreements in one contract, some judges will look at the Lease Option as a sale rather than a lease, and therefore make you go through a full foreclosure or forfeiture process versus an eviction. This will take much longer, be more expensive, and may require an attorney.

A cosigner can be an important safeguard (for the rental agreement only) if you have a weak applicant, and they have a strong parent or friend who is willing to sign with them. It works well for giving liability to someone else who will come through with the payments. I had a situation where a mother cosigned for her daughter. It was just a rental, but the daughter had terrible credit. The mother, however, had worked for General Motors for 25 to 30 years and made a good "guarantee" person for me. The daughter stuck me for nearly $5,000 in unpaid rent and damages. The mother paid for it out of her GM checks. In another case, the mother was a local Realtor in Michigan, and she asked me to help her daughter get a house. Her daughter had been through a rough time, and the mother was willing to cosign. I probably didn't even run the daughter's credit because I knew the mother was a well-known Realtor and was good for whatever might happen. The mother paid the $5,000 option fee, and the rent was $1,300. Eventually the daughter left, owing me $3,000 in unpaid rent, and the mom had to pay it off.

Having rent due on the first of the month is the easiest for most people. If a tenant moves in on the seventh, I prorate the rent for the month. My rental agreements specify late fees of $25 for the first day late and $5 per day afterwards, and the tenant, of course, must sign the agreement. The higher your rent, the higher the late fee can be. I can't reiterate enough how necessary it is to have everything in writing, spelled out in detail. That way your tenant can't say, "I never agreed to that." All you must do is point to the contract and say, "Here it is in black and white, and there's your signature underneath it."

Your other fees on the property can include a pet deposit, security deposit, cleaning fees, and the like. In a Lease Option, I usually do not require a security deposit, because if they have an extra $2,500 for a security deposit, which is refundable, I'd rather have them apply that to the option fee, which is nonrefundable. There are some good reasons and areas of the country where even a small security deposit *is* recommended. It gives the tenant something they can get back if they don't purchase. Some judges like a small amount showing as a security deposit. This way the entire amount the Tenant-Buyer is putting down won't be non-refundable. The option fee, however, does not show up on the rental agreement, because it is in the option agreement only. The option agreement is a separate document.

Your rental agreement should state the total cost to move in. For example, if there are pet or

196

cleaning fees, and/or a security deposit you will add them to the first month's rent to get the total for the rental agreement. The rental fees plus the security deposit make up the total move-in costs. The rental agreement must also show the total amount of anticipated rent for the contracted period, including prorated months. Do not put the option fee balance due on the rental agreement. You need to add that separately.

You can also state in the agreement that if the rent is more than 10 days late, the agreement may revert to a month-to-month rental (nullifying the purchase option) at the discretion of the landlord. I generally don't do this unless I want to get rid of the tenant, because when this alternative plan is set in motion it allows the tenant to move out at any time. Be sure your rental agreement states that the keys are due back within 24 hours if the tenant moves out.

Payments should be received by the due date. If they still use mail, then it should be postmarked before the first. Most likely you can set up some automatic electronic payment system with them. In my rental contracts I also specify that any bounced checks will require an additional fee. Although I start out trusting my tenants and allowing them to pay with personal checks, if one check bounces, all payments after that must be paid in certified funds or electronic payments only. I also recommend that if their rent is late twice within a 12-month period, their monthly rent will increase by $50 per month. This needs to be in the rental agreement to apply. If they are already struggling, this might be difficult to enforce, but if you have it in writing, then you can decide if you want to push for it or not.

You should specify to the tenant how their payments will be applied, and in what order:

1. Outstanding dishonored check fees.
2. Outstanding late fees chargeable to tenant.
3. Outstanding legal fees, court costs or both.
4. Outstanding utility bills that are the tenant's responsibility.
5. Any damage caused by tenant.
6. Costs for re-letting the property, if applicable.
7. Additional Lease Option fees owed.
8. Rent.

You should apply their payment toward rent last. Normally you can't evict for any of the other unpaid items, only unpaid rent. Use their money to pay for unpaid utilities, and if the rest doesn't cover the rent, you can begin eviction proceedings in most states. Again, check with your local investor group or a local real estate attorney on landlord eviction laws.

Additional Issues to Cover in Your Rental Contract

Occupancy Having any guest staying more than 14 days will be considered a breach of the agreement unless the resident tenant receives written consent from the landlord. I also don't allow them to use the premises for a home business without my permission (written into my agreement). A lot of people have home-based businesses, and that's not a concern except if they have customers coming in and out of the home, which creates a potential liability issue. Check with your Tenant-Buyer to see what kind of home-based business they will have. Marijuana growing is very popular right now. Address this clearly in your rental agreement. I don't allow any smoking in my homes, nor the growing of Marijuana on or in the property. Check the legal wording and exclusions allowed in your state/city for your rental agreements.

Pets I make sure that they sign an agreement with me regarding pets on the premises. There are certain breeds that insurance companies will not insure. Those breeds are not allowed in my rentals. No dogs comprised of the following breeds are allowed on the property by either the tenant or their guests: Akita, Alaskan Malamute, Chow, Doberman Pinscher, Irish Wolfhound, Rottweiler, Siberian Husky, Au Presa Canarias, Great Dane, Boxer, Dalmatian, Pit bull, Mastiff, Saint Bernard, German Shepard, Australian Shepard.

Entry and Inspection This gives you the right to enter the property at reasonable times and with reasonable notice to inspect the premises. It's not that you are inspecting their personal lives, but that you want to make sure the home and property, which do not yet legally belong to the Tenant-Buyer, are maintained in accordance with the rental agreement. You may also want to show the home to prospective new tenants or buyers. If the tenant decides not to exercise, you want to have the right to install a "for sale" sign on the front lawn. However, you shouldn't even step onto the lawn without calling the tenant first, as this is violating their rights to peaceful enjoyment.

Assignment and Subletting I do not let my tenants (or Tenant-Buyers) sublet or rent any portion of the premises without my prior consent. The subletter's name is not on the rental agreement.

Joint and Several Liability Anyone who signs the contract is one hundred percent responsible for all the points within the contract up to the total amount due. One time I had three men who signed the agreement and all three split later. I was only able to find one of them and I told him he was one hundred percent responsible to fulfill the agreement. He felt he should only be responsible for one-third, but this inclusion of Joint and Several Liability protects the landlord from having to find all the tenants. If one can be found, that one is one hundred percent responsible.

Maintenance, Repairs, and Alterations It is always the tenant's responsibility to maintain the residence and property in a clean and sanitary manner including fixtures, equipment, appliances, furniture, and all other furnishings. If they should choose not to exercise the purchase option down the line, the residence should be left in the same condition as originally rented, normal wear and tear excepted. Residents/tenants are responsible for changing the furnace filters and the batteries in smoke detectors on a regular basis. They should be responsible for the maintenance of the property. The tenant cannot make major changes to the structure until they own the property. I had one resident who tore off an upper decking because he decided he didn't want it, and I had to pay for it and then rebill him because

I didn't own that home. The resident also cannot paint, hang wallpaper, or make any other changes without my consent. One of my tenants repainted the inside of the home navy blue, and then left after two months. I had to sue to recoup my costs for repainting the home.

Appliances One of the things I list on the contract is all the appliances already in the home. I make it clear to the tenant (Tenant-Buyer) that all the appliances in the home are there for my convenience—in other words, they belong to me. If, therefore, one of the appliances stops working and they dispose of it without telling me and then leave the home with that appliance missing, I will bill them for it. If they want to remove the appliance, I have to agree to it and I will cross off their rental agreement with my initials and the date.

Insurance Coverage Because the owner's policy does not cover the belongings of the tenant, the owner requires the tenant to carry their own insurance against the risk of damage to their personal property. **This insurance must be in place before the tenant moves in.** This policy is where the tenant (Tenant-Buyer) also names you as *additional insured* for extra liability protection.

Security Deposit Act Make sure that the Security Deposit Act (SDA) of your own state is in your rental contract. The SDA varies by state, and you must know what the rules are for your state. You are the one providing the contract, so you are responsible for that information.

Notices Any notices must be in writing for your own protection, and not verbal. Notices should be sent to the residence address. If the tenant (Tenant-Buyer) is sending you a notice, it should be sent to the address specified in the contract (either office or post office box).

Make Sure Your Tenants Read and Understand the Agreement

It is very important that you go through the contract line by line with the tenant so that they have heard everything out loud and are fully responsible for the contents when they sign their name. Don't skip over any points of your contract, even if they begin to fidget because it takes a while. You might also ask after each point, "Do you have any questions about that?" If they want to take the contract with them to look at more closely, that is okay. If they receive it electronically, they can review it at their leisure.

Purchase Agreement—Offer to Purchase – Sales Contract

The offer to purchase should be pro-seller. Some things to consider when drafting the purchase agreement include:

- What items that were in the house will remain with the house (for example, appliances)?

- If they get an FHA or other government mortgage, the lender might stipulate improvements to the property before the loan goes through. I don't want to be responsible for that, so I say clearly in my contract that the tenant is responsible for any requirements needed to fulfill their own mortgage.

- Make it clear that the Tenant-Buyer is buying the house "as is."

- The Tenant-Buyer should have a home inspection done before moving in. If they waive their right to do so, I mark down and have them initial the date they walked through the house.

- Make sure to give the Tenant-Buyer the seller's disclosure statement. This not only becomes a part of their history, but it will then be handed off to the next buyer as a complete history of the house.

- Include the lead-based paint disclosure and the property inventory check-in/out list.

- If you are a licensed Realtor, you have to disclose this in writing.

- Advise the purchaser to seek the advice of a mortgage broker and an attorney before signing the purchase agreement.

Be Prepared for the Tenants

On the move-in date the Tenant-Buyer delivers the final balance in certified funds or electronic transfer. The day they move in, make sure the following items have been completed:

- You have a copy of their renter's insurance.
- You have enough keys for the home.
- Remove the sign and lockbox, if any.
- Make sure they have the utilities turned on in their name.
- Have the tenant walk through the home and complete the check-in/out list.
- Take pictures/video of the home.

Now that you have all this fresh in your mind, it's time to practice! Get the forms together and go through them until you know them. Bookmark this section for reference until it's memorized.

CHAPTER 14

Managing the Property and the Tenant-Buyer

It's amazing to me how many people will pay an option fee and then walk away a few months later, knowing that they have just forfeited their option fee. It is equally amazing how some people will try to get their option fee back, even though they are nonrefundable. The option fee paid is for the *right and privilege* to purchase a home within a given time frame. Whether the Tenant-Buyer (optionee) meets the terms of the option is up to them. My goal is to get people to buy, and I'll do what I can to help them, but I can't make them responsible. I can't make them close on the home either. Approximately half of my Tenant-Buyers never get to the closing table; some walk away from their option fees after only a few months of tenancy. If they forfeit their rights, that's their choice, but some Tenant-Buyers will try to get that option back any way they can.

One of the smallest houses I ever Lease Optioned was in Michigan. It was approximately 700 square feet and had what is called a Michigan basement—a cellar with a dirt floor (or rough cement), stone walls, and a low ceiling. I leased it to a man named Arnold, who moved with his wife from a larger house into this smaller one. You might say that Arnold was like a customer because this was the second home I'd rented to him, but he was a good renter, always paying his bills on time. This time they decided to do a Lease Option versus just renting the home. However, it wasn't two weeks into the rental when I got the phone call with the four dreaded words, "We have a problem." I braced myself and asked, "What's the problem?"
Arnold replied, "There's a snake in the house." I asked, "What kind of snake?"
Arnold said, "A *big* snake, like a boa or python.

Arnold and his wife now wanted their option fee back and said they were going to move out immediately. He asked me, "Wendy, do you know of any snakes in this house?" He had told me that they have found stool samples on the basement floor and had them examined by a local pet store. They had supposedly told them it was a large snake.
   I said, "Arnold, hold on just a moment."

I put him on hold and thought about it for a moment. It began to come back to me that the previous owner, a big burly guy with a lot of tattoos, did have snakes. I was a little fuzzy on it, though, because I had only been out to the house once, whereas my office manager, Amie, had done many of the visits to that home. I turned to Amie and asked, "Did the previous owner by any chance have snakes?"

She said, "Oh yes, don't you remember? He had cages full of them in the basement. And on the day that we went to close and do the walk-though, I noticed that one of the big cages was empty, so I asked him where that snake was, and he said he gave it away." We both fell on the floor laughing hysterically. We had never heard of such a thing in all our years of real estate. A big snake loose in a small house. Understandably, it was not so funny to the Tenant-Buyer.

We had no idea where to start. We had dealt with leaking roofs, flooded basements, broken furnaces, frozen pipes, anything else, but big snakes? We don't have those in Michigan!

I got back on the phone with Arnold and said, "Well, there's a chance there could be a snake in the house. Let me call the previous owner and see if he knows anything about the snake. I'll call you back." The previous owner was nowhere to be found.

Do you know how hard it is to find a snake expert in Michigan? I called animal experts, the zoo, pet shops, animal control, and exterminators, but I couldn't get help on the situation. I had my handymen go into the house and crawl through everything, including the attic, to find the snake. They couldn't find one.

In the meantime, Arnold called and said someone had gone into the home and seen the snake's tail go up into the wall from the crawl space in the basement. Arnold also told us he and his wife were moving out. Soon I received a call from their attorney asking for their option fee back. After discussing it with their attorney and several of my friends, who agreed they would not live with a snake either, I told the attorney that when I found the snake, I would gladly return the option fee.

After many more weeks of searching, we finally found a guy whom I nicknamed "Mr. Outback" because he was willing to handle any type of critter situation.

Mr. Outback said, "Look, I've got this glue that's $100 per gallon (20 years ago now), and I'm going to put it onto a plywood board and put the board on the basement floor. When the snake crawls across it, he'll get stuck, and we'll have him!"

I let him put the board down, but, doubting the success of this method, I also called the attorney back and said, "I'll tell you what: If you can get sworn affidavits from the people who examined the stool samples and from the people who saw the tail go up into the wall, I'll refund the option fee." In the meantime, my partner said, "Sell that house."

The house went back on the market, but I forgot that glue board was in the basement. An agent, Susan, was showing the house. She went into the basement, and I had forgotten about the glue board. My cell phone rang when apparently, she stepped onto the glue board. "Wendy? What is my foot stuck to in the basement?"

I said, "Oh, that's just the glue board to catch the big snake in the house!"

Susan screamed, and I couldn't stop laughing. Her shoe was completely stuck to the board. I said, "I'll pay for your shoes!" The house *did* sell not long afterwards, and I wrote on the seller's disclosure, where it asks for history of infestation, "None confirmed."

I never heard from the attorney or Arnold again. Apparently, they couldn't get sworn statements from their witnesses.

I think what may have happened in this case is that Arnold and his wife didn't like the smaller home. When the neighbors told them about the previous owner's snakes, they began to imagine noises in the walls. Regardless, with no snake, there was no refund. I could have gone after the rest of the rental agreement also, but we sold the home, so I dropped the matter. It is amazing what people will do to get out of an agreement.

Wendy's Lesson

Option fees are *not* refundable, even though some people will try to get them back. They might even make up stories to get them back.

Property Management Issues

If you have Tenant-Buyers in your home, you have certain responsibilities to them. Take care of the house and make sure it's livable, keep open lines of communication. View your sellers and Tenant-Buyers as customers. I'm tougher on the Tenant-Buyers because they mess up deals more often, while it's not usually an issue with the sellers. I still always keep my end of the bargain.

Make sure that you're keeping your Realtors, lenders, and others always informed about this Tenant-Buyer or seller (if the Realtor was involved), and that they know where to reach you if they have questions. Communication is key!

Protecting Your Privacy with Tenants

In general, you do not want your tenants or Tenant-Buyers to know where you live, so have their rent come to either an office or a post office box. In case a deal goes sour, and you have to evict them, you don't want a disgruntled, grudge-bearing Tenant-Buyer to show up on your doorstep. You must protect yourself and your family. My address is private for my family and my protection. Don't make it too easy for them to find you.

Who Is Responsible for Repairs?

One of the benefits of the Lease Option is maintenance—the Tenant-Buyer usually does it all! My Lease Option contract says that the Tenant-Buyer is responsible for all maintenance, major and minor. If I ever *do* end up doing any repairs, I'm going to add the cost to the purchase price at closing. Let them think through their own possibilities first, but if they still don't know what to do, then send your own maintenance people and recoup the cost at closing.

For example, if the Tenant-Buyer's heat goes out in the middle of a Michigan winter, it's crucial to get that fixed. On the other hand, if the air conditioner goes out in the summer, it's unpleasant but livable. Don't make your Tenant-Buyer unduly fix too much, because if you treat the tenant like an owner then the court may treat *you* like a seller. The Tenant-Buyer can claim that they've put so many dollars into the property, and the court may make you go through a forfeiture or a foreclosure versus an eviction, which in most states is more expensive and more difficult.

In a buyer's market you can put more of the responsibility for maintenance onto the *seller* (see Chapter 6 on negotiations). In a seller's market, it won't be as easy. I need to preapprove in writing any improvements my Tenant-Buyers want to do to the home.

Keep a copy of any letter regarding maintenance in the Tenant-Buyer's folder. When a Tenant-Buyer calls, everything discussed is recorded for their file. The same goes for maintenance. It's important to track everything. If the roof leaks, and someone slips and falls, accurate files will suddenly become very important! How do you think I know that one? ☺

Transition between Seller Moving Out and Tenant-Buyer Moving In

After the seller has moved out, make sure it's ready for the Tenant-Buyer. As you learn more you will ask the seller to do more before they move out, so the home is completely ready for your Tenant-Buyer without you having to pay for much, or preferably anything.

Move-in List for the Tenant-Buyer. This can include these steps:

- Change the locks.
- Carpets cleaned if needed (the seller may do this, but if they don't, you need to make sure it happens).
- New paint (if needed – or touch ups).
- Home fully cleaned
- Kitchen cabinets are cleaned out.
- Garage cleaned out.
- All appliances left behind are clean and in good working order.

Always assume that the Tenant-Buyer *won't* buy. You don't want to count those chickens before they've hatched!

Always have complete documentation of everything regarding a Tenant-Buyer moving in. The best ways to get a picture of what the home looked like at move-in are videos with the Tenant-Buyer inside and a written/signed-by-Tenant-Buyer move-in checklist. It is important that you capture on video their verbal acknowledgment of the condition of everything, whether good or bad. You also protect yourself with paper documentation of the condition of the house—documentation that they have signed. The Tenant-Buyer always thinks they're going to buy when they move in. Life sometimes throws us a curve and things happen. The Tenant-Buyer might get divorced, get relocated, lose a job, become disabled, etc. They then end up moving out of your home. And sometimes they leave damage.

If the window wasn't broken at the time of move-in but is when they move out, you will have the paper and video evidence you need to take them to court and sue for damages.

Go through the check-in/checkout sheet with the outgoing Tenant-Buyer, if you have a chance—have them check the condition of everything and sign everything. Take pictures at the same time or even video the walk-through for future reference if needed.

Maintenance on the Property

Although the option agreement states that the Tenant-Buyer is responsible for all maintenance, it is still important that you keep the place habitable and treat the current resident like a tenant/renter, not an owner. If you treat them like an owner, a judge might also treat them like an owner, which will nullify the option.

When a Good Buyer Turns Bad

Unfortunately, this business is not all perfect. There are times when you will have a Tenant-Buyer who you think is great—you are sure they will exercise their option; they have paid on time, taken care of improvements/repairs, and been nice in all dealings. Then it happens: either you don't hear from them, they miss a payment, or they start to make things difficult with repairs, complaints, and so on. They were a good tenant but now they are bad.

Try to work things out on the phone first. If this does not resolve the situation, then put any issues in writing. If you have a problem with a Tenant-Buyer that can't be resolved over the phone or in writing, then you must go to the next step: eviction and the revoking of their option to purchase. For you to be able to do this, they must have violated part of the rental agreement or the option agreement.

Such situations are why I use option contracts that are subject to the rental agreement being followed. A great clause to include in your option contract is this statement: "If any rental or option payment is made 10 days or more late, then this option can be declared null and void by Optionor." It is usually advised to revoke an option in writing *before* you evict a Tenant-Buyer. Don't try to evict at the exact same time as you revoke their option agreement. This adds only a few days to the process. Once you revoke their option, you can start the eviction, as there is then no option agreement in place. (In most parts of the country, revoking an option agreement is not necessary to evict someone; however, it's safest that way.)

To revoke an option, you can send the Tenant-Buyer a letter via both first-class mail and certified mail, both letters containing the information that the option has been revoked. The certified one is the one you want them to receive and sign for, but if they don't, you sent it first class also. I use this for extra precaution. When you send the revocation letter, you should indicate why you are revoking their option. You might want to attach a copy of their option agreement and highlight the area you are utilizing to revoke their option contract. The letter can be as simple as this:

> *Dear Joe,*
>
> *Attached is a copy of the option agreement you signed. Your rent is now 15 days overdue, and this is a violation of the option agreement. You have been late many other times also. We are now voiding your option agreement. Please be advised that you no longer have the right to buy this home.*
>
> > *Sincerely,*
> > *Wendy Patton, member Wendy Patton's LLC*

If you want to allow them to reinstate their option, you can state that in this letter:

> *Dear Joe,*
> *If you want to reinstate your Lease Option, you will need to remit the amount of $ _____ currently due, by (date).*
> > *Sincerely,*
> > *Wendy Patton, member Wendy Patton's LLC*

I recommend this statement if you want to work it out with the Tenant-Buyers. Remember to try other, softer ways to work things out first; the revocation letter should be a last resort. If this is used too early in the negotiations, the Tenant-Buyer may be angered to the point of no return.

The best advice I can give on late payers is to start eviction as soon as possible. My office starts to evict when rent is five days late. From over 35 years in this business, I have learned that tenants aren't always honest with you. I tend to want to believe them and to work with them. It was always hard for me to evict, because of my soft heart. Believing in people is my default and on occasion it turned out to bite me in the butt. Unfortunately, I've been burned many times by deceit and promises that could not be kept. After managing my own properties over many years, now I now use the services of a property manager and my stress level has gone way down. Remembering one thing can help you be firm on this policy:

Wendy's Advice on Accepting Sob Stories

> If the Tenant-Buyer doesn't pay their rent, <u>you</u> are paying it for them.

You can listen to all the sob stories you want; however, most of us can't afford to carry another family.

If you don't like playing the heavy, you can have your partner/spouse sign the contracts and you be "the manager." Then the Tenant-Buyer doesn't know you are the owner—they only think you manage the home. This way when they don't pay and they give you a sob story, you can be the good guy. Example: Tenant-Buyer hasn't paid rent due to husband being laid off, wife is pregnant, it's December and very cold outside, and it's almost Christmas. You can say, "Boy, I really feel for you. This must be a hard time for you. I would let you stay, but I have to start the eviction process, or I could lose my job. The owner is very strict on this and is tight on cash also. He/she really needs you to pay soon. Do you think you can do it?"

You don't want to have late payments from your Tenant-Buyers, so you lay out the ground rules up front about late fees. Alternatively, though, Tenant-Buyers might feel too intimidated to call their landlord with even a *legitimate* excuse about why the rent is late. It is important, therefore, to keep a rapport with the Tenant-Buyer—facilitate a comfort zone and open communication. Be friendly but not friends—at least not until the option is exercised. It's like a parent-child relationship—the parent is not the child's best friend. Being a landlord is a business. If the Tenant-Buyer doesn't pay the rent and you don't do anything about it, *you* will have to pay their rent—and that's not a smart way to run a business.

If you have an arrangement with your Tenant-Buyers that their rent is always due on the first day of the month and you don't get it, call them immediately or send a notice: "Is your rent going to be late? Call in with one of these numbers, so we will know why." When your Tenant-Buyer first moves in, you can give them a list of the most popular excuses you've had for rent being late. It's a little humor but at the same time lets them know you've heard it all before and that you'll be watching. It also shows there is a serious side to paying rent on time. You can add to your own list as you learn through the years. You won't believe the excuses you will hear.

- I lost my job.
- My dog ate the cash.
- My grandmother died.

- My grandmother died again.
- My roommate stole the money.
- My boss didn't pay me.
- My paycheck bounced.

Wendy's Tip

At the very least, Tenant-Buyer issues provide a great wealth of learning experience, and many times a good laugh! Learn to smile at the stories—it helps relieve the stress.

If you need to take legal steps to collect past-due amounts, be aware that each state has different collection procedures and sources. In Michigan I can garnish bank accounts, wages, state tax refunds, etc. In Texas, landlords can't garnish anything. You may want to use a collection service but be aware that the collection company will take 40 to 60 percent of what is recovered.

Tips to Increase Profits and Protection

1. Sometimes it pays off to find the Tenant-Buyers before you find the house! Line up some potential Tenant-Buyers, then go find the homes that will fit them in their price range and in their area. This is especially a good idea in a buyer's market.

2. Clearly define "on time" to your Tenant-Buyer, and charge for late rent. My rental agreements say that I will charge $25 plus $5 per day for late fees. Also charge court costs, state fees, legal fees, whatever your state will allow you to charge.

3. Enforce your maintenance co-pays on your rental agreement/lease. If the Tenant-Buyer is supposed to pay the first $50 of maintenance, make sure they do. Reminder this is part of the first $500 or whatever you have in your option agreement.

4. Consider increasing rent if the Tenant-Buyer is late a few times with their rent. This must be in writing, just like anything else you want to enforce.

5. Keep track of the title during transition, especially if you're not making the mortgage payment, and especially if it's a long-term contract. You want to make sure the title stays

clean and clear. Review the title work occasionally if you feel there could be something going on with the seller that might negatively affect it.

Moving a Tenant-Buyer Out When They Decide Not to Exercise

If the Tenant-Buyer decides not to buy the property, then go through the property with them and check it out.

If you had a security deposit with the Tenant-Buyer, keep in mind that in most states a security deposit cannot be used to cover normal wear and tear on the property. Usually with an Option I don't have a security deposit, because I want as much money as they have applied to their *nonrefundable* option fee, as opposed to a *refundable* security deposit. There are some areas of the country that are very pro-tenant, where you might want to put a small amount in the security deposit area on the rental agreement. Of course, if they have animals, you might also want to charge more of a security deposit. In any rental agreement, if the security deposit isn't enough to cover damages, you would have to sue the Tenant-Buyer to get recovery for the overage.

A Success Story

Years ago, when I first started with Lease Options, I Lease Optioned a property to a real estate attorney's daughter, who wanted her dad to review the contracts. It's always fine with me if an attorney reviews my contracts. But after the attorney review, the dad called me and said in a stern voice, "I'm not changing one thing." Now, if you know anything about attorneys; when you hire them to review a contract, they *always* mark it up. Somehow, I think it's how they convince you they're worth their fees.

Jokingly I said something like, "Oh no, my contracts must not be very good then." This is because they normally change everything to be "pro" their client.

He said, "No, you don't understand. My daughter made her bed, and she can lie in it. She got the bad credit herself, and she can fix it. Your contracts are tough, but they're fair. If she doesn't do her part, she'll lose her money. I'm not bailing her out anymore. I just wanted to make sure they were *fair*."

Thankfully, the daughter made her payments and ended up buying the house. That deal profited $35,000 for me. Three years after the closing I saw the daughter. She ran up and hugged me and thanked me for her home. She had recently sold it and made over $40,000 herself! She had two children and needed a larger home. This is a true win-win-win!

CHAPTER 15

Closing: The Big Payday

This is when it all comes together! This is the real estate investor's payday. If you have been working with your Tenant-Buyer from the beginning and keeping in touch with their mortgage broker, you will know when they are ready to purchase your home—when they are finally ready to close! If they want to use a mortgage broker of their own choosing, find out who it is and keep in touch with the broker so that you'll know where they stand on getting the client's mortgage closed.

Although the paperwork was signed many months earlier, often the mortgage lender may want you to change something on the contracts in order to get the mortgage approved. For example, the buyer may need more money for closing costs, so the lender may ask if you are willing to pay for some closing costs if you increase the price of the home by the same amount. I am always willing to do this, if the home can *appraise* for the new amount and the changes are fair for all parties involved.

A simultaneous or double closing is when there are two closings on the same home at the same time or usually on the same day. It is sold and bought the same day. In investor terminology it's called "an A to B and B to C closing". You, the investor, need to come up with the money to pay A before you can get the funds from C. If you don't have the money to pay A (and most of you won't), then you can use what is called Transactional Funding. Transactional Funding is easily found from a hard money lender, or a friend. I do Transactional Funding for investors in Michigan as much as I can. This funding will cost you about 2% of what you borrow. If you borrow $200,000, then you will pay $4,000 for Transactional Funding.

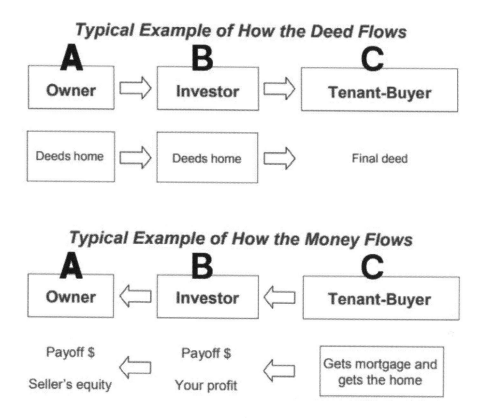

Typical Example of How the Deed Flows

A		**B**		**C**
Owner	⇨	Investor	⇨	Tenant-Buyer
Deeds home	⇨	Deeds home	⇨	Final deed

Typical Example of How the Money Flows

A		**B**		**C**
Owner	⇦	Investor	⇦	Tenant-Buyer
Payoff $ / Seller's equity	⇦	Payoff $ / Your profit	⇦	Gets mortgage and gets the home

This applies only to Lease Option deals. (With Subject-Tos you will already own the home, so there will not be a double closing.) These can be tricky with lenders that require seasoning of title (discussed in Chapter 7). It is essential to show that your interest in the title did not appear overnight. Depending on which state you're working in, closings may be handled by either a title company or an attorney. Some title companies and attorneys don't like simultaneous closings due to the fraud in the investing industry that has created the seasoning requirements. Make sure you find a title company or attorney who understands how you do this business and what you're doing. If you want a good reference, your local real estate investor group will certainly know who does this type of closing in your area. Tell them you're looking for an A to B and B to C double closing. (A is the seller, B is you, C is the Tenant-Buyer).

The are several issues with a double closing:

1. B must pay A without using C's money.

2. It costs B extra closing fees/title insurance/deed transfer fees.

3. The lender might not allow B (you) to take title and then sell to C (your Tenant-Buyer)— There might be a seasoning issue.

The good things about double closings are:

1. No changes need to be made to the agreement with the seller (A). What was signed is what you close with.

2. The seller never sees what you sold the property for. Yes, they can find out later in public record, but likely won't care by then.

To avoid the *issues* above there are some choices.

<u>For #1 above</u> – You must pay for what is called *Transactional Funding*. This is funding from a hard money lender (unless you have your own cash to pay A) which usually costs around 2% and is borrowed for a day. If you need $200,000 that would be $4,000. If you're *making* a lot of money, this might not be a big deal. The *funder* wires the funds to the closing for you to pay off the Seller (A). Then C pays *you* and you use *that* money to pay off the *funder*. Sometimes the title company may have someone who offers this service. In Michigan I offer this service. One day you may also offer this service to other investors. This expense just needs to go into the profitability worksheet to determine your profit.

<u>For #2 above</u> – When you do a double closing, not only do you need transactional funding (unless you have your own cash) but transferring title an extra time (as the middleman) will incur additional fees. The fees you incur will be title insurance, closing fees, and any deed revenue fees you might have locally.

<u>For #3 above</u> – The type of loan your Tenant-Buyer gets will determine whether "seasoning of title" will be an issue. Seasoning of title has to do with how long the seller in a transaction has been on the title prior to selling the home to a buyer. This idea of seasoning became an issue during the last downturn (2006-2010) when there were many deals involving flipping fraud.

Not every type of loan has a seasoning type of requirement. This is something to check with your Tenant-Buyers *lender* to confirm well in advance of any closing. If there is a seasoning requirement for your buyer, then you will likely have to have the deed go right from the seller (A) to the Tenant-Buyer (C). This would mean you/the investor (B) are no longer a part of the deal.

When you are out of the deal how do you protect your interest? There are multiple ways to do that. Likely you can work with the seller to put a lien on the property for your profit, OR you can do a payoff for your memorandum of option with the title company for that amount. Each deal is a bit different, but those are a couple of ideas to ponder. When we stop to take a moment and brainstorm on solutions for problems, we can come up with all sorts of ideas.

With seasoning a possible stumbling block, it is important up front that your contract with the seller can handle any type of change you might need. My contracts clearly state the seller understands that, due to the mortgage requirements of the buyer I might sell the home to later, the documents between me and them (the seller) might have to be redone. Redoing the documents will in no way affect their bottom line. If there are additional costs for any change to the seller's bottom line (what they net), I will cover those. That explains this situation in a high level, but it is something to prepare in advance.

Cheat Sheet for Double Closings:
A is the Seller/Owner
B is the Investor (you)
C is the Tenant-Buyer

Find out when the Tenant-Buyer intends to close and stay in communication with them and the seller about it until you get it down to the exact day and hour. *You* need to be the coordinator, not anyone else. You must make sure all the pieces fall into place. Coordinate the Tenant-Buyer's plans with the mortgage company. Make sure the Tenant-Buyer, the title company or attorney, and the mortgage company are all on the same page. Reconfirm with each party the day prior. It would be a shame for the deal to fall through due to a scheduling oversight.

The mortgage lender only sees one half of the transaction—the part between the investor and the Tenant-Buyer (B to C). To the lender, I am the seller. The *title* company sees *both* parts. Make sure when you are coordinating with the title company or attorney's office that they know both sides of the transaction, as they will need the paperwork on both sides. To them it is two separate files, and two closings.

The mortgage lender will need: copies of the contracts, a payoff letter (see the example at the end of this chapter), and proof of the Tenant-Buyer's payments. From the beginning, ask the Tenant-Buyer to keep copies of their canceled rent checks, or electronic payments, if possible. They WILL have to show those later. On my end I can show the rent came in from them, but likely the mortgage lender will want proof from their account to me for rent payments along with their option fee.

Normally, I do not like my buyers and sellers to meet. Though intellectually each of them know I am making a profit and each of them know I am a real estate investor, putting that dollar amount in front of them can destroy their enthusiasm. Many times, they will eventually see the numbers, but their closings will be at different times and locations.

Although it doesn't really matter who closes first with a double closing (A to B and B to C). If the buyer closes first, they will have to come back a second time. Let me illustrate why.

Scenario 1: Tenant-Buyer first. The Tenant-Buyer comes in with the mortgage papers completed but cannot receive *their* completed ownership package, because I don't have the deed yet from the seller—I can sign a deed to them, but I don't have one yet from the seller to me. They will have to come back and get their closing package *after* the seller closes with me. This is called a "dry closing," or "closing in escrow," meaning that something more must happen for it to be completed. In this case, the *seller's* and my closing must take place for it to be completed.

Though it may seem less efficient, I *prefer* to close with my Tenant-Buyer first as I find it more professional. This way, the money is at the title company or attorney's office. After that successfully closes, I will call the seller to let them know everything is fine and ready for their

215

closing. If the Tenant-Buyer doesn't close or their mortgage has a hiccup, then I delay closing with the seller. I just let them know my buyer's mortgage has a hiccup or delay. I will keep them updated.

Here is an example of a payoff letter for the lender:

To Whom It May Concern:

    Date: xx/xx/xxxx

    The payoff for <u>Tenant-Buyer's name</u> for <u>123 XYZ Street</u> is:

Purchase Price	<u>*$325,000*</u>
Less option fee paid on <u>xx/xx/xxxx</u> $5,000	*=*
Balance due as of <u>xx/xx/xxxx</u>	*$320,000*

    Please feel free to call me with any questions.

        Sincerely,
        Wendy Patton,
        Member
        Wendy Patton's, LLC
        (248) 394-0767

Add any additional expenses or repairs you paid for during the option period, outstanding utilities, repairs, etc. Don't forget to put these in the payoff letter also. If there is any unpaid rent due, do not put that on the statement listed that way or it might cause a red flag for their mortgage lender. Get them to pay that off before the letter goes out.

These items would go right under the option fee like below:

> *To Whom It May Concern:*
>
>   *Date: xx/xx/xxxx*
>
>   *The payoff for <u>Tenant-Buyer's name</u> for 123 XYZ Street*
>   *is:*
>
>   *Purchase Price*   *$325,000*
>   *Less option fee paid on xx/xx/xxxx*   –
>   *$5,000*
>   *Roof repair*
>   *+$2,500*
>   _____
>   *Balance due as of xx/xx/xxxx*   *$322,500*
>
>   *Please feel free to call me with any questions.*
>   *Sincerely,*
>   *Wendy Patton,*
>   *Member Wendy*
>   *Patton's, LLC*
>   *(248) 394-0767*

CHAPTER 16

Advanced Concepts and Strategies for Selling with Lease Options

I once bought a parcel of property on a Land Contract (contract for deed/seller financing). The property was splitable and located near me. This was quite rare for that area. One part of the property needed development and the other part had a house. The seller of the house was an older lady who had lived there for 30 years.

Because the house needed some work, I Lease Optioned it as a handyman special. Along came Steve, who was a licensed builder. Because he was a licensed builder, I had him sign all the contracts under both his personal name and his company name.

For Steve, this seemed like the perfect house. There wasn't anything wrong with the home that he wasn't capable to fix. It wasn't too far into the renovations, however, that Steve called me and said, "We got a problem—this house has been in a fire."

I was unaware of any fire, so naturally my first response was to call the seller and ask if she knew anything about a fire. The seller said that while she lived there, there had never been a fire. Now the house was built in the 1920s or 1930s, so there was a possibility that lots of things could have happened to it, but she didn't know about a fire and neither did my inspectors. Steve said, "Wendy, I can't even believe the *roof* is standing, because all the rafters are completely charred all the way up and through the decking."

I asked him what it would cost to repair, and he said $3,500 in materials. I offered to give him $3,500 off the purchase price when he exercised the contract. This had been advertised as a handyman special, so I hadn't cheated him or lied to him. How could I know what was up under the plaster? He agreed and we signed an addendum.

Everything seemed to go smoothly for months—he was making repairs and improvements, and I was sure he was going to exercise the option. Month 17 came (out of 18 on the contract), and I asked him if he'd been speaking to the lender and if he was going to get a mortgage. He said he had a little glitch in his credit, so I asked if he wanted to extend for another six months. I didn't have a problem with this because he'd been paying perfectly. But he said, "No, I'm moving next month. I don't like all this development happening around me."

Steve had known about the development when he moved in, and it was documented in the contracts that he signed. He moved out and sued me for the option money he had put down in the beginning.

Being sued is scary and nerve-wracking for most people. I don't like it myself, but I have been through it a handful of times. It's inevitable, and definitely a reason to keep excellent records on every little thing that happens with each house and every Tenant-Buyer.

In court Steve told the judge that there were many problems with the home, and he showed the judge lots of pictures of the home and of the fire damage. The judge asked him if he thought I had known about the fire. He responded, "No, I couldn't tell either, it was covered in plaster." Then the judge asked me. I said I had not known and that I did offer to pay the $3,500 to fix it. The judge looked over our contracts very briefly, and noted where it said the home was sold "as is," that it was a "handyman special", and that Steve had had the home inspected. The judge pulled her glasses down to her nose, pointed to a paragraph in my contract, and said to Steve, "Wendy did not have to offer to pay anything for the roof—she was more than fair. So, sir, I have just one question for you. What part of 'This option fee is NONREFUNDABLE' do you not understand? Case dismissed!"

Advanced Selling Strategies for Lease Options

Having mastered the basics of Lease Option deals, you might want to add some of these strategies to your tool belt.

Handyman Specials

Handyman specials are homes that are in less than perfect condition and require sweat equity to bring them up to a new level. A lot of money can be made from a handyman special. The Tenant-Buyer's overall purchase price, or option fee required, should be lower because they do the work themselves. There are more people who want this scenario then there are homes. This technique will work in most areas of the country, but not in areas where the city requires certification or landlord licensing. In those areas the city won't allow homes that aren't perfectly up to code to be rented. Sometimes these homes just need paint or a few minor changes/updates, but sometimes they may need some major repairs. In areas where the city doesn't require inspections or certifications, this can be a great way to liquidate your properties. Tenant-Buyers perceive value in the fact that they can do the sweat equity themselves. You'll make just as much money, and you won't have to go over budget on doing your own rehabbing.

One word of caution: Make sure the home is *habitable*. It must be able to be lived in, or you will have problems if the Tenant-Buyer doesn't pay and decides to fight you on rent or their Lease Option. Any judge will expect the landlord to provide a "habitable" home for their tenant. Generally, the Tenant-Buyer is going to love you because you are giving them the American dream: a nice fixer-upper.

Section 8

Section 8 is a rental-assistance program funded by the federal Housing and Urban Development department (HUD), which gives approved tenants financial assistance by paying a portion of the rent directly to the landlord. Section 8 now has a program for Lease Options. Section 8 doesn't control the particulars of how the Lease Option is set up but will make the monthly payments as with their regular program. After the Lease Option is started, they will help the Tenant-Buyer get a mortgage that will convert the Lease Option to a purchase. It's not appropriate for every Section 8 tenant, but for a select few that qualify. Talk with your local Section 8 administrators so that you have all the current information.

As a *landlord*, I love Section 8, because the rent payment, or most of it, comes directly to me from the state. This program itself, however, is not one I'm a fan of or have ever used. I feel it is putting the Tenant-Buyer in a bad situation that might later be a nightmare for them. How will they pay for a roof that will be $7500-$15,000? It just doesn't make sense to me unless it's someone in school or someone who will have a very different financial outlook soon.

Ads for Soft Rental Markets

In *soft* rental markets there will be many rentals but not many good Tenant-Buyers. In order to get a good Tenant-Buyer in your home, you will need to make your rental ads stand out. The ad needs to contain something that makes it look better than the competition's ads. One idea that I have used is to offer to rent for a few hundred dollars lower per month then market rent. When the applicants call, I give them choices. Finding out how much they can put down for an option fee will be crucial. Example: if you put $7500 down, then the rent is $1750, *but* if you put $10,000 down the rent is $1550 like the ad says. Which one works for them?

Also don't forget those Realtors during this time. Who do they know who can't get a mortgage yet? Remember the letter: "$1000 or a piece of garbage?" Work with agents during soft rental markets. The agents can use the extra cash and you can use their non-qualified buyers. It's a win/win!

Strategies for Reducing your Taxes

First of all, I must disclose that I am *not* a CPA or tax advisor. Seek the advice of one to confirm what I am sharing with you and how it applies to your situation. These are things I've learned about taxes in my many years of investing. Would you, kind of, not mind if you had to worry about paying Uncle Sam? About getting into a lower tax bracket because you're making too much money with Lease Options and Subject-Tos? When you've been investing for some time and get your pipeline filled with deals, your income will increase, and you'll need to become creative in finding ways to save on your taxes when you sell. You can always keep your properties forever, but if/when you do sell, there are tax repercussions. Here are some things that I have done to reduce taxes for myself.

Exercise Your Lease Option and Hold for Another 12 Months

If you are in a higher tax bracket, you might want to consider exercising your Lease Options with your sellers *prior* to your Tenant-Buyers exercising their options, because a simultaneous (double) closing is considered a short-term capital gain, and since you only owned it for one day, you would be taxed at your normal income rate. If you exercise your Lease Option and hold the title for more than 12 months it becomes long-term capital gains, taxed at a much lower rate. Reminder you can also do a Performance Mortgage to create long term capital gains. Unfortunately, if you sell on a Lease Option and don't do one of these techniques (Performance Mortgage or buy and hold for 12 months) the profits are likely taxed at higher rates.

Therefore, if taxes or a high tax bracket is an issue for you, consider exercising your option with the seller early (or do Subject-Tos) and then make sure your Tenant-Buyer doesn't close for another 12 months. This would give you long-term capital gains on the ownership of the property, giving you a much better tax rate on the profit. This is not a problem with Subject-Tos, as you are the owner from day one and just have to do a Lease Option for 12 months to get a long-term capital gains rate. Also note that you can put a provision in your Lease Option agreement with your Tenant-Buyer that they can only exercise after xx/xx/xxxx date. This provision must be clear and in writing if you want to prevent them from closing early and putting you into a short-term tax situation.

1031 Tax-Deferred Exchange

A 1031 exchange is an excellent way to defer your taxes and capital gains by taking the profit of your sale and rolling it into a property of higher value, or two or more properties whose combined value is higher than your sale. It's a bit more complex but that is a good high-level view. A 1031 tax-deferred exchange is a great tax strategy, but it takes a bit of planning and foresight because of the timing involved. You need to have a property/properties lined up and ready to put your profit into prior to realizing that profit.

As to the profit, *you* won't control the money yourself once you sell the property you are exchanging. A company which does 1031 exchanges will play what is called the "intermediary" between the current sale and the new property/properties and will move the money from one closing to the next *for* you. It must be done very carefully and with a qualified non-interested third party. You also can't live in the new property (at least not for a while). You need to *rent* the properties or hold them as an investment because a 1031 is for *investment* exchanges and *not personal residences*.

This strategy should be used when you need to defer your capital gains. When you're first starting out in the business, you might not be showing much income, so you won't need the 1031 technique, but do remember it exists. When you find you do need these and/or other tax lowering techniques, you know you've made it!

Use Your IRA for Lease Options and Subject-Tos

Speaking of "making it" in real estate, your retirement funds can be a key to a tax-free wealth-building strategy. There are two basic types of IRAs.

A traditional IRA is what most people have. You get a tax deduction when you put money in, but you pay taxes when you take the money out after 59 ½ years of age. You pay a penalty also if you take anything out before 59 ½.

A Roth IRA is the opposite. You don't get the tax deduction when you put the money in, but you don't pay income taxes when you take it *out* after 59 ½ years old. The Roth is tax free for life (at least at the time this book was written).

Roth IRAs are my favorite by far because I realize that what I put in the Roth IRA I will be able to significantly grow before I retire. The reason I can grow the Roth IRA is because I use an IRA custodian who is a 'Self-Directed IRA Custodian". This doesn't mean I can select my mutual fund or stocks. This means I can buy rentals, flips, apartments, land, etc. with my IRA. Imagine buying a property where you flip it and make $40,000. It likely took less then 6 months to do that. When it's in your Roth that money stays in there tax-free for you to buy more properties or invest in what you choose. A lot of people think if you make too much money you can't contribute to your Roth IRA. Yes, that is technically true, but you can always open a traditional IRA. Once you have funded the traditional IRA you then move the money to a Roth conversion. Anyone can do that no matter what your income limit is. You get the write off for the traditional and then once you convert it you pay the taxes on the amount converted. They call this the "back door" Roth approach. You can sell your Lease Options by "assigning" the Lease Option at the end, like discussed above and all of your profit goes into your Roth. Make sure you leverage this loophole and tax strategy as soon as you can afford to put some of your investments away for the future. The company I use and recommend is Equity Trust in Ohio. They are the largest in the country and have been around a very long time. If you want a contact to personally help you there, reach out to me at Info@WendyPatton.com and I can help you out. They have shielded a huge chunk of my income earned. Having them help you in the same way is a "win-win" ☺.

225

PART 5

CREATING FUTURE FINANCIAL FREEDOM—FX3

CHAPTER 17

Business Organization for Lease Option and Subject-To Investments

You might be thinking, "I have a few properties, and keeping track of what's going on isn't difficult with a few files on my desk." But apply that thinking to 175 active properties in various stages of buying and selling, renters paying late, evictions and rehabs, and you've got an administrative nightmare if you don't have systems in place. That was my life in 2003 I married my husband, Michael in 2003. He saved my life with real estate. Early in our dating life, he asked me, "Why do you have so many houses?". I replied, "Well, I like them". He then replied, "But you don't even have that many shoes!" I then thought about it for a minute and replied, "You're right! I need to go shoe shopping!" What really happened is that I downsized and kept around 50 of my best properties. Some of the 175 got paid off by selling others, and some were paid down, or money saved for when I exercised my Lease Options. The point here is once you have too many homes, think about consolidating the equity to have some of your homes free and clear while others are Lease Optioned. Simplifying was the best thing to catapult my real estate business to the next level.

Setting Up an Effective System

Whether you have only a few properties or many, you might as well set up your business as if you're planning for many properties. That way you're already in the groove for expansion.

Color Coding Your Files

Set up an online storage account like Dropbox or Google Drive to keep all your files handy. I keep my files in alphabetical order by property address, not by seller or Tenant-Buyer name. Each property should have two files: one for the Tenant-Buyer and one for the Seller. I explained how to set up each folder more in Chapter 7.

Seller Folder

The seller folder holds all the documents that you signed with the seller—the "pro-buyer" contracts. If you own the property on a Subject-To or a mortgage, all the mortgage or Subject-To documents will be put there. In the seller folder you will also put any correspondence with that seller as well as any information about the home such as title work that was done, surveys, inspections, etc.

Tenant-Buyer Folder

The Tenant-Buyer folder holds all the signed "pro-seller" contracts. It also holds all correspondence with the Tenant-Buyer, original application, credit report, copies of payments, all bills, maintenance records, all other related correspondence, and pictures of the house. This folder may even contain a video of a walkthrough of the property with the Tenant-Buyer to show the condition of the home when they moved in.

This folder should also be used to keep track of any communications with the Tenant-Buyer. Create a simple spreadsheet or word document in the folder to keep a record. Anytime one of your tenants calls, texts, or emails; make note of the communication, including what was said and what the resolution was. Document everything with dates and times, and if you send a maintenance person, make a record of who you sent and what they did to fix or not fix the problem. Property management software can track much of this for you, but you have to enter the information in the system. The data is only as good as your record keeping. Hopefully, you will never need the documentation, but if you ever do, you will have it there. Don't throw it away until years after you have sold the property to them or to someone else. I had a case where a tenant sued me a year after they moved out for a slip-and-fall case from 2.5 years earlier; however, we had all our documentation, so it never went to court. *Keep your records!* I didn't even know they were upset about it, and I would never have expected them to try that, but they did. Tenant-Buyers have a certain number of years in which they can still come back and sue you, so hope for the best and plan for the worst.

It might sound like I have gotten sued a lot or ended up in court often. With as many deals as I have done, of course I have some. It is rare that this happens, but I am sharing most of them with you so you can learn from them to protect yourself.

Software for Your Business

If you have only a few properties, you don't need any special software for keeping track of their information. A simple spreadsheet in Excel or Google will work just fine. However, if you have many properties, you may want to invest in a property management software program. Talk to someone in your real estate investors group or on one of the real estate web sites to see what program will meet your current needs. There are many property management systems on the market. See which one is rated the best and will fit your strategies and goals best.

There are also many accounting programs available. In my office, for each of my companies, we use

QuickBooks. It writes our checks or tracks electronic payments, keeps our accounts balanced, and at any time I can get an itemized report. QuickBooks has been the best for many years and still seems to be the leading bookkeeping software in the industry. At any time, I can run a report to see how my LLC, or a property is doing financially. The key is to make sure the software can track items by property so that whenever an item is paid or received, it is linked to a particular property. If you are using the appropriate software and have religiously assigned the payments and deposits, you should be able to quickly see a summary and/or detail of all income, expenses, improvements, and so on by property. In QuickBooks, using "Class Tracking," with each *class* being a particular property, you will be able to easily accomplish this.

Good bookkeeping and tracking of your numbers are a key to being successful. You must know where you always stand financially. If you don't keep organized and updated, then you won't really know where you stand. Numbers and number tracking in detail is something I learned much later in my real estate career (with Keller Williams actually) and it really changed my financial knowledge and the trajectory of all my businesses. Another advantage to good bookkeeping records is that your bill with your accountant will be much lower because so much of their work is already completed. Handing your accountant, a shoe box full of receipts is expensive and not a good way to run your business. And yes, real estate investing is a true business.

Wendy's Tip

Learn as much as you can about real estate investing, but don't forget to learn about running it like a true business. Business skills will take you to another level that most investors never get to.

Work Orders

When something goes wrong in a home, or when you have work to be completed, you will need a process to track the work and the call. The contractor must complete the work order, fill it out with details of what was completed, and then bring it back to us in order to get paid. We then scan this into the Tenant-Buyer's file. You can also create a detailed email/document which you can save in the Tenant-Buyer's file. We then follow up with the tenant, if the house is occupied, to make sure the work was completed. If so, we issue payment to the handyman. We keep a copy of the work order in the Tenant-Buyer file. The repair cost may later be added to the purchase price, depending on the terms of the Lease Option contract with the Tenant-Buyer and the extent of the repair. The seller may also be responsible, depending on what was negotiated with them.

Tenant Payment Ledger

Using a software system will help you with your ledger. However, you can also do something manually if you like. Here's an example of what one might look like:

Your Company Name:_____   Option Fee: _____

Address of Rental: _____   Lease Dates (to/from): _____

Tenant Name: _____   Water Softener:_____
                                       (amount if applicable)

Buyer Phone: _____
                                       City Water: _____

Monthly Rent:_____
                                       City Sewer: _____

Other charges:_____

Security Deposit:_____

The next section of the ledger is the payment history. In the following example, the Tenant-Buyer has had an option fee of $7,500, and their move-in date is November 1, 2XXX. The monthly rent will be $1,295, and there's a quarterly water/sewer bill of $52.50. The "Credit" column is for the Tenant-Buyer payments, the "Debit" column is what the tenant owes, and the "Balance" is the sum of the two.

You can use Excel to track their payment ledger.

Date	Description	Debit (owed)	Credit (paid)	Balance
11-1-XX	Option fee due	$1,500.00		$1,500.00
11-1-XX	November rent due	$1,095.00		$2,595.00
11-1-XX	Option fee payment		$1,500.00	$1,095.00
11-1-XX	November rent payment		$1,095.00	0.00
11-10-XX	Water/sewer bill due	$ 52.50		$ 52.50
11-23-XX	Water/sewer bill payment		$ 52.50	0.00

Using a Tenant List

If you are not using a software system to handle your rentals yet, you can track your Tenant-Buyers on a Word or Excel list. Below is a document you can use as an example for showing all of your properties. (Notice, I again organize information by property address.) This list shows the current Tenant-Buyers, their Lease Option expiration dates and what utilities they are responsible to pay. There is a column for the owner and their address (if you have purchased it on a Lease Option), and the contract expiration date. This list will allow you to know immediately who should be working on their financing and whose option is coming due soon. You can always stay ahead by checking your list on a regular basis and getting your Tenant-Buyers to a mortgage broker several months before their contract expires. You can also see when your Lease Option is coming due with your seller. I like this type of document so show me an overview of my entire business.

Property	Company	Owner Info	Lease Start	Tenant	Lease End	Rent	Utilities	Misc. Info
123 Lake Woods Waterford 48329	Your LLC	Cheryl Larati (234) 222-2343	XX/05/31	Clare Kilgore (333) 333-4444	XX/11/31	$1,995	Township water/ sewer	Lease option
123 Geneva Clarkston 48346	Your LLC	Rog & Ruth Rechy (222) 342-4444	XX/02/28	Kristin & Jesse Genola (333) 333-4444	XX/08/29	$1,795	Well, septic softener	Lease option
123 Hilltop Oxford 48371	Your other LLC	Julie Greeny (111) 222-2222	XX/03/31	Karla & Mike Westford (333) 333-4444	XX/03/31	$2,595	Sewer/ well	Lease option
123 Huntsman Lapeer 48446	Your other LLC	Brookie Cookie 123 Bliss Street Ann Arbor 48123 (333) 333-4444	XX/07/31	Bradford Shue (333) 444-3333	XX/01/31	$1,895	Township water/ sewer	Lease option

Property	Company	Owner Info	Lease Start	Tenant	Lease End	Rent	Utilities	Misc. Info
123 Hollywood Fenton 48132	Your LLC	Fifth Third Bank	XX/05/31 —. —.	Alan & Kim Wayne (333) 123-4567	XX/05/31	$1,095	Sewer/ well	Rental
321 Crescent Rochester Hills 48561	Your other LLC	Bank One	XX/07/31 —. —.	Gregory & Kim Shultz (333) 123-4567	XX/07/31	$1,495	Well, septic Softener	Rental
481 Kroft Lake Orion 48362	Your LLC	Jenpot Arat HomeOwner (222) 222-3333	XX/12/31	Jennifer Gale (333) 333-1234	XX/05/31	$1,695	Well, septic Softener	Lease Option
321 Hope St. Lake Orion	Your LLC	Crik Patton (222) 333-3333	XX/10/31	Evalyn Faith (333) 123-4678	0X/07/31	$2,495	Sewer	Lease Option
123 Blue Lake Orion	Your LLC	Michael Gott (123) 000-0000	XX/11/31	Amia and Ava Huitt	XX/11/31	$1,900	Water, Sewer	Lease Option
444 Cloud Pontiac	Your LLC	Rachel and Jake Sarahi (111) 222-3333	XX/12/01	Parker Swingale	XX/11/31	$2,100	Water, Sewer	Remtal

Keeping Necessary Documents on Hand

It is extremely important to have a digital folder (on Dropbox, Google Drive, or another platform) with documents that you will be using on a regular basis. Nothing is more annoying than needing a document and finding that you don't have it at your fingertips. Spending time searching online or through your email for a form is not worth the hassle. For instance, depending on your state, you can download tenant or legal documents from the state's web site. Save these documents to your business area (near your owner/Tenant-Buyer folders) to enable you to pull them up and tailor them as needed. You may want to create a document checklist to make sure that you have what you need each time you do a deal. The key is to get organized early on, so your business is easier later.

Good Recordkeeping Is a Must!

In addition to the two folders I've mentioned, one more file should be used to store *every* receipt for each property. These can certainly be kept online, but better yet in QuickBooks. There are always expenses that the Tenant-Buyer is not responsible for paying (advertising costs, attorney fees, insurance, etc.). Every time an invoice or bill is paid for a particular property, a copy of the invoice is scanned into QuickBooks. We note the check number or ach and date paid on each invoice. If the Tenant-Buyer is responsible for reimbursing us, a copy of the invoice is also placed in their file. At year end, these receipt files will contain all documentation needed to substantiate all expenses, improvements, etc. for that particular property. This is a simple and easy way to do it no matter what exists with technology, but obviously most documents are now stored online. Both physical and electronic files work. Just have a system and be organized.

For those items that cannot be associated with a particular property—for instance, general advertising not tied to a particular property ("We Lease Homes," "Office Manager Needed," etc.), postage, office supplies, license fees, or the like—we use a \file (or class) labeled, "General Rentals" and file receipts for those types of expenses in this file.

The last type of file used to document our bookkeeping is a file for each bank account, labeled with the LLC name and "Canceled Checks." We file all the bank statements and canceled checks for that LLC in that file. Your bank statements and photos of any cancelled checks are likely emailed to you, or you can download them to your online system unless your bank keeps them for many years where you can access them.

At year end, all files are moved to storage boxes (again online or physical). Each box is labeled with the LLC name and year. Placed in this box are all the files with the receipts for each property under that LLC, as well as the canceled check/bank statement files for that LLC. This may seem like a lot to store away, and some of it may seem redundant (a copy in the tenant file and a copy in the property receipt file), but if you are ever unfortunate enough to go through an audit, everything you need to support your tax filing is in one box, efficiently organized and easy to retrieve. You hope you will never need them, but there are times you will need a copy of a receipt and you want to be able to locate it quickly. I have been audited three times and all my audits had zero changes, because my records were so easy to find, and they were very clean. The auditor's first words when arriving to my office and getting a tour of our records was, "Wow, you are *very* organized!" You don't want to be audited, but if you are, it's nice to have someone respond that way. Most investors are unorganized.

When to Hire Someone

At some point you will need to hire someone to help in your business. When your business has grown to the point where you are no longer able to handle all the Tenant-Buyers, bookkeeping, or organization necessary to efficiently run things, or you are so busy handling the little stuff that you are not spending enough time on the real money-making end of your business, it is time to get help.

My first assistant was hired in the early 1990s. I was slammed with my Tenant-Buyers, sellers, maintenance calls, inspection meetings, bookkeeping, etc. I knew I needed help, but I didn't yet know much about hiring someone or training them properly. I was working more then 50-hour weeks in the business and was overwhelmed. My twins were still very young. I decided to run an ad to find someone. I was looking for someone who could work 20 to 40 hours a week. This was going to be a rare person; someone who didn't need full time but was willing to work it. A woman in her early 50s applied for the position. Her name was Judy. She wasn't the only applicant, but she was the one I liked best and ended up hiring. Judy rarely worked less than 40 hours a week. There was that much to do. She helped with all my showings, calls, maintenance management, rent tracking, bank runs, and more. She was my right hand.

When you are making your first hire, you're probably concerned about how much it will cost you. Likely you're not rolling in the dough just yet. Therefore, I wanted to start with a part-time person. This would protect me if it got tight with the budget. The thing that's hard for many to comprehend until they experience it, is the value another person brings to your team. It's called LEVERAGE. Leverage is so important to a business. Once Judy started, I had more time with my kids and more time to make deals with sellers. This was short-lived though.

About six months after Judy started, we realized we were *both* slammed. She was working full-time, and I was back up to 50 hours a week. It was time to hire assistant number two. Judy had a daughter-in-law named Amie who she said was amazing and super smart/hardworking. You know, all the good things you would want for someone on your team. After interviewing Amie, I decided to hire her.

Fast forward over 30 years:

Amie ended up purchasing my property management company (started in the late 90s) and has grown it to a large company. She opened a second one in Mississippi where I also had a brokerage (started in 2006). Amie and I are business partners in commercial buildings now and share office space in one of them. She manages all my rental properties. I realized I never liked to manage properties and she loved it. She is a rock star property manager in metro

Detroit – Millennium Realty, LLC in Clarkston.

Judy recently turned 80 and has worked for Amie's property management company for many years. She does some of the maintenance inspections and city property inspections for Amie. She also does showings. She's truly amazing and still a dear friend.

So, it all sounds easy after that overview of my experience, right? Well, honestly it was luck with those two. What I have learned about business and hiring since the early 1990s is so much more. Would I still have hired them knowing what I know now? Of course, but back then I didn't know the real reasons why. I just felt they were good, honest people. Note the key word: "felt". Back then I went more on my gut rather than learning how to thoroughly screen a candidate to make sure they would be a good fit. This book isn't about hiring, but this is a key to growing this business. There is a book I highly recommend: <u>The Ideal Team Player</u> by Pat Lencioni. I love his process of determining who is a good team player and why. His interview questions in the book are the ones I use as part of *my* interview process. As you grow your business, continue to learn more and more about how to hire the right person.

Don't forget to train the person once you hire them. This is often overlooked because we are so busy. This, however, is the make or break to their success in the role and you getting permanently rid of the role. Continually be a student of hiring and training your team.

Qualities to Look for in an Office Manager or Property Manager

Of the many qualities you should consider when hiring an office manager or property manager, I have discovered a few that I feel are the most essential. Pick a person who has the qualities that are most important for the job you need accomplished, and the rest of their skills will be bonuses. This individual will be your right-hand person and a key part of your team, so it is crucial that you select the right one. Here are the skills that I have found to be the most important over the years—not necessarily in order of importance:

- *Firm.* There are times when a tenant will try to push the limits of being late on rent. You want your assistant to be firm.
- *Pleasant.* Your assistant must be pleasant even when *you* want to blow up. There are times when I've wanted to lose my temper with someone on the phone, but my assistant will not blow up because they are not personally involved, so they can be non-emotional and pleasant.
- *Detailed.* This person must be very detail oriented. They will be tracking tenants' rent, late fees, option fees, correspondence, and many other items. Everything must be documented and detailed.
- *Communicative.* This person must be able to diligently convey information to all necessary parties in a timely manner. It is also important for them to discern what is important.
- *Good follow-through.* This is very important, as the little details that fall through the cracks can cost you tens of thousands of dollars and lawsuits. Making sure that

nothing falls through the cracks is critical; for example, did the gas get turned on at your vacant home in January in the Michigan area? If not, you might have an ice-skating rink in your home. How do I know? I have had some follow-through problems in the past.

- *Organized.* Following the system(s) you have in place and your checklists will be very important. Also, knowing that your assistant has things well organized, labeled, and filed, so that you can easily find things when you need them, will reduce stress for you.

- *Computer skills.* It is impossible in this day and age, to keep up with business-related information without computers. Your assistant must have computer skills. Basic word processing and spreadsheets are usually the most important parts of property management. Spreadsheets can be taught, but word processing is a must.

- *Take initiative/work independently.* Your assistant must be a self-starter. They must know what to do when you are on the road. You will be in and out of the office much of the time, or you will want the ability to be. Make sure you hire someone capable of running things if you are out of town. Can they handle calls? Make decisions? Make good judgment calls? Will they work when you are not there watching them?

After Judy and Amie, there have been many more hires. Some of my best part-time employees are women who didn't *need* their jobs; they *wanted* their jobs. This makes a huge difference in the way they perform at work. When someone *needs* to work, you would think that would be enough motivation; however, if they are not self-motivated it is not enough to keep them doing their best every day. If someone *wants* to work, that is enough motivation. This is just a guideline—I have also had several full-time employees who *did* need their jobs who were fantastic. Overall, my team has been amazing, and I could not do what I do without them.

 Wendy's Advice on Hiring

If you are hiring someone part-time, you might want to consider someone who doesn't *need* a job but, rather, someone who *wants* a job. Look for motivation. It is the key.

CHAPTER 18

Where to Go from Here:
A Step-by-Step Action Plan

> Make $120,000/year in real estate investing, part-time (10 hours per week), starting with less than $5,000 of personal net worth! Yes, it is possible with Lease Options and Subject-Tos.

Figuring out where to take that first step the day after attending an exciting seminar, or reading a great book, can be overwhelming. Many people will buy a real estate investing course and then not know what to do next, so they do nothing. They have wasted time and money learning about tools that can yield them much income if they don't use those tools.

I have asked many other speakers/educators and students around the country about this. "Where do I begin? How do I get started? What exactly do I do to implement the course I purchased?" Most courses assume you understand how to get started and what to do next, but the reality is that most people don't. You are not alone.

What I would love to leave you with after reading my book is a list of things to consider for your next steps if you want to pursue Lease Options and/or Subject-Tos.

Where to go from here:
1. Purchase my courses on Subject-To and/or Lease Options (the Arsenal includes all the Lease Option courses). These courses will give you personal help and experience of over 35 years. All of my courses have step-by-step audios to teach you how to do the business and how to fill out the forms. Reading a book is one thing but having all the contracts and knowing how to fill them out is another.

Just for you!

For reading this book, I put together a special deal just for you! When you purchase my Wealth Building Arsenal course, I will give you my Subject-To course for FREE. This is a huge savings for you. Call my office at 248-394-0767 or email me at Info@WendyPatton.com and reference this deal to get both! You can't find this deal on my website.

2. Consider hiring a Lease Option coach. Although I don't coach anymore, one of my dear friends does. Contact my office at 248-394-0767 and we can put you two in touch. There is nothing better than having a lifeline when you have a deal or questions.

3. Join your local real estate investors group if you haven't already. If you are in Michigan, hopefully you attend mine at www.MichiganRealEstateInvestors.com.

4. Set up your office with supplies and a system as discussed in the previous chapters. This is a great business. Treat it like one.

5. Create an account on Dropbox, Google Drive or similar platform if you don't have one already. Create folders for the master forms for each type of deal. This way you can copy the entire folder once you are ready to go.

6. Consider getting your real estate license – once you feel you need one to help with comps, showings, etc. Reach out to my office if you want help to find out about getting a license in your area and finding an investor-friendly office.

7. Set up your LLC once you have your business going. It is not urgent to do this before you do a deal. Do a deal! You can always move your properties to your LLC later. The important part of success is to *get started*. You engineers will know what I'm talking about here...

8. Create an email specifically for your real estate business to direct people to.

9. Purchase QuickBooks once you have a property purchased/optioned.

10. Legal Shield – www.GotLegalPlans.com to sign up for a legal plan in your state. This is a great deal which will help you with legal fees.

11. Please keep in touch with me to share your experiences doing what you learned from my book and courses. I would love to share those stories with others in the future.

12. Please give my book a review on Amazon! I appreciate it very much.

> ### Wendy's Big Picture Advice for Lease Options and Subject-To's
>
> - Don't assume the economy will always remain strong. (For the first 15 years I invested, I didn't know anything different than a seller's market. We always had appreciation; everything was hot.). Then the marked tanked!
>
> - Pace yourself (with money and time), so you don't burn out. Buying too many properties too fast can leave you with too much to handle. Figure out how many houses you can handle based on your current circumstances. Control your growth.
>
> - Be careful choosing homes. Eventually you will have more homes than you will be able to handle. Don't get sloppy. Continue to evaluate each deal on its own. Always cherry pick your deals.
>
> - Find good Tenant-Buyers.
>
> - Practice good management techniques.
>
> - Don't let anyone tell you that you can't do it!
>
> - Cash the checks and live happily ever after!

The sacrifices we make, make us!

Not only is this all possible for anyone, but it is easy if you follow a system and step-by-step instructions. If you don't have those yet, check out my website.

Sacrifice is essential when you want to be successful. Are you willing to sacrifice something to build wealth and your financial future? Many people wish they could make money, yet they won't do what it takes. These are the same people who continue to believe they will someday win big in the lottery. They want the money thrown in their lap.

I have made lots of sacrifices over the years. When I first started to invest in real estate in 1985, I was 21 years old. I owned several rental properties. My friends would go out on the weekend and party while I spent my weekends painting, cleaning, driving by my homes, looking at new ones, etc.   While I was *building* wealth for the future, they were *spending* theirs. Many nights I would eat popcorn for dinner, when I had spent my paycheck on paint for one of my homes. Learning how to be a frugal shopper was key. Using coupons, keeping my heat low/AC high— all to save money and build for the future. I spent years traveling on weekends or did late evening meetings or conference calls. This meant time away from my family, and they realized that building for the future affected them also. TV wasn't part of my life.

Today I don't sacrifice like I used to. It's now time to enjoy the fruits of my labor and the sacrifices that my husband and my kids made.

Hopefully you have gotten a lot out of this book, which was first published in 2005. It was one of the hardest things I've ever done. I had 3 months from my publisher to have it completed from scratch. *This* time, I updated it with no deadlines. *This* time it wasn't stressful but was very fulfilling. My wish for you is that you will discover the same love for real estate that I have had over the years, and that you will one day share *your* knowledge and experience with others.

To Your Success,

Wendy Patton

P.S. Please, keep in touch! AND... Thanks for reading my book!

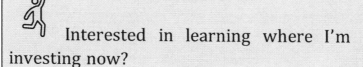 Interested in learning where I'm investing now?

Call my office at 248-394-0767 or email me at Info@WendyPatton.com to receive information on where I am currently investing and if there is an opportunity for you as well.

 Download My Bonuses for FREE!!

I have included a few special documents (BONUSES) with the purchase of this book. You can download my Buying on a Subject-To Checklist, Buying on a Lease Option Checklist, and the Claim of Interest by following the instructions on www.WendyPatton.com/Bonus

GLOSSARY

Below are some terms and definitions for real estate investors. These are Wendy Patton's definitions—not Webster's.

1031 Exchange an IRS code that allows a person to exchange their like kind property for another property of equal or greater value and defer (not avoid) the capital gains on the first property.

CMA Comparative Market Analysis. Realtors use these to show the value of the home to a seller.

Double Dip Realtors usually divide commissions 50/50 : 50 percent to the agent who works with the seller (the listing agent) and 50 percent to the agent who works with the buyer (the buyer's agent). A double dip is when a Realtor is able to work with both the buyer and seller and collect the entire commission.

Due-on-Sale a clause in most mortgages that says if the owner sells the property or conveys interest in it to anyone, the bank can call the entire mortgage due immediately. It is rare that this happens, but both Lease Options and Subject-Tos can violate due-on-sale clauses by giving an interest in the property.

Earnest Money is money given in good faith by a purchaser of a home; a deposit to purchase a home. Applied to the purchase price at closing or forfeited if the purchaser backs out. Not normally used with a Lease Option but could be with a Subject-To.

Escrow (1) Escrow accounts are non-interest bearing bank accounts in which you can deposit earnest money received on a property. (2) Escrow can also be a way of closing on a property. To "close in escrow" means that the title company or attorney prepares all the paperwork but does not release any of the originals to anyone until something else happens (i.e., another deed is brought in to the title company and shown, another $200 is received from the buyer, etc.).

Foreclosure When someone owns a home and they can't or don't pay the mortgage payments, the bank will "foreclose" on the home, taking it back from the owner. In some states the owner would have a redemption period after the foreclosure or Sheriff's sale. In most states there is no redemption time. The redemption time gives the owner time to "redeem" the title of their property, but they must pay the entire balance in full in order to redeem. Most owners can't do this without selling to another person or investor. Once foreclosure is started on a seller, only a few lenders will refinance the property for the seller.

FSBO (pronounced FIZZ-bo) an acronym for "for sale by owner," referring to properties that are sold without a Realtor, but by the owner individually.

Land Contract aka "contract for deed". The seller in effect becomes the bank and only transfers the deed when the buyer's contract is paid in full.

Land Trust is a way to hold title to a home that camouflages the ownership. This is not an asset protection tool but tied in with LLCs it can be very effective in asset protection and camouflage. This is used primarily so that no one will know the real identity of the owner. It is also used many times to avoid due-on-sale, seasoning, and the like. Many investors use this technique to hold properties. It works like a company and can be named as simply as, "Joe Smith's Land Trust." You can deed your property into it and thereby prevent the due-on-sales. Liens can't be attached to it. I don't use it with my sellers because most of them would find it scary and confusing, but it is a legitimate way to operate.

Lease Option Read the book! ☺

Lease Purchase This is similar to a Lease Option; however, a Lease Purchase has no option. Technically the buyer is guaranteeing the purchase of the home. Lease Purchases work well only when the buyer can make this guarantee or when you as an investor will guarantee the closing. It is a lease with a purchase agreement (no option agreement).

Memorandum of Option a document that records the buyer's interest in the property. It prevents the seller from selling the home or refinancing during the option period.

MLS Multiple Listing Service—a database and computer system which contains all of the homes listed by Realtors. In most states only licensed Realtors can access this data

Option An option gives an optionee a right to exercise a privilege. It gives the optionee the right or privilege to buy, within a given time period, for a given price. Options are used heavily in real estate, but many options are used in commercial real estate (i.e., you option a piece of property on the corner of two busy highways, then find a buyer, like Walmart, to come and develop it. That is when you would exercise your option. If you don't find a buyer, then you wouldn't exercise your option). A purchase agreement is technically an option to buy a property, but with a short time frame.

Performance Mortgage A Performance Mortgage is similar to a regular mortgage on the seller's property and is used to guarantee that they will sell you the property. It gives you a lien/mortgage on the property (but only on a dollar figure) if they don't perform and sell the home to you. It's only based on performance. It puts you on title, so if their first mortgage goes into foreclosure, you would be notified because you are a mortgage holder.

PITI principal, interest, taxes, and insurance—a full mortgage payment

PI principal and interest payment. Taxes and insurance are paid by the owner directly. This happens when a buyer puts 20%, or more, down on their mortgage. The bank will then allow the buyer to pay these bills themselves.

PMI private mortgage insurance. This is usually required on all mortgages that have less than 20 percent down. It is normally a monthly payment added to the mortgage payment, insuring that part of the loan (the part that is greater than 80 percent of the original purchase price) for the lender.

Rehabbing a property is when a person buys a fixer-upper and renovates it, making the property look new and beautiful. Each level of rehab is determined by the investor and price range of the home. A rehabber would not rehab a million-dollar home the same way they would rehab a $100,000 home

Retail Value market value—the price at which Realtors list and sell homes

Sandwich Lease Option A Sandwich Lease Option is where you have a Lease Option with the seller, and you sell the home on a Lease Option to another buyer. You are in the middle.

Seasoning is the time between when an investor buys a property and sells it. Seasoning starts when you record the deed. Whenever you record a deed, hand-carry it to the courthouse immediately or work with a title company to e-record it.

Seller Financing When the seller acts like the bank to finance the purchase to a buyer. They would get a mortgage and a note signed by the buyer (just like a bank would).

Seller Holdback typically a second mortgage on a home the seller is selling. The buyer gets a mortgage for the majority of the sales price, then the seller holds a second mortgage for the balance or some portion remaining. This is another type of seller financing. Most lenders will not allow this any longer. This industry, and its standards, are always changing.

Short Sale When a bank is owed a certain amount of money on a home, but the owner is having financial issues and the balance of the mortgage is more than the home is worth. The bank would "short" what is owed and take less to consider the mortgage paid in full.

Subject-To Read the book ☺

Title Insurance insures the clear ownership and title for the purchaser or the lender in the case of a lender policy.

Transactional Funding is funding used for many Sandwich Lease Option closings or double closings with wholesalers. This is funding to pay A (the seller) because you can't use the money from C (the Tenant-Buyer) to pay A.

RESOURCES

1. Wendy Patton: www.WendyPatton.com

2. Credit Reports: check out my website resources page to see who I am currently using

3. Credit Repair: check out my website resources page to see who I am currently using

4. Lease Option Coaching: contact my office at 248-394-0767 or by emailing me at

   Info@WendyPatton.com

5. Legal Shield: www.GotLegalPlans.com Great legal plans to help save you

   money!

6. Fair Housing Act: www.usdoj.gov/crt/housing/title8.htm

7. Michigan Real Estate Investors: www.MichiganRealEstateInvestors.com

8. National Real Estate Investors Association: (to find a group)

   http://www.nationalreia.com

9. Rental listings:

   a. www.Rent.com

   b. www.Zillow.com

   c. www.Apartments.com

   d. www.Facebook.com

   e. www.Trulia.com

   f. www.HotPads.com

10. Self-directed IRAS: Equity Trust (email us at Info@WendyPatton.com for who to contact)

12. Becoming a Real Estate Agent: You can download your free copy of my book on how to

become a real estate agent at www.WendyPatton.com - also email me at

Info@WendyPatton.com as I'd love to help you find an investor friendly brokerage near you.

Made in the USA
Columbia, SC
05 July 2023

20044382R00148